U.S. Department of Justice

~~Attorney Work Product // May Contain Material Protected Under Fed. R. Crim. P. 6(e)~~

Report On The Investigation Into Russian Interference In The 2016 Presidential Election

Volume I of II

Special Counsel Robert S. Mueller, III

Submitted Pursuant to 28 C.F.R. § 600.8(c)

Washington, D.C.

March 2019

U.S. Department of Justice

~~Attorney Work Product // May Contain Material Protected Under Fed. R. Crim. P. 6(e)~~

TABLE OF CONTENTS – VOLUME I

U.S. Department of Justice

~~Attorney Work Product // May Contain Material Protected Under Fed. R. Crim. P. 6(e)~~

U.S. Department of Justice

~~Attorney Work Product // May Contain Material Protected Under Fed. R. Crim. P. 6(e)~~

U.S. Department of Justice

~~Attorney Work Product // May Contain Material Protected Under Fed. R. Crim. P. 6(e)~~

INTRODUCTION TO VOLUME I

This report is submitted to the Attorney General pursuant to 28 C.F.R. § 600.8(c), which states that, "[a]t the conclusion of the Special Counsel's work, he . . . shall provide the Attorney General a confidential report explaining the prosecution or declination decisions [the Special Counsel] reached."

The Russian government interfered in the 2016 presidential election in sweeping and systematic fashion. Evidence of Russian government operations began to surface in mid-2016. In June, the Democratic National Committee and its cyber response team publicly announced that Russian hackers had compromised its computer network. Releases of hacked materials—hacks that public reporting soon attributed to the Russian government—began that same month. Additional releases followed in July through the organization WikiLeaks, with further releases in October and November.

In late July 2016, soon after WikiLeaks's first release of stolen documents, a foreign government contacted the FBI about a May 2016 encounter with Trump Campaign foreign policy advisor George Papadopoulos. Papadopoulos had suggested to a representative of that foreign government that the Trump Campaign had received indications from the Russian government that it could assist the Campaign through the anonymous release of information damaging to Democratic presidential candidate Hillary Clinton. That information prompted the FBI on July 31, 2016, to open an investigation into whether individuals associated with the Trump Campaign were coordinating with the Russian government in its interference activities.

That fall, two federal agencies jointly announced that the Russian government "directed recent compromises of e-mails from US persons and institutions, including US political organizations," and, "[t]hese thefts and disclosures are intended to interfere with the US election process." After the election, in late December 2016, the United States imposed sanctions on Russia for having interfered in the election. By early 2017, several congressional committees were examining Russia's interference in the election.

Within the Executive Branch, these investigatory efforts ultimately led to the May 2017 appointment of Special Counsel Robert S. Mueller, III. The order appointing the Special Counsel authorized him to investigate "the Russian government's efforts to interfere in the 2016 presidential election," including any links or coordination between the Russian government and individuals associated with the Trump Campaign.

As set forth in detail in this report, the Special Counsel's investigation established that Russia interfered in the 2016 presidential election principally through two operations. First, a Russian entity carried out a social media campaign that favored presidential candidate Donald J. Trump and disparaged presidential candidate Hillary Clinton. Second, a Russian intelligence service conducted computer-intrusion operations against entities, employees, and volunteers working on the Clinton Campaign and then released stolen documents. The investigation also identified numerous links between the Russian government and the Trump Campaign. Although the investigation established that the Russian government perceived it would benefit from a Trump presidency and worked to secure that outcome, and that the Campaign expected it would benefit

U.S. Department of Justice

~~Attorney Work Product~~ // ~~May Contain Material Protected Under Fed. R. Crim. P. 6(e)~~

electorally from information stolen and released through Russian efforts, the investigation did not establish that members of the Trump Campaign conspired or coordinated with the Russian government in its election interference activities.

* * *

Below we describe the evidentiary considerations underpinning statements about the results of our investigation and the Special Counsel's charging decisions, and we then provide an overview of the two volumes of our report.

The report describes actions and events that the Special Counsel's Office found to be supported by the evidence collected in our investigation. In some instances, the report points out the absence of evidence or conflicts in the evidence about a particular fact or event. In other instances, when substantial, credible evidence enabled the Office to reach a conclusion with confidence, the report states that the investigation established that certain actions or events occurred. A statement that the investigation did not establish particular facts does not mean there was no evidence of those facts.

In evaluating whether evidence about collective action of multiple individuals constituted a crime, we applied the framework of conspiracy law, not the concept of "collusion." In so doing, the Office recognized that the word "collud[e]" was used in communications with the Acting Attorney General confirming certain aspects of the investigation's scope and that the term has frequently been invoked in public reporting about the investigation. But collusion is not a specific offense or theory of liability found in the United States Code, nor is it a term of art in federal criminal law. For those reasons, the Office's focus in analyzing questions of joint criminal liability was on conspiracy as defined in federal law. In connection with that analysis, we addressed the factual question whether members of the Trump Campaign "coordinat[ed]"—a term that appears in the appointment order—with Russian election interference activities. Like collusion, "coordination" does not have a settled definition in federal criminal law. We understood coordination to require an agreement—tacit or express—between the Trump Campaign and the Russian government on election interference. That requires more than the two parties taking actions that were informed by or responsive to the other's actions or interests. We applied the term coordination in that sense when stating in the report that the investigation did not establish that the Trump Campaign coordinated with the Russian government in its election interference activities.

* * *

The report on our investigation consists of two volumes:

Volume I describes the factual results of the Special Counsel's investigation of Russia's interference in the 2016 presidential election and its interactions with the Trump Campaign. Section I describes the scope of the investigation. Sections II and III describe the principal ways Russia interfered in the 2016 presidential election. Section IV describes links between the Russian

U.S. Department of Justice

~~Attorney Work Product // May Contain Material Protected Under Fed. R. Crim. P. 6(e)~~

government and individuals associated with the Trump Campaign. Section V sets forth the Special Counsel's charging decisions.

Volume II addresses the President's actions towards the FBI's investigation into Russia's interference in the 2016 presidential election and related matters, and his actions towards the Special Counsel's investigation. Volume II separately states its framework and the considerations that guided that investigation.

U.S. Department of Justice

~~Attorney Work Product // May Contain Material Protected Under Fed. R. Crim. P. 6(e)~~

EXECUTIVE SUMMARY TO VOLUME I

RUSSIAN SOCIAL MEDIA CAMPAIGN

The Internet Research Agency (IRA) carried out the earliest Russian interference operations identified by the investigation—a social media campaign designed to provoke and amplify political and social discord in the United States. The IRA was based in St. Petersburg, Russia, and received funding from Russian oligarch Yevgeniy Prigozhin and companies he controlled. Prigozhin is widely reported to have ties to Russian President Vladimir Putin, Harm to Ongoing Matter

In mid-2014, the IRA sent employees to the United States on an intelligence-gathering mission with instructions Harm to Ongoing Matter

The IRA later used social media accounts and interest groups to sow discord in the U.S. political system through what it termed "information warfare." The campaign evolved from a generalized program designed in 2014 and 2015 to undermine the U.S. electoral system, to a targeted operation that by early 2016 favored candidate Trump and disparaged candidate Clinton. The IRA's operation also included the purchase of political advertisements on social media in the names of U.S. persons and entities, as well as the staging of political rallies inside the United States. To organize those rallies, IRA employees posed as U.S. grassroots entities and persons and made contact with Trump supporters and Trump Campaign officials in the United States. The investigation did not identify evidence that any U.S. persons conspired or coordinated with the IRA. Section II of this report details the Office's investigation of the Russian social media campaign.

RUSSIAN HACKING OPERATIONS

At the same time that the IRA operation began to focus on supporting candidate Trump in early 2016, the Russian government employed a second form of interference: cyber intrusions (hacking) and releases of hacked materials damaging to the Clinton Campaign. The Russian intelligence service known as the Main Intelligence Directorate of the General Staff of the Russian Army (GRU) carried out these operations.

In March 2016, the GRU began hacking the email accounts of Clinton Campaign volunteers and employees, including campaign chairman John Podesta. In April 2016, the GRU hacked into the computer networks of the Democratic Congressional Campaign Committee (DCCC) and the Democratic National Committee (DNC). The GRU stole hundreds of thousands of documents from the compromised email accounts and networks. Around the time that the DNC announced in mid-June 2016 the Russian government's role in hacking its network, the GRU began disseminating stolen materials through the fictitious online personas "DCLeaks" and "Guccifer 2.0." The GRU later released additional materials through the organization WikiLeaks.

4

U.S. Department of Justice

~~Attorney Work Product~~ // ~~May Contain Material Protected Under Fed. R. Crim. P. 6(e)~~

The presidential campaign of Donald J. Trump ("Trump Campaign" or "Campaign") showed interest in WikiLeaks's releases of documents and welcomed their potential to damage candidate Clinton. Beginning in June 2016, ▮Harm to Ongoing Matter▮ forecast to senior Campaign officials that WikiLeaks would release information damaging to candidate Clinton. WikiLeaks's first release came in July 2016. Around the same time, candidate Trump announced that he hoped Russia would recover emails described as missing from a private server used by Clinton when she was Secretary of State (he later said that he was speaking sarcastically). ▮Harm to Ongoing Matter▮ WikiLeaks began releasing Podesta's stolen emails on October 7, 2016, less than one hour after a U.S. media outlet released video considered damaging to candidate Trump. Section III of this Report details the Office's investigation into the Russian hacking operations, as well as other efforts by Trump Campaign supporters to obtain Clinton-related emails.

RUSSIAN CONTACTS WITH THE CAMPAIGN

The social media campaign and the GRU hacking operations coincided with a series of contacts between Trump Campaign officials and individuals with ties to the Russian government. The Office investigated whether those contacts reflected or resulted in the Campaign conspiring or coordinating with Russia in its election-interference activities. Although the investigation established that the Russian government perceived it would benefit from a Trump presidency and worked to secure that outcome, and that the Campaign expected it would benefit electorally from information stolen and released through Russian efforts, the investigation did not establish that members of the Trump Campaign conspired or coordinated with the Russian government in its election interference activities.

The Russian contacts consisted of business connections, offers of assistance to the Campaign, invitations for candidate Trump and Putin to meet in person, invitations for Campaign officials and representatives of the Russian government to meet, and policy positions seeking improved U.S.-Russian relations. Section IV of this Report details the contacts between Russia and the Trump Campaign during the campaign and transition periods, the most salient of which are summarized below in chronological order.

2015. Some of the earliest contacts were made in connection with a Trump Organization real-estate project in Russia known as Trump Tower Moscow. Candidate Trump signed a Letter of Intent for Trump Tower Moscow by November 2015, and in January 2016 Trump Organization executive Michael Cohen emailed and spoke about the project with the office of Russian government press secretary Dmitry Peskov. The Trump Organization pursued the project through at least June 2016, including by considering travel to Russia by Cohen and candidate Trump.

Spring 2016. Campaign foreign policy advisor George Papadopoulos made early contact with Joseph Mifsud, a London-based professor who had connections to Russia and traveled to Moscow in April 2016. Immediately upon his return to London from that trip, Mifsud told Papadopoulos that the Russian government had "dirt" on Hillary Clinton in the form of thousands

U.S. Department of Justice

~~Attorney Work Product // May Contain Material Protected Under Fed. R. Crim. P. 6(e)~~

of emails. One week later, in the first week of May 2016, Papadopoulos suggested to a representative of a foreign government that the Trump Campaign had received indications from the Russian government that it could assist the Campaign through the anonymous release of information damaging to candidate Clinton. Throughout that period of time and for several months thereafter, Papadopoulos worked with Mifsud and two Russian nationals to arrange a meeting between the Campaign and the Russian government. No meeting took place.

Summer 2016. Russian outreach to the Trump Campaign continued into the summer of 2016, as candidate Trump was becoming the presumptive Republican nominee for President. On June 9, 2016, for example, a Russian lawyer met with senior Trump Campaign officials Donald Trump Jr., Jared Kushner, and campaign chairman Paul Manafort to deliver what the email proposing the meeting had described as "official documents and information that would incriminate Hillary." The materials were offered to Trump Jr. as "part of Russia and its government's support for Mr. Trump." The written communications setting up the meeting showed that the Campaign anticipated receiving information from Russia that could assist candidate Trump's electoral prospects, but the Russian lawyer's presentation did not provide such information.

Days after the June 9 meeting, on June 14, 2016, a cybersecurity firm and the DNC announced that Russian government hackers had infiltrated the DNC and obtained access to opposition research on candidate Trump, among other documents.

In July 2016, Campaign foreign policy advisor Carter Page traveled in his personal capacity to Moscow and gave the keynote address at the New Economic School. Page had lived and worked in Russia between 2003 and 2007. After returning to the United States, Page became acquainted with at least two Russian intelligence officers, one of whom was later charged in 2015 with conspiracy to act as an unregistered agent of Russia. Page's July 2016 trip to Moscow and his advocacy for pro-Russian foreign policy drew media attention. The Campaign then distanced itself from Page and, by late September 2016, removed him from the Campaign.

July 2016 was also the month WikiLeaks first released emails stolen by the GRU from the DNC. On July 22, 2016, WikiLeaks posted thousands of internal DNC documents revealing information about the Clinton Campaign. Within days, there was public reporting that U.S. intelligence agencies had "high confidence" that the Russian government was behind the theft of emails and documents from the DNC. And within a week of the release, a foreign government informed the FBI about its May 2016 interaction with Papadopoulos and his statement that the Russian government could assist the Trump Campaign. On July 31, 2016, based on the foreign government reporting, the FBI opened an investigation into potential coordination between the Russian government and individuals associated with the Trump Campaign.

Separately, on August 2, 2016, Trump campaign chairman Paul Manafort met in New York City with his long-time business associate Konstantin Kilimnik, who the FBI assesses to have ties to Russian intelligence. Kilimnik requested the meeting to deliver in person a peace plan for Ukraine that Manafort acknowledged to the Special Counsel's Office was a "backdoor" way for Russia to control part of eastern Ukraine; both men believed the plan would require candidate Trump's assent to succeed (were he to be elected President). They also discussed the status of the

U.S. Department of Justice

~~Attorney Work Product // May Contain Material Protected Under Fed. R. Crim. P. 6(e)~~

Trump Campaign and Manafort's strategy for winning Democratic votes in Midwestern states. Months before that meeting, Manafort had caused internal polling data to be shared with Kilimnik, and the sharing continued for some period of time after their August meeting.

Fall 2016. On October 7, 2016, the media released video of candidate Trump speaking in graphic terms about women years earlier, which was considered damaging to his candidacy. Less than an hour later, WikiLeaks made its second release: thousands of John Podesta's emails that had been stolen by the GRU in late March 2016. The FBI and other U.S. government institutions were at the time continuing their investigation of suspected Russian government efforts to interfere in the presidential election. That same day, October 7, the Department of Homeland Security and the Office of the Director of National Intelligence issued a joint public statement "that the Russian Government directed the recent compromises of e-mails from US persons and institutions, including from US political organizations." Those "thefts" and the "disclosures" of the hacked materials through online platforms such as WikiLeaks, the statement continued, "are intended to interfere with the US election process."

Post-2016 Election. Immediately after the November 8 election, Russian government officials and prominent Russian businessmen began trying to make inroads into the new administration. The most senior levels of the Russian government encouraged these efforts. The Russian Embassy made contact hours after the election to congratulate the President-Elect and to arrange a call with President Putin. Several Russian businessmen picked up the effort from there.

Kirill Dmitriev, the chief executive officer of Russia's sovereign wealth fund, was among the Russians who tried to make contact with the incoming administration. In early December, a business associate steered Dmitriev to Erik Prince, a supporter of the Trump Campaign and an associate of senior Trump advisor Steve Bannon. Dmitriev and Prince later met face-to-face in January 2017 in the Seychelles and discussed U.S.-Russia relations. During the same period, another business associate introduced Dmitriev to a friend of Jared Kushner who had not served on the Campaign or the Transition Team. Dmitriev and Kushner's friend collaborated on a short written reconciliation plan for the United States and Russia, which Dmitriev implied had been cleared through Putin. The friend gave that proposal to Kushner before the inauguration, and Kushner later gave copies to Bannon and incoming Secretary of State Rex Tillerson.

On December 29, 2016, then-President Obama imposed sanctions on Russia for having interfered in the election. Incoming National Security Advisor Michael Flynn called Russian Ambassador Sergey Kislyak and asked Russia not to escalate the situation in response to the sanctions. The following day, Putin announced that Russia would not take retaliatory measures in response to the sanctions at that time. Hours later, President-Elect Trump tweeted, "Great move on delay (by V. Putin)." The next day, on December 31, 2016, Kislyak called Flynn and told him the request had been received at the highest levels and Russia had chosen not to retaliate as a result of Flynn's request.

* * *

On January 6, 2017, members of the intelligence community briefed President-Elect Trump on a joint assessment—drafted and coordinated among the Central Intelligence Agency, FBI, and

U.S. Department of Justice

~~Attorney Work Product~~ // ~~May Contain Material Protected Under Fed. R. Crim. P. 6(e)~~

National Security Agency—that concluded with high confidence that Russia had intervened in the election through a variety of means to assist Trump's candidacy and harm Clinton's. A declassified version of the assessment was publicly released that same day.

Between mid-January 2017 and early February 2017, three congressional committees—the House Permanent Select Committee on Intelligence (HPSCI), the Senate Select Committee on Intelligence (SSCI), and the Senate Judiciary Committee (SJC)—announced that they would conduct inquiries, or had already been conducting inquiries, into Russian interference in the election. Then-FBI Director James Comey later confirmed to Congress the existence of the FBI's investigation into Russian interference that had begun before the election. On March 20, 2017, in open-session testimony before HPSCI, Comey stated:

> I have been authorized by the Department of Justice to confirm that the FBI, as part of our counterintelligence mission, is investigating the Russian government's efforts to interfere in the 2016 presidential election, and that includes investigating the nature of any links between individuals associated with the Trump campaign and the Russian government and whether there was any coordination between the campaign and Russia's efforts. . . . As with any counterintelligence investigation, this will also include an assessment of whether any crimes were committed.

The investigation continued under then-Director Comey for the next seven weeks until May 9, 2017, when President Trump fired Comey as FBI Director—an action which is analyzed in Volume II of the report.

On May 17, 2017, Acting Attorney General Rod Rosenstein appointed the Special Counsel and authorized him to conduct the investigation that Comey had confirmed in his congressional testimony, as well as matters arising directly from the investigation, and any other matters within the scope of 28 C.F.R. § 600.4(a), which generally covers efforts to interfere with or obstruct the investigation.

President Trump reacted negatively to the Special Counsel's appointment. He told advisors that it was the end of his presidency, sought to have Attorney General Jefferson (Jeff) Sessions unrecuse from the Russia investigation and to have the Special Counsel removed, and engaged in efforts to curtail the Special Counsel's investigation and prevent the disclosure of evidence to it, including through public and private contacts with potential witnesses. Those and related actions are described and analyzed in Volume II of the report.

* * *

THE SPECIAL COUNSEL'S CHARGING DECISIONS

In reaching the charging decisions described in Volume I of the report, the Office determined whether the conduct it found amounted to a violation of federal criminal law chargeable under the Principles of Federal Prosecution. *See* Justice Manual § 9-27.000 *et seq.* (2018). The standard set forth in the Justice Manual is whether the conduct constitutes a crime; if so, whether admissible evidence would probably be sufficient to obtain and sustain a conviction;

U.S. Department of Justice

~~Attorney Work Product // May Contain Material Protected Under Fed. R. Crim. P. 6(e)~~

and whether prosecution would serve a substantial federal interest that could not be adequately served by prosecution elsewhere or through non-criminal alternatives. *See* Justice Manual § 9-27.220.

Section V of the report provides detailed explanations of the Office's charging decisions, which contain three main components.

First, the Office determined that Russia's two principal interference operations in the 2016 U.S. presidential election—the social media campaign and the hacking-and-dumping operations—violated U.S. criminal law. Many of the individuals and entities involved in the social media campaign have been charged with participating in a conspiracy to defraud the United States by undermining through deceptive acts the work of federal agencies charged with regulating foreign influence in U.S. elections, as well as related counts of identity theft. *See United States v. Internet Research Agency, et al.*, No. 18-cr-32 (D.D.C.). Separately, Russian intelligence officers who carried out the hacking into Democratic Party computers and the personal email accounts of individuals affiliated with the Clinton Campaign conspired to violate, among other federal laws, the federal computer-intrusion statute, and they have been so charged. *See United States v. Netyksho, et al.*, No. 18-cr-215 (D.D.C.). Harm to Ongoing Matter

Personal Privacy

Second, while the investigation identified numerous links between individuals with ties to the Russian government and individuals associated with the Trump Campaign, the evidence was not sufficient to support criminal charges. Among other things, the evidence was not sufficient to charge any Campaign official as an unregistered agent of the Russian government or other Russian principal. And our evidence about the June 9, 2016 meeting and WikiLeaks's releases of hacked materials was not sufficient to charge a criminal campaign-finance violation. Further, the evidence was not sufficient to charge that any member of the Trump Campaign conspired with representatives of the Russian government to interfere in the 2016 election.

Third, the investigation established that several individuals affiliated with the Trump Campaign lied to the Office, and to Congress, about their interactions with Russian-affiliated individuals and related matters. Those lies materially impaired the investigation of Russian election interference. The Office charged some of those lies as violations of the federal false-statements statute. Former National Security Advisor Michael Flynn pleaded guilty to lying about his interactions with Russian Ambassador Kislyak during the transition period. George Papadopoulos, a foreign policy advisor during the campaign period, pleaded guilty to lying to investigators about, *inter alia*, the nature and timing of his interactions with Joseph Mifsud, the professor who told Papadopoulos that the Russians had dirt on candidate Clinton in the form of thousands of emails. Former Trump Organization attorney Michael Cohen pleaded guilty to making false statements to Congress about the Trump Moscow project. Harm to Ongoing Matter

And in February 2019, the U.S. District Court for the District of Columbia found that

U.S. Department of Justice

~~Attorney Work-Product // May Contain Material Protected Under Fed. R. Crim. P. 6(e)~~

Manafort lied to the Office and the grand jury concerning his interactions and communications with Konstantin Kilimnik about Trump Campaign polling data and a peace plan for Ukraine.

* * *

The Office investigated several other events that have been publicly reported to involve potential Russia-related contacts. For example, the investigation established that interactions between Russian Ambassador Kislyak and Trump Campaign officials both at the candidate's April 2016 foreign policy speech in Washington, D.C., and during the week of the Republican National Convention were brief, public, and non-substantive. And the investigation did not establish that one Campaign official's efforts to dilute a portion of the Republican Party platform on providing assistance to Ukraine were undertaken at the behest of candidate Trump or Russia. The investigation also did not establish that a meeting between Kislyak and Sessions in September 2016 at Sessions's Senate office included any more than a passing mention of the presidential campaign.

The investigation did not always yield admissible information or testimony, or a complete picture of the activities undertaken by subjects of the investigation. Some individuals invoked their Fifth Amendment right against compelled self-incrimination and were not, in the Office's judgment, appropriate candidates for grants of immunity. The Office limited its pursuit of other witnesses and information—such as information known to attorneys or individuals claiming to be members of the media—in light of internal Department of Justice policies. *See, e.g.,* Justice Manual §§ 9-13.400, 13.410. Some of the information obtained via court process, moreover, was presumptively covered by legal privilege and was screened from investigators by a filter (or "taint") team. Even when individuals testified or agreed to be interviewed, they sometimes provided information that was false or incomplete, leading to some of the false-statements charges described above. And the Office faced practical limits on its ability to access relevant evidence as well—numerous witnesses and subjects lived abroad, and documents were held outside the United States.

Further, the Office learned that some of the individuals we interviewed or whose conduct we investigated—including some associated with the Trump Campaign—deleted relevant communications or communicated during the relevant period using applications that feature encryption or that do not provide for long-term retention of data or communications records. In such cases, the Office was not able to corroborate witness statements through comparison to contemporaneous communications or fully question witnesses about statements that appeared inconsistent with other known facts.

Accordingly, while this report embodies factual and legal determinations that the Office believes to be accurate and complete to the greatest extent possible, given these identified gaps, the Office cannot rule out the possibility that the unavailable information would shed additional light on (or cast in a new light) the events described in the report.

U.S. Department of Justice

~~Attorney Work Product // May Contain Material Protected Under Fed. R. Crim. P. 6(e)~~

I. THE SPECIAL COUNSEL'S INVESTIGATION

On May 17, 2017, Deputy Attorney General Rod J. Rosenstein—then serving as Acting Attorney General for the Russia investigation following the recusal of former Attorney General Jeff Sessions on March 2, 2016—appointed the Special Counsel "to investigate Russian interference with the 2016 presidential election and related matters." Office of the Deputy Att'y Gen., Order No. 3915-2017, *Appointment of Special Counsel to Investigate Russian Interference with the 2016 Presidential Election and Related Matters*, May 17, 2017) ("Appointment Order"). Relying on "the authority vested" in the Acting Attorney General, "including 28 U.S.C. §§ 509, 510, and 515," the Acting Attorney General ordered the appointment of a Special Counsel "in order to discharge [the Acting Attorney General's] responsibility to provide supervision and management of the Department of Justice, and to ensure a full and thorough investigation of the Russian government's efforts to interfere in the 2016 presidential election." Appointment Order (introduction). "The Special Counsel," the Order stated, "is authorized to conduct the investigation confirmed by then-FBI Director James B. Comey in testimony before the House Permanent Select Committee on Intelligence on March 20, 2017," including:

> (i) any links and/or coordination between the Russian government and individuals associated with the campaign of President Donald Trump; and

> (ii) any matters that arose or may arise directly from the investigation; and

> (iii) any other matters within the scope of 28 C.F.R. § 600.4(a).

Appointment Order ¶ (b). Section 600.4 affords the Special Counsel "the authority to investigate and prosecute federal crimes committed in the course of, and with intent to interfere with, the Special Counsel's investigation, such as perjury, obstruction of justice, destruction of evidence, and intimidation of witnesses." 28 C.F.R. § 600.4(a). The authority to investigate "any matters that arose . . . directly from the investigation," Appointment Order ¶ (b)(ii), covers similar crimes that may have occurred during the course of the FBI's confirmed investigation before the Special Counsel's appointment. "If the Special Counsel believes it is necessary and appropriate," the Order further provided, "the Special Counsel is authorized to prosecute federal crimes arising from the investigation of these matters." *Id.* ¶ (c). Finally, the Acting Attorney General made applicable "Sections 600.4 through 600.10 of Title 28 of the Code of Federal Regulations." *Id.* ¶ (d).

The Acting Attorney General further clarified the scope of the Special Counsel's investigatory authority in two subsequent memoranda. A memorandum dated August 2, 2017, explained that the Appointment Order had been "worded categorically in order to permit its public release without confirming specific investigations involving specific individuals." It then confirmed that the Special Counsel had been authorized since his appointment to investigate allegations that three Trump campaign officials—Carter Page, Paul Manafort, and George Papadopoulos—"committed a crime or crimes by colluding with Russian government officials with respect to the Russian government's efforts to interfere with the 2016 presidential election." The memorandum also confirmed the Special Counsel's authority to investigate certain other matters, including two additional sets of allegations involving Manafort (crimes arising from payments he received from the Ukrainian government and crimes arising from his receipt of loans

U.S. Department of Justice

~~Attorney Work Product // May Contain Material Protected Under Fed. R. Crim. P. 6(e)~~

from a bank whose CEO was then seeking a position in the Trump Administration); allegations that Papadopoulos committed a crime or crimes by acting as an unregistered agent of the Israeli government; and four sets of allegations involving Michael Flynn, the former National Security Advisor to President Trump.

On October 20, 2017, the Acting Attorney General confirmed in a memorandum the Special Counsel's investigative authority as to several individuals and entities. First, "as part of a full and thorough investigation of the Russian government's efforts to interfere in the 2016 presidential election," the Special Counsel was authorized to investigate "the pertinent activities of Michael Cohen, Richard Gates, ████████████, Roger Stone, and ██ ██" "Confirmation of the authorization to investigate such individuals," the memorandum stressed, "does not suggest that the Special Counsel has made a determination that any of them has committed a crime." Second, with respect to Michael Cohen, the memorandum recognized the Special Counsel's authority to investigate "leads relate[d] to Cohen's establishment and use of Essential Consultants LLC to, *inter alia*, receive funds from Russian-backed entities." Third, the memorandum memorialized the Special Counsel's authority to investigate individuals and entities who were possibly engaged in "jointly undertaken activity" with existing subjects of the investigation, including Paul Manafort. Finally, the memorandum described an FBI investigation opened before the Special Counsel's appointment into "allegations that [then-Attorney General Jeff Sessions] made false statements to the United States Senate[,]" and confirmed the Special Counsel's authority to investigate that matter.

The Special Counsel structured the investigation in view of his power and authority "to exercise all investigative and prosecutorial functions of any United States Attorney." 28 C.F.R. § 600.6. Like a U.S. Attorney's Office, the Special Counsel's Office considered a range of classified and unclassified information available to the FBI in the course of the Office's Russia investigation, and the Office structured that work around evidence for possible use in prosecutions of federal crimes (assuming that one or more crimes were identified that warranted prosecution). There was substantial evidence immediately available to the Special Counsel at the inception of the investigation in May 2017 because the FBI had, by that time, already investigated Russian election interference for nearly 10 months. The Special Counsel's Office exercised its judgment regarding what to investigate and did not, for instance, investigate every public report of a contact between the Trump Campaign and Russian-affiliated individuals and entities.

The Office has concluded its investigation into links and coordination between the Russian government and individuals associated with the Trump Campaign. Certain proceedings associated with the Office's work remain ongoing. After consultation with the Office of the Deputy Attorney General, the Office has transferred responsibility for those remaining issues to other components of the Department of Justice and FBI. Appendix D lists those transfers.

Two district courts confirmed the breadth of the Special Counsel's authority to investigate Russia election interference and links and/or coordination with the Trump Campaign. *See United States v. Manafort*, 312 F. Supp. 3d 60, 79-83 (D.D.C. 2018); *United States v. Manafort*, 321 F. Supp. 3d 640, 650-655 (E.D. Va. 2018). In the course of conducting that investigation, the Office periodically identified evidence of potential criminal activity that was outside the scope of the Special Counsel's authority established by the Acting Attorney General. After consultation with

U.S. Department of Justice

~~Attorney Work Product // May Contain Material Protected Under Fed. R. Crim. P. 6(e)~~

the Office of the Deputy Attorney General, the Office referred that evidence to appropriate law enforcement authorities, principally other components of the Department of Justice and to the FBI. Appendix D summarizes those referrals.

* * *

To carry out the investigation and prosecution of the matters assigned to him, the Special Counsel assembled a team that at its high point included 19 attorneys—five of whom joined the Office from private practice and 14 on detail or assigned from other Department of Justice components. These attorneys were assisted by a filter team of Department lawyers and FBI personnel who screened materials obtained via court process for privileged information before turning those materials over to investigators; a support staff of three paralegals on detail from the Department's Antitrust Division; and an administrative staff of nine responsible for budget, finance, purchasing, human resources, records, facilities, security, information technology, and administrative support. The Special Counsel attorneys and support staff were co-located with and worked alongside approximately 40 FBI agents, intelligence analysts, forensic accountants, a paralegal, and professional staff assigned by the FBI to assist the Special Counsel's investigation. Those "assigned" FBI employees remained under FBI supervision at all times; the matters on which they assisted were supervised by the Special Counsel.[1]

During its investigation the Office issued more than 2,800 subpoenas under the auspices of a grand jury sitting in the District of Columbia; executed nearly 500 search-and-seizure warrants; obtained more than 230 orders for communications records under 18 U.S.C. § 2703(d); obtained almost 50 orders authorizing use of pen registers; made 13 requests to foreign governments pursuant to Mutual Legal Assistance Treaties; and interviewed approximately 500 witnesses, including almost 80 before a grand jury.

* * *

From its inception, the Office recognized that its investigation could identify foreign intelligence and counterintelligence information relevant to the FBI's broader national security mission. FBI personnel who assisted the Office established procedures to identify and convey such information to the FBI. The FBI's Counterintelligence Division met with the Office regularly for that purpose for most of the Office's tenure. For more than the past year, the FBI also embedded personnel at the Office who did not work on the Special Counsel's investigation, but whose purpose was to review the results of the investigation and to send—in writing—summaries of foreign intelligence and counterintelligence information to FBIHQ and FBI Field Offices. Those communications and other correspondence between the Office and the FBI contain information derived from the investigation, not all of which is contained in this Volume. This Volume is a summary. It contains, in the Office's judgment, that information necessary to account for the Special Counsel's prosecution and declination decisions and to describe the investigation's main factual results.

---

[1] FBI personnel assigned to the Special Counsel's Office were required to adhere to all applicable federal law and all Department and FBI regulations, guidelines, and policies. An FBI attorney worked on FBI-related matters for the Office, such as FBI compliance with all FBI policies and procedures, including the FBI's Domestic Investigations and Operations Guide (DIOG). That FBI attorney worked under FBI legal supervision, not the Special Counsel's supervision.

13

U.S. Department of Justice

~~Attorney Work Product // May Contain Material Protected Under Fed. R. Crim. P. 6(e)~~

II. RUSSIAN "ACTIVE MEASURES" SOCIAL MEDIA CAMPAIGN

The first form of Russian election influence came principally from the Internet Research Agency, LLC (IRA), a Russian organization funded by Yevgeniy Viktorovich Prigozhin and companies he controlled, including Concord Management and Consulting LLC and Concord Catering (collectively "Concord").[2] The IRA conducted social media operations targeted at large U.S. audiences with the goal of sowing discord in the U.S. political system.[3] These operations constituted "active measures" (активные мероприятия), a term that typically refers to operations conducted by Russian security services aimed at influencing the course of international affairs.[4]

The IRA and its employees began operations targeting the United States as early as 2014. Using fictitious U.S. personas, IRA employees operated social media accounts and group pages designed to attract U.S. audiences. These groups and accounts, which addressed divisive U.S. political and social issues, falsely claimed to be controlled by U.S. activists. Over time, these social media accounts became a means to reach large U.S. audiences. IRA employees travelled to the United States in mid-2014 on an intelligence-gathering mission to obtain information and photographs for use in their social media posts.

IRA employees posted derogatory information about a number of candidates in the 2016 U.S. presidential election. By early to mid-2016, IRA operations included supporting the Trump Campaign and disparaging candidate Hillary Clinton. The IRA made various expenditures to carry out those activities, including buying political advertisements on social media in the names of U.S. persons and entities. Some IRA employees, posing as U.S. persons and without revealing their Russian association, communicated electronically with individuals associated with the Trump Campaign and with other political activists to seek to coordinate political activities, including the staging of political rallies.[5] The investigation did not identify evidence that any U.S. persons knowingly or intentionally coordinated with the IRA's interference operation.

By the end of the 2016 U.S. election, the IRA had the ability to reach millions of U.S. persons through their social media accounts. Multiple IRA-controlled Facebook groups and

---

[2] The Office is aware of reports that other Russian entities engaged in similar active measures operations targeting the United States. Some evidence collected by the Office corroborates those reports, and the Office has shared that evidence with other offices in the Department of Justice and FBI.

[3] **Harm to Ongoing Matter**
see also SM-2230634, serial 44 (analysis). The FBI case number cited here, and other FBI case numbers identified in the report, should be treated as law enforcement sensitive given the context. The report contains additional law enforcement sensitive information.

[4] As discussed in Part V below, the active measures investigation has resulted in criminal charges against 13 individual Russian nationals and three Russian entities, principally for conspiracy to defraud the United States, in violation of 18 U.S.C. § 371. *See* Volume I, Section V.A, *infra*; Indictment, *United States v. Internet Research Agency, et al.*, 1:18-cr-32 (D.D.C. Feb. 16, 2018), Doc. 1 ("*Internet Research Agency Indictment*").

[5] *Internet Research Agency* Indictment ¶¶ 52, 54, 55(a), 56, 74; **Harm to Ongoing Matter**

U.S. Department of Justice

~~Attorney Work Product // May Contain Material Protected Under Fed. R. Crim. P. 6(e)~~

Instagram accounts had hundreds of thousands of U.S. participants. IRA-controlled Twitter accounts separately had tens of thousands of followers, including multiple U.S. political figures who retweeted IRA-created content. In November 2017, a Facebook representative testified that Facebook had identified 470 IRA-controlled Facebook accounts that collectively made 80,000 posts between January 2015 and August 2017. Facebook estimated the IRA reached as many as 126 million persons through its Facebook accounts.[6] In January 2018, Twitter announced that it had identified 3,814 IRA-controlled Twitter accounts and notified approximately 1.4 million people Twitter believed may have been in contact with an IRA-controlled account.[7]

A. Structure of the Internet Research Agency

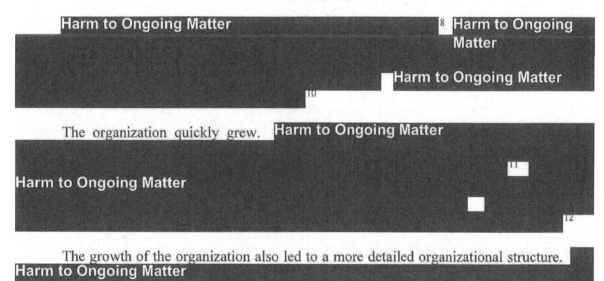

Harm to Ongoing Matter   [8] Harm to Ongoing Matter

Harm to Ongoing Matter

The organization quickly grew. Harm to Ongoing Matter

Harm to Ongoing Matter

The growth of the organization also led to a more detailed organizational structure.

Harm to Ongoing Matter

---

[6] *Social Media Influence in the 2016 U.S. Election, Hearing Before the Senate Select Committee on Intelligence*, 115th Cong. 13 (11/1/17) (testimony of Colin Stretch, General Counsel of Facebook) ("We estimate that roughly 29 million people were served content in their News Feeds directly from the IRA's 80,000 posts over the two years. Posts from these Pages were also shared, liked, and followed by people on Facebook, and, as a result, three times more people may have been exposed to a story that originated from the Russian operation. Our best estimate is that approximately 126 million people may have been served content from a Page associated with the IRA at some point during the two-year period."). The Facebook representative also testified that Facebook had identified 170 Instagram accounts that posted approximately 120,000 pieces of content during that time. Facebook did not offer an estimate of the audience reached via Instagram.

[7] Twitter, Update on Twitter's Review of the 2016 US Election (Jan. 31, 2018).

[8] *See* SM-2230634, serial 92.

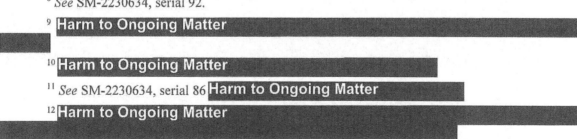

[9] Harm to Ongoing Matter

[10] Harm to Ongoing Matter

[11] *See* SM-2230634, serial 86 Harm to Ongoing Matter

[12] Harm to Ongoing Matter

Harm to Ongoing Matter

[3]

Two individuals headed the IRA's management: its general director, Mikhail Bystrov, and its executive director, Mikhail Burchik. Harm to Ongoing Matter

[14] Harm to Ongoing Matter

[15]

As early as the spring of 2014, the IRA began to hide its funding and activities. Harm to Ongoing Matter

[16]

The IRA's U.S. operations are part of a larger set of interlocking operations known as "Project Lakhta," Harm to Ongoing Matter

[7] Harm to Ongoing Matter

[18]

B. Funding and Oversight from Concord and Prigozhin

Until at least February 2018, Yevgeniy Viktorovich Prigozhin and two Concord companies funded the IRA. Prigozhin is a wealthy Russian businessman who served as the head of Concord.

---

[13] Harm to Ongoing Matter

[14] *See, e.g.,* SM-2230634, serials 9, 113 & 180 Harm to Ongoing Matter
.

[15] Harm to Ongoing Matter

[16] Harm to Ongoing Matter

See SM-2230634, serials 131 & 204.

[17] Harm to Ongoing Matter

[18] Harm to Ongoing Matter

U.S. Department of Justice

~~Attorney Work Product // May Contain Material Protected Under Fed. R. Crim. P. 6(e)~~

Harm to Ongoing Matter

  Prigozhin was sanctioned by the U.S. Treasury Department in December 2016,[19] **Harm to Ongoing Matter**

[20] **Harm to Ongoing Matter**

[1] Numerous media sources have reported on Prigozhin's ties to Putin, and the two have appeared together in public photographs.[22]

Harm to Ongoing Matter

[23] **Harm to Ongoing Matter**

Harm to Ongoing Matter

[4] **Harm to Ongoing Matter**

[5] **Harm to Ongoing Matter**

Harm to Ongoing Matter

---

[19] U.S. Treasury Department, "Treasury Sanctions Individuals and Entities in Connection with Russia's Occupation of Crimea and the Conflict in Ukraine" (Dec. 20, 2016).

[20] **Harm to Ongoing Matter**

[21] **Harm to Ongoing Matter**

[22] *See, e.g.*, Neil MacFarquhar, *Yevgeny Prigozhin, Russian Oligarch Indicted by U.S., Is Known as "Putin's Cook"*, New York Times (Feb. 16, 2018).

[23] **Harm to Ongoing Matter**

[24] **Harm to Ongoing Matter**

[25] **Harm to Ongoing Matter** *see also* SM-2230634, serial 113 HOM

U.S. Department of Justice

~~Attorney Work Product // May Contain Material Protected Under Fed. R. Crim. P. 6(e)~~

Harm to Ongoing Matter

Harm to Ongoing Matter

[26] Harm to Ongoing Matter

[27]

Harm to Ongoing Matter

Harm to Ongoing Matter

[28]

Harm to Ongoing Matter

---

[26] Harm to Ongoing Matter

[27] Harm to Ongoing Matter

[28] The term "troll" refers to internet users—in this context, paid operatives—who post inflammatory or otherwise disruptive content on social media or other websites.

U.S. Department of Justice

~~Attorney Work Product // May Contain Material Protected Under Fed. R. Crim. P. 6(e)~~

IRA employees were aware that Prigozhin was involved in the IRA's U.S. operations,

Harm to Ongoing Matter

Harm to Ongoing Matter[29]

[30] In May 2016, IRA employees, claiming to be U.S. social activists and administrators of Facebook groups, recruited U.S. persons to hold signs (including one in front of the White House) that read "Happy 55th Birthday Dear Boss," as an homage to Prigozhin (whose 55th birthday was on June 1, 2016).[31]

Harm to Ongoing Matter[32]

Harm to Ongoing Matter

C. The IRA Targets U.S. Elections

1. The IRA Ramps Up U.S. Operations As Early As 2014

The IRA's U.S. operations sought to influence public opinion through online media and forums. By the spring of 2014, the IRA began to consolidate U.S. operations within a single general department, known internally as the "Translator" (Переводчик) department. **Harm to Ongoing Matter**

IRA subdivided the Translator Department into different responsibilities, ranging from operations on different social media platforms to analytics to

---

[29] **Investigative Technique** *See* SM-2230634, serials 131 & 204.

[30] *See* SM-2230634, serial 156.

[31] *Internet Research Agency* Indictment ¶ 12(b); *see also* 5/26/16 Facebook Messages, ID 1479936895656747 (United Muslims of America) & **Personal Privacy**

[32] **Harm to Ongoing Matter** *see also* SM-2230634, serial 189. **Harm to Ongoing Matter**

graphics and IT.

Harm to Ongoing Matter

[33] Harm to Ongoing Matter

[34]

Harm to Ongoing Matter

U.S. Department of Justice

~~Attorney Work Product // May Contain Material Protected Under Fed. R. Crim. P. 6(e)~~

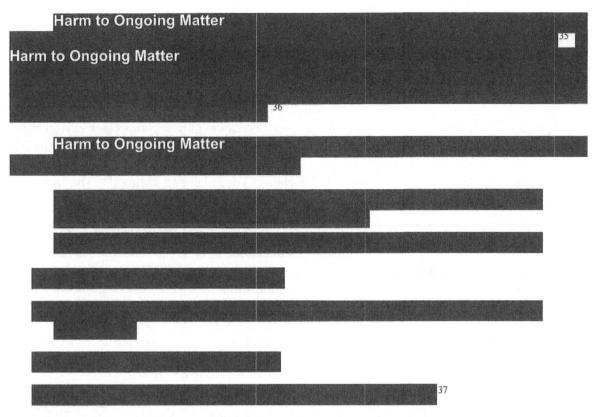

IRA employees also traveled to the United States on intelligence-gathering missions. In June 2014, four IRA employees applied to the U.S. Department of State to enter the United States, while lying about the purpose of their trip and claiming to be four friends who had met at a party.[38] Ultimately, two IRA employees—Anna Bogacheva and Aleksandra Krylova—received visas and entered the United States on June 4, 2014.

Prior to traveling, Krylova and Bogacheva compiled itineraries and instructions for the trip. **Harm to Ongoing Matter**

Harm to Ongoing Matter

---

[35] **Harm to Ongoing Matter**

[36] **Harm to Ongoing Matter**

[37] **Harm to Ongoing Matter**

[38] *See* SM-2230634, serials 150 & 172 **Harm to Ongoing Matter**

[39] **Harm to Ongoing Matter**

Harm to Ongoing Matter
Harm to Ongoing Matter
[40]
[41]

2. U.S. Operations Through IRA-Controlled Social Media Accounts

Dozens of IRA employees were responsible for operating accounts and personas on different U.S. social media platforms. The IRA referred to employees assigned to operate the social media accounts as "specialists."[42] Starting as early as 2014, the IRA's U.S. operations included social media specialists focusing on Facebook, YouTube, and Twitter.[43] The IRA later added specialists who operated on Tumblr and Instagram accounts.[44]

Initially, the IRA created social media accounts that pretended to be the personal accounts of U.S. persons.[45] By early 2015, the IRA began to create larger social media groups or public social media pages that claimed (falsely) to be affiliated with U.S. political and grassroots organizations. In certain cases, the IRA created accounts that mimicked real U.S. organizations. For example, one IRA-controlled Twitter account, @TEN_GOP, purported to be connected to the Tennessee Republican Party.[46] More commonly, the IRA created accounts in the names of fictitious U.S. organizations and grassroots groups and used these accounts to pose as anti-immigration groups, Tea Party activists, Black Lives Matter protestors, and other U.S. social and political activists.

The IRA closely monitored the activity of its social media accounts.
Harm to Ongoing Matter

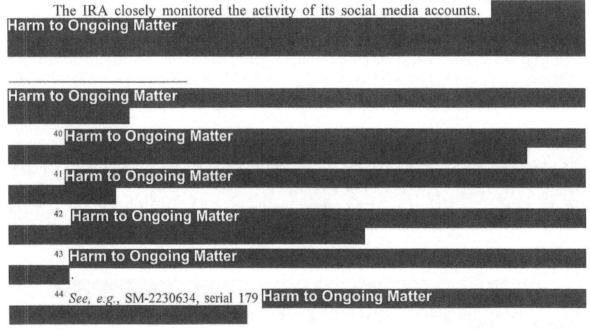

Harm to Ongoing Matter

[40] **Harm to Ongoing Matter**

[41] **Harm to Ongoing Matter**

[42] **Harm to Ongoing Matter**

[43] **Harm to Ongoing Matter**

[44] *See, e.g.,* SM-2230634, serial 179 **Harm to Ongoing Matter**

[45] *See, e.g.,* Facebook ID 100011390466802 (Alex Anderson); Facebook ID 100009626173204 (Andrea Hansen); Facebook ID 100009728618427 (Gary Williams); Facebook ID 100013640043337 (Lakisha Richardson).

[46] The account claimed to be the "Unofficial Twitter of Tennessee Republicans" and made posts that appeared to be endorsements of the state political party. *See, e.g.,* @TEN_GOP, 4/3/16 Tweet ("Tennessee GOP backs @realDonaldTrump period #makeAmericagreatagain #tngop #tennessee #gop").

Harm to Ongoing Matter

Harm to Ongoing Matter

Harm to Ongoing Matter

By February 2016, internal IRA documents referred to support for the Trump Campaign and opposition to candidate Clinton.[49] For example, HOM directions to IRA operators Harm to Ongoing Matter "Main idea: Use any opportunity to criticize Hillary [Clinton] and the rest (except Sanders and Trump - we support them)."[50] Harm to Ongoing Matter

The focus on the U.S. presidential campaign continued throughout 2016. In HOM 2016 internal HOM reviewing the IRA-controlled Facebook group "Secured Borders," the

---

[47] Harm to Ongoing Matter

[48] *See, e.g.*, SM-2230634 serial 131 HOM .

[49] The IRA posted content about the Clinton candidacy before Clinton officially announced her presidential campaign. IRA-controlled social media accounts criticized Clinton's record as Secretary of State and promoted various critiques of her candidacy. The IRA also used other techniques. Harm to Ongoing Matter *See* SM-2230634, serial 70.

[50] Harm to Ongoing Matter

author criticized the "lower number of posts dedicated to criticizing Hillary Clinton" and reminded the Facebook specialist "it is imperative to intensify criticizing Hillary Clinton."[51]

IRA employees also acknowledged that their work focused on influencing the U.S. presidential election. Harm to Ongoing Matter

Harm to Ongoing Matter

[52]

3. U.S. Operations Through Facebook

Many IRA operations used Facebook accounts created and operated by its specialists. Harm to Ongoing Matter

Harm to Ongoing Matter

[53]

Harm to Ongoing Matter

[4] IRA Facebook groups active during the 2016 campaign covered a range of political issues and included purported conservative

---

[51] Harm to Ongoing Matter

[52] Harm to Ongoing Matter

[53] Harm to Ongoing Matter

[54] Harm to Ongoing Matter

U.S. Department of Justice

~~Attorney Work Product // May Contain Material Protected Under Fed. R. Crim. P. 6(e)~~

groups (with names such as "Being Patriotic," "Stop All Immigrants," "Secured Borders," and "Tea Party News"), purported Black social justice groups ("Black Matters," "Blacktivist," and "Don't Shoot Us"), LGBTQ groups ("LGBT United"), and religious groups ("United Muslims of America").

Throughout 2016, IRA accounts published an increasing number of materials supporting the Trump Campaign and opposing the Clinton Campaign. For example, on May 31, 2016, the operational account "Matt Skiber" began to privately message dozens of pro-Trump Facebook groups asking them to help plan a "pro-Trump rally near Trump Tower."[55]

To reach larger U.S. audiences, the IRA purchased advertisements from Facebook that promoted the IRA groups on the newsfeeds of U.S. audience members. According to Facebook, the IRA purchased over 3,500 advertisements, and the expenditures totaled approximately $100,000.[56]

During the U.S. presidential campaign, many IRA-purchased advertisements explicitly supported or opposed a presidential candidate or promoted U.S. rallies organized by the IRA (discussed below). As early as March 2016, the IRA purchased advertisements that overtly opposed the Clinton Campaign. For example, on March 18, 2016, the IRA purchased an advertisement depicting candidate Clinton and a caption that read in part, "If one day God lets this liar enter the White House as a president – that day would be a real national tragedy."[57] Similarly, on April 6, 2016, the IRA purchased advertisements for its account "Black Matters" calling for a "flashmob" of U.S. persons to "take a photo with #HillaryClintonForPrison2016 or #nohillary2016."[58] IRA-purchased advertisements featuring Clinton were, with very few exceptions, negative.[59]

IRA-purchased advertisements referencing candidate Trump largely supported his campaign. The first known IRA advertisement explicitly endorsing the Trump Campaign was purchased on April 19, 2016. The IRA bought an advertisement for its Instagram account "Tea Party News" asking U.S. persons to help them "make a patriotic team of young Trump supporters" by uploading photos with the hashtag "#KIDS4TRUMP."[60] In subsequent months, the IRA purchased dozens of advertisements supporting the Trump Campaign, predominantly through the Facebook groups "Being Patriotic," "Stop All Invaders," and "Secured Borders."

---

[55] 5/31/16 Facebook Message, ID 100009922908461 (Matt Skiber) to ID ███████
5/31/16 Facebook Message, ID 100009922908461 (Matt Skiber) to ID
███████████ Personal Privacy ██████████

[56] *Social Media Influence in the 2016 U.S. Election, Hearing Before the Senate Select Committee on Intelligence*, 115th Cong. 13 (11/1/17) (testimony of Colin Stretch, General Counsel of Facebook).

[57] 3/18/16 Facebook Advertisement ID 6045505152575.

[58] 4/6/16 Facebook Advertisement ID 6043740225319.

[59] *See* SM-2230634, serial 213 (documenting politically-oriented advertisements from the larger set provided by Facebook).

[60] 4/19/16 Facebook Advertisement ID 6045151094235.

U.S. Department of Justice

~~Attorney Work Product // May Contain Material Protected Under Fed. R. Crim. P. 6(e)~~

Collectively, the IRA's social media accounts reached tens of millions of U.S. persons. Individual IRA social media accounts attracted hundreds of thousands of followers. For example, at the time they were deactivated by Facebook in mid-2017, the IRA's "United Muslims of America" Facebook group had over 300,000 followers, the "Don't Shoot Us" Facebook group had over 250,000 followers, the "Being Patriotic" Facebook group had over 200,000 followers, and the "Secured Borders" Facebook group had over 130,000 followers.[61] According to Facebook, in total the IRA-controlled accounts made over 80,000 posts before their deactivation in August 2017, and these posts reached at least 29 million U.S persons and "may have reached an estimated 126 million people."[62]

4. U.S. Operations Through Twitter

A number of IRA employees assigned to the Translator Department served as Twitter specialists. Harm to Ongoing Matter

[63]

The IRA's Twitter operations involved two strategies. First, IRA specialists operated certain Twitter accounts to create individual U.S. personas, Harm to Ongoing Matter

[4] Separately, the IRA operated a network of automated Twitter accounts (commonly referred to as a bot network) that enabled the IRA to amplify existing content on Twitter.

a. Individualized Accounts

Harm to Ongoing Matter

[65] Harm to Ongoing Matter

---

[61] *See* Facebook ID 1479936895656747 (United Muslims of America); Facebook ID 1157233400960126 (Don't Shoot); Facebook ID 1601685693432389 (Being Patriotic); Facebook ID 757183957716200 (Secured Borders). Harm to Ongoing Matter

Harm to Ongoing Matter

Harm to Ongoing Matter

[62] *Social Media Influence in the 2016 U.S. Election, Hearing Before the Senate Select Committee on Intelligence*, 115th Cong. 13 (11/1/17) (testimony of Colin Stretch, General Counsel of Facebook).

[63] Harm to Ongoing Matter

[64] Harm to Ongoing Matter

[65] Harm to Ongoing Matter

U.S. Department of Justice

~~Attorney Work Product // May Contain Material Protected Under Fed. R. Crim. P. 6(e)~~

Harm to Ongoing Matter [66]

The IRA operated individualized Twitter accounts similar to the operation of its Facebook accounts, by continuously posting original content to the accounts while also communicating with U.S. Twitter users directly (through public tweeting or Twitter's private messaging).

The IRA used many of these accounts to attempt to influence U.S. audiences on the election. Individualized accounts used to influence the U.S. presidential election included @TEN_GOP (described above); @jenn_abrams (claiming to be a Virginian Trump supporter with 70,000 followers); @Pamela_Moore13 (claiming to be a Texan Trump supporter with 70,000 followers); and @America_1st_ (an anti-immigration persona with 24,000 followers).[67] In May 2016, the IRA created the Twitter account @march_for_trump, which promoted IRA-organized rallies in support of the Trump Campaign (described below).[68]

Using these accounts and others, the IRA provoked reactions from users and the media. Multiple IRA-posted tweets gained popularity.[70] U.S. media outlets also quoted tweets from IRA-controlled accounts and attributed them to the reactions of real U.S. persons.[71] Similarly, numerous high-

---

[66] **Harm to Ongoing Matter**

[67] Other individualized accounts included @MissouriNewsUS (an account with 3,800 followers that posted pro-Sanders and anti-Clinton material).

[68] *See* @march_for_trump, 5/30/16 Tweet (first post from account).

[69] **Harm to Ongoing Matter**

[70] For example, one IRA account tweeted, "To those people, who hate the Confederate flag. Did you know that the flag and the war wasn't about slavery, it was all about money." The tweet received over 40,000 responses. @Jenn_Abrams 4/24/17 (2:37 p.m.) Tweet.

[71] Josephine Lukito & Chris Wells, *Most Major Outlets Have Used Russian Tweets as Sources for Partisan Opinion: Study*, Columbia Journalism Review (Mar. 8, 2018); *see also Twitter Steps Up to Explain #NewYorkValues to Ted Cruz*, Washington Post (Jan. 15, 2016) (citing IRA tweet); *People Are Slamming the CIA for Claiming Russia Tried to Help Donald Trump*, U.S. News & World Report (Dec. 12, 2016).

U.S. Department of Justice

~~Attorney Work Product // May Contain Material Protected Under Fed. R. Crim. P. 6(e)~~

profile U.S. persons, including former Ambassador Michael McFaul,[72] Roger Stone,[73] Sean Hannity,[74] and Michael Flynn Jr.,[75] retweeted or responded to tweets posted to these IRA-controlled accounts. Multiple individuals affiliated with the Trump Campaign also promoted IRA tweets (discussed below).

b. IRA Botnet Activities

In January 2018, Twitter publicly identified 3,814 Twitter accounts associated with the IRA.[79] According to Twitter, in the ten weeks before the 2016 U.S. presidential election, these accounts posted approximately 175,993 tweets, "approximately 8.4% of which were election-

---

[72] @McFaul 4/30/16 Tweet (responding to tweet by @Jenn_Abrams).

[73] @RogerJStoneJr 5/30/16 Tweet (retweeting @Pamela_Moore13); @RogerJStoneJr 4/26/16 Tweet (same).

[74] @seanhannity 6/21/17 Tweet (retweeting @Pamela_Moore13).

[75] @mflynnJR 6/22/17 Tweet ("RT @Jenn_Abrams: This is what happens when you add the voice over of an old documentary about mental illness onto video of SJWs. . .").

[76] A botnet refers to a network of private computers or accounts controlled as a group to send specific automated messages. On the Twitter network, botnets can be used to promote and republish ("retweet") specific tweets or hashtags in order for them to gain larger audiences.

[77] Harm to Ongoing Matter

[78] Harm to Ongoing Matter

[79] Eli Rosenberg, *Twitter to Tell 677,000 Users they Were Had by the Russians. Some Signs Show the Problem Continues*, Washington Post (Jan. 19, 2019).

U.S. Department of Justice

Attorney Work Product // May Contain Material Protected Under Fed. R. Crim. P. 6(e)

related."[80] Twitter also announced that it had notified approximately 1.4 million people who Twitter believed may have been in contact with an IRA-controlled account.[81]

5. U.S. Operations Involving Political Rallies

The IRA organized and promoted political rallies inside the United States while posing as U.S. grassroots activists. First, the IRA used one of its preexisting social media personas (Facebook groups and Twitter accounts, for example) to announce and promote the event. The IRA then sent a large number of direct messages to followers of its social media account asking them to attend the event. From those who responded with interest in attending, the IRA then sought a U.S. person to serve as the event's coordinator. In most cases, the IRA account operator would tell the U.S. person that they personally could not attend the event due to some preexisting conflict or because they were somewhere else in the United States.[82] The IRA then further promoted the event by contacting U.S. media about the event and directing them to speak with the coordinator.[83] After the event, the IRA posted videos and photographs of the event to the IRA's social media accounts.[84]

The Office identified dozens of U.S. rallies organized by the IRA. The earliest evidence of a rally was a "confederate rally" in November 2015.[85] The IRA continued to organize rallies even after the 2016 U.S. presidential election. The attendance at rallies varied. Some rallies appear to have drawn few (if any) participants, while others drew hundreds. The reach and success of these rallies was closely monitored [Harm to Ongoing Matter]

---

[80] Twitter, "Update on Twitter's Review of the 2016 US Election" (updated Jan. 31, 2018). Twitter also reported identifying 50,258 automated accounts connected to the Russian government, which tweeted more than a million times in the ten weeks before the election.

[81] Twitter, "Update on Twitter's Review of the 2016 US Election" (updated Jan. 31, 2018).

[82] 8/20/16 Facebook Message, ID 100009922908461 (Matt Skiber) to ID [redacted].

[83] See, e.g., 7/21/16 Email, joshmilton024@gmail.com to [redacted]; 7/21/16 Email, joshmilton024@gmail.com to [Personal Privacy]

[84] @march_for_trump 6/25/16 Tweet (posting photos from rally outside Trump Tower).

[85] Instagram ID 2228012168 (Stand For Freedom) 11/3/15 Post ("Good evening buds! Well I am planning to organize a confederate rally [. . .] in Houston on the 14 of November and I want more people to attend.").

Harm to Ongoing Matter

Harm to Ongoing Matter

U.S. Department of Justice

~~Attorney Work Product // May Contain Material Protected Under Fed. R. Crim. P. 6(e)~~

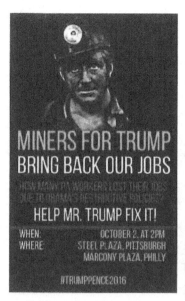

*IRA Poster for Pennsylvania
Rallies organized by the IRA*

From June 2016 until the end of the presidential campaign, almost all of the U.S. rallies organized by the IRA focused on the U.S. election, often promoting the Trump Campaign and opposing the Clinton Campaign. Pro-Trump rallies included three in New York; a series of pro-Trump rallies in Florida in August 2016; and a series of pro-Trump rallies in October 2016 in Pennsylvania. The Florida rallies drew the attention of the Trump Campaign, which posted about the Miami rally on candidate Trump's Facebook account (as discussed below).[86]

Many of the same IRA employees who oversaw the IRA's social media accounts also conducted the day-to-day recruiting for political rallies inside the United States. **Harm to Ongoing Matter**

[87]

6. Targeting and Recruitment of U.S. Persons

As early as 2014, the IRA instructed its employees to target U.S. persons who could be used to advance its operational goals. Initially, recruitment focused on U.S. persons who could amplify the content posted by the IRA. **Harm to Ongoing Matter**

Harm to Ongoing Matter

[88]

IRA employees frequently used **Investigative Technique** Twitter, Facebook, and Instagram to contact and recruit U.S. persons who followed the group. The IRA recruited U.S. persons from across the political spectrum. For example, the IRA targeted the family of **Personal Privacy** and a number of black social justice activists

---

[86] The pro-Trump rallies were organized through multiple Facebook, Twitter, and email accounts. *See, e.g.,* Facebook ID 100009922908461 (Matt Skiber); Facebook ID 1601685693432389 (Being Patriotic); Twitter Account @march_for_trump; beingpatriotic@gmail.com. (Rallies were organized in New York on June 25, 2016; Florida on August 20, 2016; and Pennsylvania on October 2, 2016.)

[87] **Harm to Ongoing Matter**

[88] **Harm to Ongoing Matter**

U.S. Department of Justice

~~Attorney Work Product // May Contain Material Protected Under Fed. R. Crim. P. 6(e)~~

while posing as a grassroots group called "Black Matters US."[89] In February 2017, the persona "Black Fist" (purporting to want to teach African-Americans to protect themselves when contacted by law enforcement) hired a self-defense instructor in New York to offer classes sponsored by Black Fist. The IRA also recruited moderators of conservative social media groups to promote IRA-generated content,[90] as well as recruited individuals to perform political acts (such as walking around New York City dressed up as Santa Claus with a Trump mask).[91]

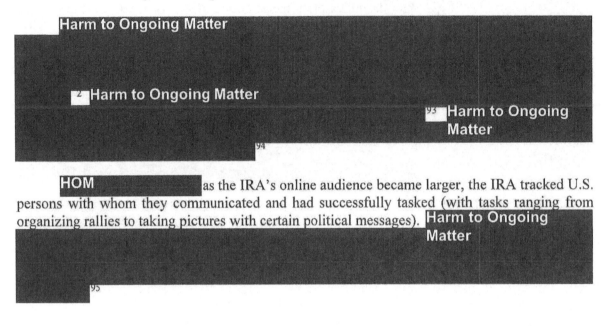

HOM as the IRA's online audience became larger, the IRA tracked U.S. persons with whom they communicated and had successfully tasked (with tasks ranging from organizing rallies to taking pictures with certain political messages). Harm to Ongoing Matter [95]

---

[89] 3/11/16 Facebook Advertisement ID 6045078289928, 5/6/16 Facebook Advertisement ID 6051652423528, 10/26/16 Facebook Advertisement ID 6055238604687; 10/27/16 Facebook Message, ID [Personal Privacy] & ID 100011698576461 (Taylor Brooks).

[90] 8/19/16 Facebook Message, ID 100009922908461 (Matt Skiber) to ID [PP]

[91] 12/8/16 Email, robot@craigslist.org to beingpatriotic@gmail.com (confirming Craigslist advertisement).

[92] 8/18-19/16 Twitter DMs, @march_for_trump & [PP]

[93] *See, e.g.,* 11/11-27/16 Facebook Messages, ID 100011698576461 (Taylor Brooks) & ID [Personal Privacy] (arranging to pay for plane tickets and for a bull horn).

[94] *See, e.g.,* 9/10/16 Facebook Message, ID 100009922908461 (Matt Skiber) & ID [Personal Privacy] (discussing payment for rally supplies); 8/18/16 Twitter DM, @march_for_trump to [PP] (discussing payment for construction materials).

[95] Harm to Ongoing Matter

U.S. Department of Justice

~~Attorney Work Product // May Contain Material Protected Under Fed. R. Crim. P. 6(e)~~

Harm to Ongoing Matter

7. Interactions and Contacts with the Trump Campaign

The investigation identified two different forms of connections between the IRA and members of the Trump Campaign. (The investigation identified no similar connections between the IRA and the Clinton Campaign.) First, on multiple occasions, members and surrogates of the Trump Campaign promoted—typically by linking, retweeting, or similar methods of reposting— pro-Trump or anti-Clinton content published by the IRA through IRA-controlled social media accounts. Additionally, in a few instances, IRA employees represented themselves as U.S. persons to communicate with members of the Trump Campaign in an effort to seek assistance and coordination on IRA-organized political rallies inside the United States.

a. *Trump Campaign Promotion of IRA Political Materials*

Among the U.S. "leaders of public opinion" targeted by the IRA were various members and surrogates of the Trump Campaign. In total, Trump Campaign affiliates promoted dozens of tweets, posts, and other political content created by the IRA.

- Posts from the IRA-controlled Twitter account @TEN_GOP were cited or retweeted by multiple Trump Campaign officials and surrogates, including Donald J. Trump Jr.,[96] Eric

---

[96] *See, e.g.,* @DonaldJTrumpJr 10/26/16 Tweet ("RT @TEN_GOP: BREAKING Thousands of names changed on voter rolls in Indiana. Police investigating #VoterFraud. #DrainTheSwamp."); @DonaldJTrumpJr 11/2/16 Tweet ("RT @TEN_GOP: BREAKING: #VoterFraud by counting tens of thousands of ineligible mail in Hillary votes being reported in Broward County, Florida."); @DonaldJTrumpJr 11/8/16 Tweet ("RT @TEN_GOP: This vet passed away last month before he could vote for Trump. Here he is in his #MAGA hat. #voted #ElectionDay."). Trump Jr. retweeted additional @TEN_GOP content subsequent to the election.

U.S. Department of Justice

~~Attorney Work Product // May Contain Material Protected Under Fed. R. Crim. P. 6(e)~~

Trump,[97] Kellyanne Conway,[98] Brad Parscale,[99] and Michael T. Flynn.[100] These posts included allegations of voter fraud,[101] as well as allegations that Secretary Clinton had mishandled classified information.[102]

- A November 7, 2016 post from the IRA-controlled Twitter account @Pamela_Moore13 was retweeted by Donald J. Trump Jr.[103]

- On September 19, 2017, President Trump's personal account @realDonaldTrump responded to a tweet from the IRA-controlled account @10_gop (the backup account of @TEN_GOP, which had already been deactivated by Twitter). The tweet read: "We love you, Mr. President!"[104]

IRA employees monitored the reaction of the Trump Campaign and, later, Trump Administration officials to their tweets. For example, on August 23, 2016, the IRA-controlled persona "Matt Skiber" Facebook account sent a message to a U.S. Tea Party activist, writing that "Mr. Trump posted about our event in Miami! This is great!"[105] The IRA employee included a screenshot of candidate Trump's Facebook account, which included a post about the August 20, 2016 political rallies organized by the IRA.

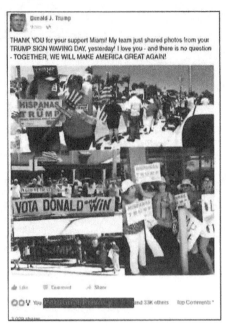

Screenshot of Trump Facebook Account (from Matt Skiber)

---

[97] @EricTrump 10/20/16 Tweet ("RT @TEN_GOP: BREAKING Hillary shuts down press conference when asked about DNC Operatives corruption & #VoterFraud #debatenight #TrumpB").

[98] @KellyannePolls 11/6/16 Tweet ("RT @TEN_GOP: Mother of jailed sailor: 'Hold Hillary to same standards as my son on Classified info' #hillarysemail #WeinerGate.").

[99] @parscale 10/15/16 Tweet ("Thousands of deplorables chanting to the media: 'Tell The Truth!' RT if you are also done w/ biased Media! #FridayFeeling").

[100] @GenFlynn 11/7/16 (retweeting @TEN_GOP post that included in part "@realDonaldTrump & @mike_pence will be our next POTUS & VPOTUS.").

[101] @TEN_GOP 10/11/16 Tweet ("North Carolina finds 2,214 voters over the age of 110!!").

[102] @TEN_GOP 11/6/16 Tweet ("Mother of jailed sailor: 'Hold Hillary to same standards as my son on classified info #hillaryemail #WeinerGate.'").

[103] @DonaldJTrumpJr 11/7/16 Tweet ("RT @Pamela_Moore13: Detroit residents speak out against the failed policies of Obama, Hillary & democrats . . . .").

[104] @realDonaldTrump 9/19/17 (7:33 p.m.) Tweet ("THANK YOU for your support Miami! My team just shared photos from your TRUMP SIGN WAVING DAY, yesterday! I love you – and there is no question – TOGETHER, WE WILL MAKE AMERICA GREAT AGAIN!").

[105] 8/23/16 Facebook Message, ID 100009922908461 (Matt Skiber) to ID

U.S. Department of Justice

~~Attorney Work Product // May Contain Material Protected Under Fed. R. Crim. P. 6(e)~~

Harm to Ongoing Matter

[106]

b. Contact with Trump Campaign Officials in Connection to Rallies

Starting in June 2016, the IRA contacted different U.S. persons affiliated with the Trump Campaign in an effort to coordinate pro-Trump IRA-organized rallies inside the United States. In all cases, the IRA contacted the Campaign while claiming to be U.S. political activists working on behalf of a conservative grassroots organization. The IRA's contacts included requests for signs and other materials to use at rallies,[107] as well as requests to promote the rallies and help coordinate logistics.[108] While certain campaign volunteers agreed to provide the requested support (for example, agreeing to set aside a number of signs), the investigation has not identified evidence that any Trump Campaign official understood the requests were coming from foreign nationals.

* * *

In sum, the investigation established that Russia interfered in the 2016 presidential election through the "active measures" social media campaign carried out by the IRA, an organization funded by Prigozhin and companies that he controlled. As explained further in Volume I, Section V.A, *infra*, the Office concluded (and a grand jury has alleged) that Prigozhin, his companies, and IRA employees violated U.S. law through these operations, principally by undermining through deceptive acts the work of federal agencies charged with regulating foreign influence in U.S. elections.

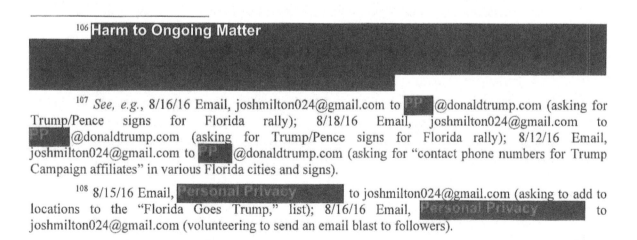

---

[106] **Harm to Ongoing Matter**

[107] *See, e.g.,* 8/16/16 Email, joshmilton024@gmail.com to [PP] @donaldtrump.com (asking for Trump/Pence signs for Florida rally); 8/18/16 Email, joshmilton024@gmail.com to [PP] @donaldtrump.com (asking for Trump/Pence signs for Florida rally); 8/12/16 Email, joshmilton024@gmail.com to [PP] @donaldtrump.com (asking for "contact phone numbers for Trump Campaign affiliates" in various Florida cities and signs).

[108] 8/15/16 Email, [Personal Privacy] to joshmilton024@gmail.com (asking to add to locations to the "Florida Goes Trump," list); 8/16/16 Email, [Personal Privacy] to joshmilton024@gmail.com (volunteering to send an email blast to followers).

U.S. Department of Justice

~~Attorney Work Product~~ // ~~May Contain Material Protected Under Fed. R. Crim. P. 6(e)~~

III. RUSSIAN HACKING AND DUMPING OPERATIONS

Beginning in March 2016, units of the Russian Federation's Main Intelligence Directorate of the General Staff (GRU) hacked the computers and email accounts of organizations, employees, and volunteers supporting the Clinton Campaign, including the email account of campaign chairman John Podesta. Starting in April 2016, the GRU hacked into the computer networks of the Democratic Congressional Campaign Committee (DCCC) and the Democratic National Committee (DNC). The GRU targeted hundreds of email accounts used by Clinton Campaign employees, advisors, and volunteers. In total, the GRU stole hundreds of thousands of documents from the compromised email accounts and networks.[109] The GRU later released stolen Clinton Campaign and DNC documents through online personas, "DCLeaks" and "Guccifer 2.0," and later through the organization WikiLeaks. The release of the documents was designed and timed to interfere with the 2016 U.S. presidential election and undermine the Clinton Campaign.

The Trump Campaign showed interest in the WikiLeaks releases and, in the summer and fall of 2016, Harm to Ongoing Matter After HOM WikiLeaks's first Clinton-related release HOM , the Trump Campaign stayed in contact HOM about WikiLeaks's activities. The investigation was unable to resolve Harm to Ongoing Matter WikiLeaks's release of the stolen Podesta emails on October 7, 2016, the same day a video from years earlier was published of Trump using graphic language about women.

A. GRU Hacking Directed at the Clinton Campaign

1. GRU Units Target the Clinton Campaign

Two military units of the GRU carried out the computer intrusions into the Clinton Campaign, DNC, and DCCC: Military Units 26165 and 74455.[110] Military Unit 26165 is a GRU cyber unit dedicated to targeting military, political, governmental, and non-governmental organizations outside of Russia, including in the United States.[111] The unit was sub-divided into departments with different specialties. One department, for example, developed specialized malicious software ("malware"), while another department conducted large-scale spearphishing campaigns.[112] Investigative Technique a bitcoin mining operation to

---

[109] As discussed in Section V below, our Office charged 12 GRU officers for crimes arising from the hacking of these computers, principally with conspiring to commit computer intrusions, in violation of 18 U.S.C. §§1030 and 371. *See* Volume I, Section V.B, *infra*; Indictment, *United States v. Netyksho*, No. 1:18-cr-215 (D.D.C. July 13, 2018), Doc. 1 ("*Netyksho* Indictment").

[110] *Netyksho* Indictment ¶ 1.

[111] Separate from this Office's indictment of GRU officers, in October 2018 a grand jury sitting in the Western District of Pennsylvania returned an indictment charging certain members of Unit 26165 with hacking the U.S. Anti-Doping Agency, the World Anti-Doping Agency, and other international sport associations. *United States v. Aleksei Sergeyevich Morenets*, No. 18-263 (W.D. Pa.).

[112] A spearphishing email is designed to appear as though it originates from a trusted source, and solicits information to enable the sender to gain access to an account or network, or causes the recipient to

U.S. Department of Justice

~~Attorney Work Product // May Contain Material Protected Under Fed. R. Crim. P. 6(e)~~

secure bitcoins used to purchase computer infrastructure used in hacking operations.[113]

Military Unit 74455 is a related GRU unit with multiple departments that engaged in cyber operations. Unit 74455 assisted in the release of documents stolen by Unit 26165, the promotion of those releases, and the publication of anti-Clinton content on social media accounts operated by the GRU. Officers from Unit 74455 separately hacked computers belonging to state boards of elections, secretaries of state, and U.S. companies that supplied software and other technology related to the administration of U.S. elections.[114]

Beginning in mid-March 2016, Unit 26165 had primary responsibility for hacking the DCCC and DNC, as well as email accounts of individuals affiliated with the Clinton Campaign:[115]

- Unit 26165 used ▮IT▮ ▮▮▮▮▮▮▮▮ to learn about ▮Investigative Technique▮ different Democratic websites, including democrats.org, hillaryclinton.com, dnc.org, and dccc.org. ▮Investigative Technique▮ ▮▮▮▮▮▮▮▮▮ began before the GRU had obtained any credentials or gained access to these networks, indicating that the later DCCC and DNC intrusions were not crimes of opportunity but rather the result of targeting.[116]

- GRU officers also sent hundreds of spearphishing emails to the work and personal email accounts of Clinton Campaign employees and volunteers. Between March 10, 2016 and March 15, 2016, Unit 26165 appears to have sent approximately 90 spearphishing emails to email accounts at hillaryclinton.com. Starting on March 15, 2016, the GRU began targeting Google email accounts used by Clinton Campaign employees, along with a smaller number of dnc.org email accounts.[117]

The GRU spearphishing operation enabled it to gain access to numerous email accounts of Clinton Campaign employees and volunteers, including campaign chairman John Podesta, junior volunteers assigned to the Clinton Campaign's advance team, informal Clinton Campaign advisors, and a DNC employee.[118] GRU officers stole tens of thousands of emails from spearphishing victims, including various Clinton Campaign-related communications.

---

download malware that enables the sender to gain access to an account or network. *Netyksho* Indictment ¶ 10.

[113] Bitcoin mining consists of unlocking new bitcoins by solving computational problems. ▮IT▮ ▮▮▮▮ kept its newly mined coins in an account on the bitcoin exchange platform CEX.io. To make purchases, the GRU routed funds into other accounts through transactions designed to obscure the source of funds. *Netyksho* Indictment ¶ 62.

[114] *Netyksho* Indictment ¶ 69.

[115] *Netyksho* Indictment ¶ 9.

[116] *See* SM-2589105, serials 144 & 495.

[117] ▮Investigative Technique▮ ▮▮▮▮▮▮▮▮▮▮

[118] ▮Investigative Technique▮

U.S. Department of Justice

Attorney Work Product // May Contain Material Protected Under Fed. R. Crim. P. 6(e)

2. Intrusions into the DCCC and DNC Networks

a. *Initial Access*

By no later than April 12, 2016, the GRU had gained access to the DCCC computer network using the credentials stolen from a DCCC employee who had been successfully spearphished the week before. Over the ensuing weeks, the GRU traversed the network, identifying different computers connected to the DCCC network. By stealing network access credentials along the way (including those of IT administrators with unrestricted access to the system), the GRU compromised approximately 29 different computers on the DCCC network.[119]

Approximately six days after first hacking into the DCCC network, on April 18, 2016, GRU officers gained access to the DNC network via a virtual private network (VPN) connection[120] between the DCCC and DNC networks.[121] Between April 18, 2016 and June 8, 2016, Unit 26165 compromised more than 30 computers on the DNC network, including the DNC mail server and shared file server.[122]

b. *Implantation of Malware on DCCC and DNC Networks*

Unit 26165 implanted on the DCCC and DNC networks two types of customized malware,[123] known as "X-Agent" and "X-Tunnel"; Mimikatz, a credential-harvesting tool; and rar.exe, a tool used in these intrusions to compile and compress materials for exfiltration. X-Agent was a multi-function hacking tool that allowed Unit 26165 to log keystrokes, take screenshots, and gather other data about the infected computers (*e.g.*, file directories, operating systems).[124] X-Tunnel was a hacking tool that created an encrypted connection between the victim DCCC/DNC computers and GRU-controlled computers outside the DCCC and DNC networks that was capable of large-scale data transfers.[125] GRU officers then used X-Tunnel to exfiltrate stolen data from the victim computers.

---

[119] Investigative Technique

[120] A VPN extends a private network, allowing users to send and receive data across public networks (such as the internet) as if the connecting computer was directly connected to the private network. The VPN in this case had been created to give a small number of DCCC employees access to certain databases housed on the DNC network. Therefore, while the DCCC employees were outside the DNC's private network, they could access parts of the DNC network from their DCCC computers.

[121] Investigative Technique
SM-2589105-HACK, serial 5.

[122] Investigative Technique
M-2589105-HACK, serial 5.

[123] "Malware" is short for malicious software, and here refers to software designed to allow a third party to infiltrate a computer without the consent or knowledge of the computer's user or operator.

[124] Investigative Technique

[125] Investigative Technique

U.S. Department of Justice

~~Attorney Work Product // May Contain Material Protected Under Fed. R. Crim. P. 6(e)~~

To operate X-Agent and X-Tunnel on the DCCC and DNC networks, Unit 26165 officers set up a group of computers outside those networks to communicate with the implanted malware.[126] The first set of GRU-controlled computers, known by the GRU as "middle servers," sent and received messages to and from malware on the DNC/DCCC networks. The middle servers, in turn, relayed messages to a second set of GRU-controlled computers, labeled internally by the GRU as an "AMS Panel." The AMS Panel ▚Investigative Technique▚ served as a nerve center through which GRU officers monitored and directed the malware's operations on the DNC/DCCC networks.[127]

The AMS Panel used to control X-Agent during the DCCC and DNC intrusions was housed on a leased computer located near ▚IT▚ Arizona.[128] ▚Investigative Technique▚

[129]

▚Investigative Technique▚

▚Investigative Technique▚

---

[126] In connection with these intrusions, the GRU used computers (virtual private networks, dedicated servers operated by hosting companies, etc.) that it leased from third-party providers located all over the world. The investigation identified rental agreements and payments for computers located in, *inter alia,* ▚Investigative Technique▚ all of which were used in the operations targeting the U.S. election.

[127] *Netyksho* Indictment ¶ 25.

[128] *Netyksho* Indictment ¶ 24(c).

[129] *Netyksho* Indictment ¶ 24(b).

The Arizona-based AMS Panel also stored thousands of files containing keylogging sessions captured through X-Agent. These sessions were captured as GRU officers monitored DCCC and DNC employees' work on infected computers regularly between April 2016 and June 2016. Data captured in these keylogging sessions included passwords, internal communications between employees, banking information, and sensitive personal information.

c. Theft of Documents from DNC and DCCC Networks

Officers from Unit 26165 stole thousands of documents from the DCCC and DNC networks, including significant amounts of data pertaining to the 2016 U.S. federal elections. Stolen documents included internal strategy documents, fundraising data, opposition research, and emails from the work inboxes of DNC employees.[130]

The GRU began stealing DCCC data shortly after it gained access to the network. On April 14, 2016 (approximately three days after the initial intrusion) GRU officers downloaded rar.exe onto the DCCC's document server. The following day, the GRU searched one compromised DCCC computer for files containing search terms that included "Hillary," "DNC," "Cruz," and "Trump."[131] On April 25, 2016, the GRU collected and compressed PDF and Microsoft documents from folders on the DCCC's shared file server that pertained to the 2016 election.[132] The GRU appears to have compressed and exfiltrated over 70 gigabytes of data from this file server.[133]

The GRU also stole documents from the DNC network shortly after gaining access. On April 22, 2016, the GRU copied files from the DNC network to GRU-controlled computers. Stolen documents included the DNC's opposition research into candidate Trump.[134] Between approximately May 25, 2016 and June 1, 2016, GRU officers accessed the DNC's mail server from a GRU-controlled computer leased inside the United States.[135] During these connections,

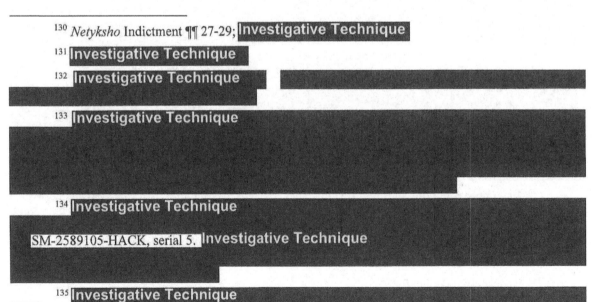

[130] *Netyksho* Indictment ¶¶ 27-29; Investigative Technique

[131] Investigative Technique

[132] Investigative Technique

[133] Investigative Technique

[134] Investigative Technique

SM-2589105-HACK, serial 5. Investigative Technique

[135] Investigative Technique

   See SM-2589105-GJ, serial 649. As part of its investigation, the FBI later received images of DNC servers and copies of relevant traffic logs. *Netyksho* Indictment ¶¶ 28-29.

U.S. Department of Justice

~~Attorney Work Product // May Contain Material Protected Under Fed. R. Crim. P. 6(e)~~

Unit 26165 officers appear to have stolen thousands of emails and attachments, which were later released by WikiLeaks in July 2016.[136]

B. Dissemination of the Hacked Materials

The GRU's operations extended beyond stealing materials, and included releasing documents stolen from the Clinton Campaign and its supporters. The GRU carried out the anonymous release through two fictitious online personas that it created—DCLeaks and Guccifer 2.0—and later through the organization WikiLeaks.

1. DCLeaks

The GRU began planning the releases at least as early as April 19, 2016, when Unit 26165 registered the domain dcleaks.com through a service that anonymized the registrant.[137] Unit 26165 paid for the registration using a pool of bitcoin that it had mined.[138] The dcleaks.com landing page pointed to different tranches of stolen documents, arranged by victim or subject matter. Other dcleaks.com pages contained indexes of the stolen emails that were being released (bearing the sender, recipient, and date of the email). To control access and the timing of releases, pages were sometimes password-protected for a period of time and later made unrestricted to the public.

Starting in June 2016, the GRU posted stolen documents onto the website dcleaks.com, including documents stolen from a number of individuals associated with the Clinton Campaign. These documents appeared to have originated from personal email accounts (in particular, Google and Microsoft accounts), rather than the DNC and DCCC computer networks. DCLeaks victims included an advisor to the Clinton Campaign, a former DNC employee and Clinton Campaign employee, and four other campaign volunteers.[139] The GRU released through dcleaks.com thousands of documents, including personal identifying and financial information, internal correspondence related to the Clinton Campaign and prior political jobs, and fundraising files and information.[140]

---

[136] *Netyksho* Indictment ¶ 29. The last-in-time DNC email released by WikiLeaks was dated May 25, 2016, the same period of time during which the GRU gained access to the DNC's email server. *Netyksho* Indictment ¶ 45.

[137] *Netyksho* Indictment ¶ 35. Approximately a week before the registration of dcleaks.com, the same actors attempted to register the website electionleaks.com using the same domain registration service. **Investigative Technique**

[138] *See* SM-2589105, serial 181; *Netyksho* Indictment ¶ 21(a).

[139] **Investigative Technique**

[140] *See, e.g.*, Internet Archive, "https://dcleaks.com/" (archive date Nov. 10, 2016). Additionally, DCLeaks released documents relating to **Personal Privacy**, emails belonging to **PP**, and emails from 2015 relating to Republican Party employees (under the portfolio name "The United States Republican Party"). "The United States Republican Party" portfolio contained approximately 300 emails from a variety of GOP members, PACs, campaigns, state parties, and businesses dated between May and October 2015. According to open-source reporting, these victims shared the same

U.S. Department of Justice

~~Attorney Work Product // May Contain Material Protected Under Fed. R. Crim. P. 6(e)~~

GRU officers operated a Facebook page under the DCLeaks moniker, which they primarily used to promote releases of materials.[141] The Facebook page was administered through a small number of preexisting GRU-controlled Facebook accounts.[142]

GRU officers also used the DCLeaks Facebook account, the Twitter account @dcleaks_, and the email account dcleaksproject@gmail.com to communicate privately with reporters and other U.S. persons. GRU officers using the DCLeaks persona gave certain reporters early access to archives of leaked files by sending them links and passwords to pages on the dcleaks.com website that had not yet become public. For example, on July 14, 2016, GRU officers operating under the DCLeaks persona sent a link and password for a non-public DCLeaks webpage to a U.S. reporter via the Facebook account.[143] Similarly, on September 14, 2016, GRU officers sent reporters Twitter direct messages from @dcleaks_, with a password to another non-public part of the dcleaks.com website.[144]

The DCLeaks.com website remained operational and public until March 2017.

2. Guccifer 2.0

On June 14, 2016, the DNC and its cyber-response team announced the breach of the DNC network and suspected theft of DNC documents. In the statements, the cyber-response team alleged that Russian state-sponsored actors (which they referred to as "Fancy Bear") were responsible for the breach.[145] Apparently in response to that announcement, on June 15, 2016, GRU officers using the persona Guccifer 2.0 created a WordPress blog. In the hours leading up to the launch of that WordPress blog, GRU officers logged into a Moscow-based server used and managed by Unit 74455 and searched for a number of specific words and phrases in English, including "some hundred sheets," "illuminati," and "worldwide known." Approximately two hours after the last of those searches, Guccifer 2.0 published its first post, attributing the DNC server hack to a lone Romanian hacker and using several of the unique English words and phrases that the GRU officers had searched for that day.[146]

Tennessee-based web-hosting company, called Smartech Corporation. William Bastone, *RNC E-Mail Was, In Fact, Hacked By Russians*, The Smoking Gun (Dec. 13, 2016).

[141] *Netyksho* Indictment ¶ 38.

[142] *See, e.g.,* Facebook Account 100008825623541 (Alice Donovan).

[143] 7/14/16 Facebook Message, ID 793058100795341 (DC Leaks) to ID ▓▓▓Personal Privacy▓▓▓

[144] *See, e.g.,* 9/14/16 Twitter DM, @dcleaks_ to ▓▓▓Personal Privacy▓▓▓ ; 9/14/16 Twitter DM, @dcleaks_ to ▓▓▓Personal Privacy▓▓▓ . The messages read: "Hi https://t.co/QTvKUjQcOx pass: KvFsg%*14@gPgu& enjoy ;)."

[145] Dmitri Alperovitch, *Bears in the Midst: Intrusion into the Democratic National Committee*, CrowdStrike Blog (June 14, 2016). CrowdStrike updated its post after the June 15, 2016 post by Guccifer 2.0 claiming responsibility for the intrusion.

[146] *Netyksho* Indictment ¶¶ 41-42.

That same day, June 15, 2016, the GRU also used the Guccifer 2.0 WordPress blog to begin releasing to the public documents stolen from the DNC and DCCC computer networks. The Guccifer 2.0 persona ultimately released thousands of documents stolen from the DNC and DCCC in a series of blog posts between June 15, 2016 and October 18, 2016.[147] Released documents included opposition research performed by the DNC (including a memorandum analyzing potential criticisms of candidate Trump), internal policy documents (such as recommendations on how to address politically sensitive issues), analyses of specific congressional races, and fundraising documents. Releases were organized around thematic issues, such as specific states (*e.g.*, Florida and Pennsylvania) that were perceived as competitive in the 2016 U.S. presidential election.

Beginning in late June 2016, the GRU also used the Guccifer 2.0 persona to release documents directly to reporters and other interested individuals. Specifically, on June 27, 2016, Guccifer 2.0 sent an email to the news outlet The Smoking Gun offering to provide "exclusive access to some leaked emails linked [to] Hillary Clinton's staff."[148] The GRU later sent the reporter a password and link to a locked portion of the dcleaks.com website that contained an archive of emails stolen by Unit 26165 from a Clinton Campaign volunteer in March 2016.[149] That the Guccifer 2.0 persona provided reporters access to a restricted portion of the DCLeaks website tends to indicate that both personas were operated by the same or a closely-related group of people.[150]

The GRU continued its release efforts through Guccifer 2.0 into August 2016. For example, on August 15, 2016, the Guccifer 2.0 persona sent a candidate for the U.S. Congress documents related to the candidate's opponent.[151] On August 22, 2016, the Guccifer 2.0 persona transferred approximately 2.5 gigabytes of Florida-related data stolen from the DCCC to a U.S. blogger covering Florida politics.[152] On August 22, 2016, the Guccifer 2.0 persona sent a U.S. reporter documents stolen from the DCCC pertaining to the Black Lives Matter movement.[153]

---

[147] Releases of documents on the Guccifer 2.0 blog occurred on June 15, 2016; June 20, 2016; June 21, 2016; July 6, 2016; July 14, 2016; August 12, 2016; August 15, 2016; August 21, 2016; August 31, 2016; September 15, 2016; September 23, 2016; October 4, 2016; and October 18, 2016.

[148] 6/27/16 Email, guccifer20@aol.fr to ▉▉▉▉▉ Personal Privacy ▉▉▉▉▉ (subject "leaked emails"); ▉▉▉▉ IT ▉▉▉▉ .

[149] 6/27/16 Email, guccifer20@aol.fr to ▉▉▉▉▉ Personal Privacy ▉▉▉▉▉ (subject "leaked emails"); ▉▉▉ IT ▉▉▉ ; *see also* 6/27/16 Email, guccifer20@aol.fr to ▉▉▉▉ Personal Privacy ▉▉▉▉ (subject "leaked emails"); IT ▉▉▉▉▉▉▉▉▉ (claiming DCLeaks was a "Wikileaks sub project").

[150] Before sending the reporter the link and password to the closed DCLeaks website, and in an apparent effort to deflect attention from the fact that DCLeaks and Guccifer 2.0 were operated by the same organization, the Guccifer 2.0 persona sent the reporter an email stating that DCLeaks was a "Wikileaks sub project" and that Guccifer 2.0 had asked DCLeaks to release the leaked emails with "closed access" to give reporters a preview of them.

[151] *Netyksho* Indictment ¶ 43(a).

[152] *Netyksho* Indictment ¶ 43(b).

[153] *Netyksho* Indictment ¶ 43(c).

U.S. Department of Justice

~~Attorney Work Product // May Contain Material Protected Under Fed. R. Crim. P. 6(e)~~

The GRU was also in contact through the Guccifer 2.0 persona with **HOM** a former Trump Campaign member **Harm to Ongoing Matter** ▮

[154] In early August 2016, **HOM** Twitter's suspension of the Guccifer 2.0 Twitter account. After it was reinstated, GRU officers posing as Guccifer 2.0 wrote **HOM** via private message, "thank u for writing back . . . do u find anyt[h]ing interesting in the docs i posted?" On August 17, 2016, the GRU added, "please tell me if i can help u anyhow . . . it would be a great pleasure to me." On September 9, 2016, the GRU—again posing as Guccifer 2.0—referred to a stolen DCCC document posted online and asked **HOM** "what do u think of the info on the turnout model for the democrats entire presidential campaign." **HOM** responded, "pretty standard."[155] The investigation did not identify evidence of other communications between **HOM** and Guccifer 2.0.

3. Use of WikiLeaks

In order to expand its interference in the 2016 U.S. presidential election, the GRU units transferred many of the documents they stole from the DNC and the chairman of the Clinton Campaign to WikiLeaks. GRU officers used both the DCLeaks and Guccifer 2.0 personas to communicate with WikiLeaks through Twitter private messaging and through encrypted channels, including possibly through WikiLeaks's private communication system.

a. WikiLeaks's Expressed Opposition Toward the Clinton Campaign

WikiLeaks, and particularly its founder Julian Assange, privately expressed opposition to candidate Clinton well before the first release of stolen documents. In November 2015, Assange wrote to other members and associates of WikiLeaks that "[w]e believe it would be much better for GOP to win . . . Dems+Media+liberals woudl [sic] then form a block to reign in their worst qualities. . . . With Hillary in charge, GOP will be pushing for her worst qualities., dems+media+neoliberals will be mute. . . . She's a bright, well connected, sadisitic sociopath."[156]

In March 2016, WikiLeaks released a searchable archive of approximately 30,000 Clinton emails that had been obtained through FOIA litigation.[157] While designing the archive, one WikiLeaks member explained the reason for building the archive to another associate:

---

[154] **HOM**

[155] **Harm to Ongoing Matter**

[156] 11/19/15 Twitter Group Chat, Group ID 594242937858486276, @WikiLeaks et al. Assange also wrote that, "GOP will generate a lot oposition [sic], including through dumb moves. Hillary will do the same thing, but co-opt the liberal opposition and the GOP opposition. Hence hillary has greater freedom to start wars than the GOP and has the will to do so." *Id.*

[157] WikiLeaks, "Hillary Clinton Email Archive," *available at* https://wikileaks.org/clinton-emails/.

U.S. Department of Justice

~~Attorney Work Product~~ // ~~May Contain Material Protected Under Fed. R. Crim. P. 6(e)~~

[W]e want this repository to become "the place" to search for background on hillary's plotting at the state department during 2009-2013. . . . Firstly because its useful and will annoy Hillary, but secondly because we want to be seen to be a resource/player in the US election, because eit [sic] may en[]courage people to send us even more important leaks.[158]

b. WikiLeaks's First Contact with Guccifer 2.0 and DCLeaks

Shortly after the GRU's first release of stolen documents through dcleaks.com in June 2016, GRU officers also used the DCLeaks persona to contact WikiLeaks about possible coordination in the future release of stolen emails. On June 14, 2016, @dcleaks_ sent a direct message to @WikiLeaks, noting, "You announced your organization was preparing to publish more Hillary's emails. We are ready to support you. We have some sensitive information too, in particular, her financial documents. Let's do it together. What do you think about publishing our info at the same moment? Thank you."[159] Investigative Technique

Around the same time, WikiLeaks initiated communications with the GRU persona Guccifer 2.0 shortly after it was used to release documents stolen from the DNC. On June 22, 2016, seven days after Guccifer 2.0's first releases of stolen DNC documents, WikiLeaks used Twitter's direct message function to contact the Guccifer 2.0 Twitter account and suggest that Guccifer 2.0 "[s]end any new material [stolen from the DNC] here for us to review and it will have a much higher impact than what you are doing."[160]

On July 6, 2016, WikiLeaks again contacted Guccifer 2.0 through Twitter's private messaging function, writing, "if you have anything hillary related we want it in the next tweo [sic] days prefable [sic] because the DNC is approaching and she will solidify bernie supporters behind her after." The Guccifer 2.0 persona responded, "ok . . . i see." WikiLeaks also explained, "we think trump has only a 25% chance of winning against hillary . . . so conflict between bernie and hillary is interesting."[161]

c. The GRU's Transfer of Stolen Materials to WikiLeaks

Both the GRU and WikiLeaks sought to hide their communications, which has limited the Office's ability to collect all of the communications between them. Thus, although it is clear that the stolen DNC and Podesta documents were transferred from the GRU to WikiLeaks, Investigative Technique

---

[158] 3/14/16 Twitter DM, @WikiLeaks to ▮▮▮▮▮▮ Less than two weeks earlier, the same account had been used to send a private message opposing the idea of Clinton "in whitehouse with her bloodlutt and amitions [sic] of empire with hawkish liberal-interventionist appointees." 11/19/15 Twitter Group Chat, Group ID 594242937858486276, @WikiLeaks et al.

[159] 6/14/16 Twitter DM, @dcleaks_ to @WikiLeaks.

[160] *Netyksho* Indictment ¶ 47(a).

[161] 7/6/16 Twitter DMs, @WikiLeaks & @guccifer_2.

U.S. Department of Justice

~~Attorney Work Product~~ // ~~May Contain Material Protected Under Fed. R. Crim. P. 6(e)~~

The Office was able to identify when the GRU (operating through its personas Guccifer 2.0 and DCLeaks) transferred some of the stolen documents to WikiLeaks through online archives set up by the GRU. Assange had access to the internet from the Ecuadorian Embassy in London, England. ▮Investigative Technique▮

[62]

On July 14, 2016, GRU officers used a Guccifer 2.0 email account to send WikiLeaks an email bearing the subject "big archive" and the message "a new attempt."[163] The email contained an encrypted attachment with the name "wk dnc link1.txt.gpg."[164] Using the Guccifer 2.0 Twitter account, GRU officers sent WikiLeaks an encrypted file and instructions on how to open it.[165] On July 18, 2016, WikiLeaks confirmed in a direct message to the Guccifer 2.0 account that it had "the 1Gb or so archive" and would make a release of the stolen documents "this week."[166] On July 22, 2016, WikiLeaks released over 20,000 emails and other documents stolen from the DNC computer networks.[167] The Democratic National Convention began three days later.

Similar communications occurred between WikiLeaks and the GRU-operated persona DCLeaks. On September 15, 2016, @dcleaks wrote to @WikiLeaks, "hi there! I'm from DC Leaks. How could we discuss some submission-related issues? Am trying to reach out to you via your secured chat but getting no response. I've got something that might interest you. You won't be disappointed, I promise."[168] The WikiLeaks account responded, "Hi there," without further elaboration. The @dcleaks_ account did not respond immediately.

The same day, the Twitter account @guccifer_2 sent @dcleaks_ a direct message, which is the first known contact between the personas.[169] During subsequent communications, the

[162] Investigative Technique

---

[163] This was not the GRU's first attempt at transferring data to WikiLeaks. On June 29, 2016, the GRU used a Guccifer 2.0 email account to send a large encrypted file to a WikiLeaks email account. 6/29/16 Email, guccifer2@mail.com ▮IT▮ (The email appears to have been undelivered.)

[164] *See* SM-2589105-DCLEAKS, serial 28 (analysis).

[165] 6/27/16 Twitter DM, @Guccifer_2 to @WikiLeaks.

[166] 7/18/16 Twitter DM, @Guccifer_2 & @WikiLeaks.

[167] "DNC Email Archive," WikiLeaks (Jul. 22, 2016), *available at* https://wikileaks.org/dnc-emails.

[168] 9/15/16 Twitter DM, @dcleaks_ to @WikiLeaks.

[169] 9/15/16 Twitter DM, @guccifer_2 to @dcleaks_.

U.S. Department of Justice

~~Attorney Work Product // May Contain Material Protected Under Fed. R. Crim. P. 6(e)~~

Guccifer 2.0 persona informed DCLeaks that WikiLeaks was trying to contact DCLeaks and arrange for a way to speak through encrypted emails.[170]

An analysis of the metadata collected from the WikiLeaks site revealed that the stolen Podesta emails show a creation date of September 19, 2016.[171] Based on information about Assange's computer and its possible operating system, this date may be when the GRU staged the stolen Podesta emails for transfer to WikiLeaks (as the GRU had previously done in July 2016 for the DNC emails).[172] The WikiLeaks site also released PDFs and other documents taken from Podesta that were attachments to emails in his account; these documents had a creation date of October 2, 2016, which appears to be the date the attachments were separately staged by WikiLeaks on its site.[173]

Beginning on September 20, 2016, WikiLeaks and DCLeaks resumed communications in a brief exchange. On September 22, 2016, a DCLeaks email account dcleaksproject@gmail.com sent an email to a WikiLeaks account with the subject "Submission" and the message "Hi from DCLeaks." The email contained a PGP-encrypted message with the filename "wiki_mail.txt.gpg."[174] ██Investigative Technique██ The email, however, bears a number of similarities to the July 14, 2016 email in which GRU officers used the Guccifer 2.0 persona to give WikiLeaks access to the archive of DNC files. On September 22, 2016 (the same day of DCLeaks' email to WikiLeaks), the Twitter account @dcleaks sent a single message to @WikiLeaks with the string of characters ██Investigative Technique██

The Office cannot rule out that stolen documents were transferred to WikiLeaks through intermediaries who visited during the summer of 2016. For example, public reporting identified Andrew Müller-Maguhn as a WikiLeaks associate who may have assisted with the transfer of these stolen documents to WikiLeaks.[175] ██Investigative Technique██

---

[170] *See* SM-2589105-DCLEAKS, serial 28; 9/15/16 Twitter DM, @Guccifer_2 & @WikiLeaks.

[171] *See* SM-2284941, serials 63 & 64 ██Investigative Technique██

[172] ██Investigative Technique██ At the time, certain Apple operating systems used a setting that left a downloaded file's creation date the same as the creation date shown on the host computer. This would explain why the creation date on WikiLeaks's version of the files was still September 19, 2016. *See* SM-2284941, serial 62 ██Investigative Technique██

[173] When WikiLeaks saved attachments separately from the stolen emails, its computer system appears to have treated each attachment as a new file and given it a new creation date. *See* SM-2284941, serials 63 & 64.

[174] *See* 9/22/16 Email, dcleaksproject@gmail.com ██IT██

[175] Ellen Nakashima et al., *A German Hacker Offers a Rare Look Inside the Secretive World of Julian Assange and WikiLeaks*, Washington Post (Jan. 17, 2018).

U.S. Department of Justice

~~Attorney Work Product // May Contain Material Protected Under Fed. R. Crim. P. 6(e)~~

Investigative Technique [176]

On October 7, 2016, WikiLeaks released the first emails stolen from the Podesta email account. In total, WikiLeaks released 33 tranches of stolen emails between October 7, 2016 and November 7, 2016. The releases included private speeches given by Clinton;[177] internal communications between Podesta and other high-ranking members of the Clinton Campaign;[178] and correspondence related to the Clinton Foundation.[179] In total, WikiLeaks released over 50,000 documents stolen from Podesta's personal email account. The last-in-time email released from Podesta's account was dated March 21, 2016, two days after Podesta received a spearphishing email sent by the GRU.

d. WikiLeaks Statements Dissembling About the Source of Stolen Materials

As reports attributing the DNC and DCCC hacks to the Russian government emerged, WikiLeaks and Assange made several public statements apparently designed to obscure the source of the materials that WikiLeaks was releasing. The file-transfer evidence described above and other information uncovered during the investigation discredit WikiLeaks's claims about the source of material that it posted.

Beginning in the summer of 2016, Assange and WikiLeaks made a number of statements about Seth Rich, a former DNC staff member who was killed in July 2016. The statements about Rich implied falsely that he had been the source of the stolen DNC emails. On August 9, 2016, the @WikiLeaks Twitter account posted: "ANNOUNCE: WikiLeaks has decided to issue a US$20k reward for information leading to conviction for the murder of DNC staffer Seth Rich."[180] Likewise, on August 25, 2016, Assange was asked in an interview, "Why are you so interested in Seth Rich's killer?" and responded, "We're very interested in anything that might be a threat to alleged Wikileaks sources." The interviewer responded to Assange's statement by commenting, "I know you don't want to reveal your source, but it certainly sounds like you're suggesting a man who leaked information to WikiLeaks was then murdered." Assange replied, "If there's someone who's potentially connected to our publication, and that person has been murdered in suspicious

[176] Investigative Technique

[177] Personal Privacy

[178] Personal Privacy

[179] *Netyksho* Indictment ¶ 43.

[180] @WikiLeaks 8/9/16 Tweet.

U.S. Department of Justice

~~Attorney Work Product // May Contain Material Protected Under Fed. R. Crim. P. 6(e)~~

circumstances, it doesn't necessarily mean that the two are connected. But it is a very serious matter...that type of allegation is very serious, as it's taken very seriously by us."[181]

After the U.S. intelligence community publicly announced its assessment that Russia was behind the hacking operation, Assange continued to deny that the Clinton materials released by WikiLeaks had come from Russian hacking. According to media reports, Assange told a U.S. congressman that the DNC hack was an "inside job," and purported to have "physical proof" that Russians did not give materials to Assange.[182]

C. Additional GRU Cyber Operations

While releasing the stolen emails and documents through DCLeaks, Guccifer 2.0, and WikiLeaks, GRU officers continued to target and hack victims linked to the Democratic campaign and, eventually, to target entities responsible for election administration in several states.

1. <u>Summer and Fall 2016 Operations Targeting Democrat-Linked Victims</u>

On July 27, 2016, Unit 26165 targeted email accounts connected to candidate Clinton's personal office ▮▮▮▮▮▮▮. Earlier that day, candidate Trump made public statements that included the following: "Russia, if you're listening, I hope you're able to find the 30,000 emails that are missing. I think you will probably be rewarded mightily by our press."[183] The "30,000 emails" were apparently a reference to emails described in media accounts as having been stored on a personal server that candidate Clinton had used while serving as Secretary of State.

Within approximately five hours of Trump's statement, GRU officers targeted for the first time Clinton's personal office. After candidate Trump's remarks, Unit 26165 created and sent malicious links targeting 15 email accounts at the domain ▮▮▮▮▮ including an email account belonging to Clinton aide ▮▮▮▮▮▮ The investigation did not find evidence of earlier GRU attempts to compromise accounts hosted on this domain. It is unclear how the GRU was able to identify these email accounts, which were not public.[184]

Unit 26165 officers also hacked into a DNC account hosted on a cloud-computing service ▮▮▮▮▮▮▮▮▮▮▮▮▮▮▮▮ On September 20, 2016, the GRU began to generate copies of the DNC data using ▮▮▮ function designed to allow users to produce backups of databases (referred to ▮▮▮ as "snapshots"). The GRU then stole those snapshots by moving

---

[181] *See Assange: "Murdered DNC Staffer Was 'Potential' WikiLeaks Source,"* Fox News (Aug. 25, 2016)(containing video of Assange interview by Megyn Kelly).

[182] M. Raju & Z. Cohen, *A GOP Congressman's Lonely Quest Defending Julian Assange*, CNN (May 23, 2018).

[183] "Donald Trump on Russian & Missing Hillary Clinton Emails," YouTube Channel C-SPAN, Posted 7/27/16, *available at* https://www.youtube.com/watch?v=3kxG8uJUsWU (starting at 0:41).

[184] Investigative Technique ▮▮▮▮▮▮▮▮▮▮▮▮▮▮▮▮▮▮▮▮▮▮▮▮▮▮▮▮

U.S. Department of Justice

~~Attorney Work Product // May Contain Material Protected Under Fed. R. Crim. P. 6(e)~~

them to 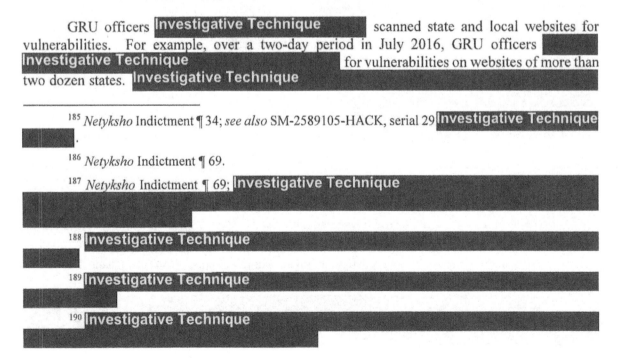[PP] account that they controlled; from there, the copies were moved to GRU-controlled computers. The GRU stole approximately 300 gigabytes of data from the DNC cloud-based account.[185]

2. Intrusions Targeting the Administration of U.S. Elections

In addition to targeting individuals involved in the Clinton Campaign, GRU officers also targeted individuals and entities involved in the administration of the elections. Victims included U.S. state and local entities, such as state boards of elections (SBOEs), secretaries of state, and county governments, as well as individuals who worked for those entities.[186] The GRU also targeted private technology firms responsible for manufacturing and administering election-related software and hardware, such as voter registration software and electronic polling stations.[187] The GRU continued to target these victims through the elections in November 2016. While the investigation identified evidence that the GRU targeted these individuals and entities, the Office did not investigate further. The Office did not, for instance, obtain or examine servers or other relevant items belonging to these victims. The Office understands that the FBI, the U.S. Department of Homeland Security, and the states have separately investigated that activity.

By at least the summer of 2016, GRU officers sought access to state and local computer networks by exploiting known software vulnerabilities on websites of state and local governmental entities. GRU officers, for example, targeted state and local databases of registered voters using a technique known as "SQL injection," by which malicious code was sent to the state or local website in order to run commands (such as exfiltrating the database contents).[188] In one instance in approximately June 2016, the GRU compromised the computer network of the Illinois State Board of Elections by exploiting a vulnerability in the SBOE's website. The GRU then gained access to a database containing information on millions of registered Illinois voters,[189] and extracted data related to thousands of U.S. voters before the malicious activity was identified.[190]

GRU officers [Investigative Technique] scanned state and local websites for vulnerabilities. For example, over a two-day period in July 2016, GRU officers [redacted] [Investigative Technique] for vulnerabilities on websites of more than two dozen states. [Investigative Technique]

---

[185] *Netyksho* Indictment ¶ 34; *see also* SM-2589105-HACK, serial 29 [Investigative Technique] [redacted].

[186] *Netyksho* Indictment ¶ 69.

[187] *Netyksho* Indictment ¶ 69; [Investigative Technique]

[188] [Investigative Technique]

[189] [Investigative Technique]

[190] [Investigative Technique]

Investigative Technique

Similar IT   for vulnerabilities continued through the election.

Unit 74455 also sent spearphishing emails to public officials involved in election administration and personnel at companies involved in voting technology. In August 2016, GRU officers targeted employees of   , a voting technology company that developed software used by numerous U.S. counties to manage voter rolls, and installed malware on the company network. Similarly, in November 2016, the GRU sent spearphishing emails to over 120 email accounts used by Florida county officials responsible for administering the 2016 U.S. election.[191] The spearphishing emails contained an attached Word document coded with malicious software (commonly referred to as a Trojan) that permitted the GRU to access the infected computer.[192] The FBI was separately responsible for this investigation. We understand the FBI believes that this operation enabled the GRU to gain access to the network of at least one Florida county government. The Office did not independently verify that belief and, as explained above, did not undertake the investigative steps that would have been necessary to do so.

D. Trump Campaign and the Dissemination of Hacked Materials

The Trump Campaign showed interest in WikiLeaks's releases of hacked materials throughout the summer and fall of 2016. Harm to Ongoing Matter

1. HOM

a. *Background*

Harm to Ongoing Matter

---

[191] *Netyksho* Indictment ¶ 76; Investigative Technique

[192] Investigative Technique

U.S. Department of Justice

~~Attorney Work Product // May Contain Material Protected Under Fed. R. Crim. P. 6(e)~~

b. Contacts with the Campaign about WikiLeaks

Harm to Ongoing Matter

Harm to Ongoing Matter [93]

On June 12, 2016, Assange claimed in a televised interview to "have emails relating to Hillary Clinton which are pending publication,"[194] but provided no additional context.

In debriefings with the Office, former deputy campaign chairman Rick Gates said that,

Harm to Ongoing Matter

Harm to Ongoing Matter [195]

Gates recalled candidate Trump being generally frustrated that the Clinton emails had not been found.[196]

Paul Manafort, who would later become campaign chairman, Harm to Ongoing Matter [197] Harm to Ongoing Matter [198]

---

[193] Harm to Ongoing Matter

[194] *See* Mahita Gajanan, *Julian Assange Timed DNC Email Release for Democratic Convention*, Time (July 27, 2016) (quoting the June 12, 2016 television interview).

[195] In February 2018, Gates pleaded guilty, pursuant to a plea agreement, to a superseding criminal information charging him with conspiring to defraud and commit multiple offenses (*i.e.*, tax fraud, failure to report foreign bank accounts, and acting as an unregistered agent of a foreign principal) against the United States, as well as making false statements to our Office. Superseding Criminal Information, *United States v. Richard W. Gates III*, 1:17-cr-201 (D.D.C. Feb. 23, 2018), Doc. 195 ("*Gates* Superseding Criminal Information"); Plea Agreement, *United States v. Richard W. Gates III*, 1:17-cr-201 (D.D.C. Feb. 23, 2018), Doc. 205 ("*Gates* Plea Agreement"). Gates has provided information and in-court testimony that the Office has deemed to be reliable.

[196] Gates 10/25/18 302, at 1-2.

[197] As explained further in Volume I, Section IV.A.8, *infra*, Manafort entered into a plea agreement with our Office. We determined that he breached the agreement by being untruthful in proffer sessions and before the grand jury. We have generally recounted his version of events in this report only when his statements are sufficiently corroborated to be trustworthy; to identify issues on which Manafort's untruthful responses may themselves be of evidentiary value; or to provide Manafort's explanations for certain events, even when we were unable to determine whether that explanation was credible. His account appears here principally because it aligns with those of other witnesses.

[198] Grand Jury

U.S. Department of Justice

~~Attorney Work Product // May Contain Material Protected Under Fed. R. Crim. P. 6(e)~~

Michael Cohen, former executive vice president of the Trump Organization and special counsel to Donald J. Trump,[199] told the Office that he recalled an incident in which he was in candidate Trump's office in Trump Tower **Harm to Ongoing Matter**

Harm to Ongoing Matter [200]

[201] Cohen further told the Office that, after WikiLeaks's subsequent release of stolen DNC emails in July 2016, candidate Trump said to Cohen something to the effect of, **HOM** [202]

Harm to Ongoing Matter

According to Gates, Manafort expressed excitement about the release **HOM** [203] Manafort, for his part, told the Office that, shortly after WikiLeaks's July 22 release, Manafort also spoke with candidate Trump **Harm to Ongoing Matter**

[204] **Harm to Ongoing Matter**

[205] Manafort also **HOM** wanted to be kept apprised of any

---

[199] In November 2018, Cohen pleaded guilty pursuant to a plea agreement to a single-count information charging him with making false statements to Congress, in violation of 18 U.S.C. § 1001(a) & (c). He had previously pleaded guilty to several other criminal charges brought by the U.S. Attorney's Office in the Southern District of New York, after a referral from this Office. In the months leading up to his false-statements guilty plea, Cohen met with our Office on multiple occasions for interviews and provided information that the Office has generally assessed to be reliable and that is included in this report.

[200] **HOM**

[201] **Harm to Ongoing Matter**

[202] Cohen 9/18/18 302, at 10. **Harm to Ongoing Matter**

Harm to Ongoing Matter

Harm to Ongoing Matter

[203] Gates 10/25/18 302 (serial 241), at 4.

[204] Grand Jury

[205] Grand Jury

developments with WikiLeaks and separately told Gates to keep in touch `HOM` about future WikiLeaks releases.[206]

According to Gates, by the late summer of 2016, the Trump Campaign was planning a press strategy, a communications campaign, and messaging based on the possible release of Clinton emails by WikiLeaks.[207] `Harm to Ongoing Matter`
`[208]` `Harm to Ongoing Matter` while Trump and Gates were driving to LaGuardia Airport. `Harm to Ongoing Matter` , shortly after the call candidate Trump told Gates that more releases of damaging information would be coming.[209]

`Harm to Ongoing Matter`

[10]

c. `Harm to Ongoing Matter`

`Harm to Ongoing Matter`

[11]

Corsi is an author who holds a doctorate in political science.[212] In 2016, Corsi also worked for the media outlet WorldNetDaily (WND). `Harm to Ongoing Matter`

[13]

---

[206] `Grand Jury`

[207] Gates 4/10/18 302, at 3; Gates 4/11/18 302, at 1-2 (SM-2180998); Gates 10/25/18 302, at 2.

[208] `HOM`

[209] Gates 10/25/18 302 (serial 241), at 4.

[210] `HOM`

[211] `HOM`

[212] Corsi first rose to public prominence in August 2004 when he published his book *Unfit for Command: Swift Boat Veterans Speak Out Against John Kerry*. In the 2008 election cycle, Corsi gained prominence for being a leading proponent of the allegation that Barack Obama was not born in the United States. Corsi told the Office that Donald Trump expressed interest in his writings, and that he spoke with Trump on the phone on at least six occasions. Corsi 9/6/18 302, at 3.

[213] Corsi 10/31/18 302, at 2; `Grand Jury` Corsi was first interviewed on September 6, 2018 at the Special Counsel's offices in Washington, D.C. He was accompanied by counsel throughout the interview. Corsi was subsequently interviewed on September 17, 2018; September 21, 2018; October 31, 2018; November 1, 2018; and November 2, 2018. Counsel was

Harm to Ongoing Matter

[14] Corsi told the Office during interviews that he "must have" previously discussed Assange with Malloch.[215]

Harm to Ongoing Matter

[216] **Harm to Ongoing Matter**

[217]

Grand Jury

According to Malloch, Corsi asked him to put Corsi in touch with Assange, whom Corsi wished to interview. Malloch recalled that Corsi also suggested that individuals in the "orbit" of U.K. politician Nigel Farage might be able to contact Assange and asked if Malloch knew them. Malloch told Corsi that he would think about the request but made no actual attempt to connect Corsi with Assange.[218]

Harm to Ongoing Matter

[19]

Harm to Ongoing Matter

[20]

---

present for all interviews, and the interviews beginning on September 21, 2018 were conducted pursuant to a proffer agreement that precluded affirmative use of his statements against him in limited circumstances.

[214] **HOM**

[215] Corsi 10/31/18 302, at 4.

[216] **HOM**

[217] **HOM**

[218] **Grand Jury** Malloch denied ever communicating with Assange or WikiLeaks, stating that he did not pursue the request to contact Assange because he believed he had no connections to Assange. **Grand Jury**

[219] **HOM**

[220] **Harm to Ongoing Matter**

Malloch stated to investigators that beginning in or about August 2016, he and Corsi had multiple FaceTime discussions about WikiLeaks Harm to Ongoing Matter had made a connection to Assange and that the hacked emails of John Podesta would be released prior to Election Day and would be helpful to the Trump Campaign. In one conversation in or around August or September 2016, Corsi told Malloch that the release of the Podesta emails was coming, after which "we" were going to be in the driver's seat.[221]

Harm to Ongoing Matter

[222] Harm to Ongoing Matter

[23] Harm to Ongoing Matter

[24] Harm to Ongoing Matter

[225]

Harm to Ongoing Matter

[226] Harm to Ongoing Matter

[27] Harm to Ongoing Matter

[228])

Harm to Ongoing Matter

[229] Harm to Ongoing Matter

---

[221] Grand Jury

[222] Harm to Ongoing Matter

[223] Harm to Ongoing Matter

[224] Harm to Ongoing Matter

[225] Harm to Ongoing Matter

[226] Harm to Ongoing Matter

[227] Harm to Ongoing Matter

[228] HOM

[229] Harm to Ongoing Matter

U.S. Department of Justice

Attorney Work Product // May Contain Material Protected Under Fed. R. Crim. P. 6(e)

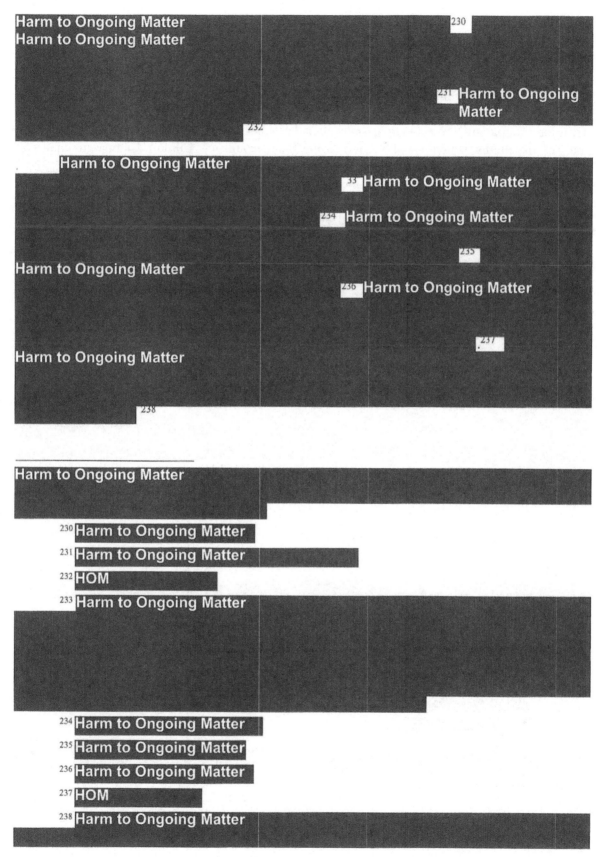

Harm to Ongoing Matter
Harm to Ongoing Matter 230

231 Harm to Ongoing Matter

232

Harm to Ongoing Matter

33 Harm to Ongoing Matter

234 Harm to Ongoing Matter

255

236 Harm to Ongoing Matter

Harm to Ongoing Matter

237

Harm to Ongoing Matter

238

Harm to Ongoing Matter

230 Harm to Ongoing Matter
231 Harm to Ongoing Matter
232 HOM
233 Harm to Ongoing Matter

234 Harm to Ongoing Matter
235 Harm to Ongoing Matter
236 Harm to Ongoing Matter
237 HOM
238 Harm to Ongoing Matter

U.S. Department of Justice

~~Attorney Work Product // May Contain Material Protected Under Fed. R. Crim. P. 6(e)~~

d. WikiLeaks's October 7, 2016 Release of Stolen Podesta Emails

On October 7, 2016, four days after the Assange press conference HOM ███████████████████, the Washington Post published an *Access Hollywood* video that captured comments by candidate Trump some years earlier and that was expected to adversely affect the Campaign.[239] Less than an hour after the video's publication, WikiLeaks released the first set of emails stolen by the GRU from the account of Clinton Campaign chairman John Podesta.

Harm to Ongoing Matter

[240] Harm to Ongoing Matter

[241] Harm to Ongoing Matter

[242]

Harm to Ongoing Matter
[243] Harm to Ongoing Matter

Corsi said that, because he had no direct means of communicating with WikiLeaks, he told members of the news site WND—who were participating on a conference call with him that day—to reach Assange immediately.[244] Corsi claimed that the pressure was

---

Harm to Ongoing Matter

[239] Candidate Trump can be heard off camera making graphic statements about women.

[240] HOM

[241] HOM

[242] HOM

[243] HOM

[244] In a later November 2018 interview, Corsi stated Harm to Ongoing Matter ███████████████████ that he believed Malloch was on the call but then focused on other individuals who were on the call-invitation, which Malloch was not. (Separate travel records show that at the time of the call, Malloch was aboard a transatlantic flight). Corsi at one point stated that after WikiLeaks's release of stolen emails on October 7, 2016, he concluded Malloch had gotten in contact with Assange. Corsi 11/1/18 302, at 6.

U.S. Department of Justice

~~Attorney Work Product // May Contain Material Protected Under Fed. R. Crim. P. 6(e)~~

enormous and recalled telling the conference call the *Access Hollywood* tape was coming.[245] Corsi stated that he was convinced that his efforts had caused WikiLeaks to release the emails when they did.[246] In a later November 2018 interview, Corsi stated that he thought that he had told people on a WND conference call about the forthcoming tape and had sent out a tweet asking whether anyone could contact Assange, but then said that maybe he had done nothing.[247]

The Office investigated Corsi's allegations about the events of October 7, 2016 but found little corroboration for his allegations about the day.[248] Harm to Ongoing Matter
[249] Harm to Ongoing Matter

[250] However, the phone records themselves do not indicate that the conversation was with any of the reporters who broke the *Access Hollywood* story, and the Office has not otherwise been able to identify the substance of the conversation. Harm to Ongoing Matter

.[251] However, the Office has not identified any conference call participant, or anyone who spoke to Corsi that day, who says that they received non-public information about the tape from Corsi or acknowledged having contacted a member of WikiLeaks on October 7, 2016 after a conversation with Corsi.

e. Donald Trump Jr. Interaction with WikiLeaks

Donald Trump Jr. had direct electronic communications with WikiLeaks during the campaign period. On September 20, 2016, an individual named Jason Fishbein sent WikiLeaks the password for an unlaunched website focused on Trump's "unprecedented and dangerous" ties

---

[245] During the same interview, Corsi also suggested that he may have sent out public tweets because he knew Assange was reading his tweets. Our Office was unable to find evidence of any such tweets.

[246] Corsi 9/21/18 302, at 6-7.

[247] Corsi 11/1/18 302, at 6.

[248] Harm to Ongoing Matter Grand Jury

[249] Harm to Ongoing Matter

[250] HOM Grand Jury Harm to Ongoing Matter

[251] HOM Grand Jury Harm to Ongoing Matter Grand Jury
Harm to Ongoing Matter

U.S. Department of Justice

~~Attorney Work Product // May Contain Material Protected Under Fed. R. Crim. P. 6(e)~~

to Russia, PutinTrump.org.[252] WikiLeaks publicly tweeted: "'Let's bomb Iraq' Progress for America PAC to launch "PutinTrump.org' at 9:30am. Oops pw is 'putintrump' putintrump.org." Several hours later, WikiLeaks sent a Twitter direct message to Donald Trump Jr., "A PAC run anti-Trump site putintrump.org is about to launch. The PAC is a recycled pro-Iraq war PAC. We have guessed the password. It is 'putintrump.' See 'About' for who is behind it. Any comments?"[253]

Several hours later, Trump Jr. emailed a variety of senior campaign staff:

Guys I got a weird Twitter DM from wikileaks. See below. I tried the password and it works and the about section they reference contains the next pic in terms of who is behind it. Not sure if this is anything but it seems like it's really wikileaks asking me as I follow them and it is a DM. Do you know the people mentioned and what the conspiracy they are looking for could be? These are just screen shots but it's a fully built out page claiming to be a PAC let me know your thoughts and if we want to look into it.[254]

Trump Jr. attached a screenshot of the "About" page for the unlaunched site PutinTrump.org. The next day (after the website had launched publicly), Trump Jr. sent a direct message to WikiLeaks: "Off the record, I don't know who that is but I'll ask around. Thanks."[255]

On October 3, 2016, WikiLeaks sent another direct message to Trump Jr., asking "you guys" to help disseminate a link alleging candidate Clinton had advocated using a drone to target Julian Assange. Trump Jr. responded that he already "had done so," and asked, "what's behind this Wednesday leak I keep reading about?"[256] WikiLeaks did not respond.

On October 12, 2016, WikiLeaks wrote again that it was "great to see you and your dad talking about our publications. Strongly suggest your dad tweets this link if he mentions us wlsearch.tk."[257] WikiLeaks wrote that the link would help Trump in "digging through" leaked emails and stated, "we just released Podesta emails Part 4."[258] Two days later, Trump Jr. publicly tweeted the wlsearch.tk link.[259]

---

[252] 9/20/16 Twitter DM, @JasonFishbein to @WikiLeaks; *see* JF00587 (9/21/16 Messages, ▨▨ @jabber.cryptoparty.is & ▨▨ @jabber.cryptoparty.is); Fishbein 9/5/18 302, at 4. When interviewed by our Office, Fishbein produced what he claimed to be logs from a chatroom in which the participants discussed U.S. politics; one of the other participants had posted the website and password that Fishbein sent to WikiLeaks.

[253] 9/20/16 Twitter DM, @WikiLeaks to @DonaldJTrumpJr.

[254] TRUMPORG_28_000629-33 (9/21/16 Email, Trump Jr. to Conway et al. (subject "Wikileaks")).

[255] 9/21/16 Twitter DM, @DonaldJTrumpJr to @WikiLeaks.

[256] 10/3/16 Twitter DMs, @DonaldJTrumpJr & @WikiLeaks.

[257] At the time, the link took users to a WikiLeaks archive of stolen Clinton Campaign documents.

[258] 10/12/16 Twitter DM, @WikiLeaks to @DonaldJTrumpJr.

[259] @DonaldJTrumpJr 10/14/16 (6:34 a.m.) Tweet.

U.S. Department of Justice

~~Attorney Work Product // May Contain Material Protected Under Fed. R. Crim. P. 6(e)~~

2. Other Potential Campaign Interest in Russian Hacked Materials

Throughout 2016, the Trump Campaign expressed interest in Hillary Clinton's private email server and whether approximately 30,000 emails from that server had in fact been permanently destroyed, as reported by the media. Several individuals associated with the Campaign were contacted in 2016 about various efforts to obtain the missing Clinton emails and other stolen material in support of the Trump Campaign. Some of these contacts were met with skepticism, and nothing came of them; others were pursued to some degree. The investigation did not find evidence that the Trump Campaign recovered any such Clinton emails, or that these contacts were part of a coordinated effort between Russia and the Trump Campaign.

a. Henry Oknyansky (a/k/a Henry Greenberg)

In the spring of 2016, Trump Campaign advisor Michael Caputo learned through a Florida-based Russian business partner that another Florida-based Russian, Henry Oknyansky (who also went by the name Henry Greenberg), claimed to have information pertaining to Hillary Clinton. Caputo notified Roger Stone and brokered communication between Stone and Oknyansky. Oknyansky and Stone set up a May 2016 in-person meeting.[260]

Oknyansky was accompanied to the meeting by Alexei Rasin, a Ukrainian associate involved in Florida real estate. At the meeting, Rasin offered to sell Stone derogatory information on Clinton that Rasin claimed to have obtained while working for Clinton. Rasin claimed to possess financial statements demonstrating Clinton's involvement in money laundering with Rasin's companies. According to Oknyansky, Stone asked if the amounts in question totaled millions of dollars but was told it was closer to hundreds of thousands. Stone refused the offer, stating that Trump would not pay for opposition research.[261]

Oknyansky claimed to the Office that Rasin's motivation was financial. According to Oknyansky, Rasin had tried unsuccessfully to shop the Clinton information around to other interested parties, and Oknyansky would receive a cut if the information was sold.[262] Rasin is noted in public source documents as the director and/or registered agent for a number of Florida companies, none of which appears to be connected to Clinton. The Office found no other evidence that Rasin worked for Clinton or any Clinton-related entities.

In their statements to investigators, Oknyansky and Caputo had contradictory recollections about the meeting. Oknyansky claimed that Caputo accompanied Stone to the meeting and provided an introduction, whereas Caputo did not tell us that he had attended and claimed that he was never told what information Oknyansky offered. Caputo also stated that he was unaware Oknyansky sought to be paid for the information until Stone informed him after the fact.[263]

---

[260] Caputo 5/2/18 302, at 4; Oknyansky 7/13/18 302, at 1.

[261] Oknyansky 7/13/18 302, at 1-2.

[262] Oknyansky 7/13/18 302, at 2.

[263] Caputo 5/2/18 302, at 4; Oknyansky 7/13/18 302, at 1.

U.S. Department of Justice

~~Attorney Work Product // May Contain Material Protected Under Fed. R. Crim. P. 6(e)~~

The Office did not locate Rasin in the United States, although the Office confirmed Rasin had been issued a Florida driver's license. The Office otherwise was unable to determine the content and origin of the information he purportedly offered to Stone. Finally, the investigation did not identify evidence of a connection between the outreach or the meeting and Russian interference efforts.

b. Campaign Efforts to Obtain Deleted Clinton Emails

After candidate Trump stated on July 27, 2016, that he hoped Russia would "find the 30,000 emails that are missing," Trump asked individuals affiliated with his Campaign to find the deleted Clinton emails.[264] Michael Flynn—who would later serve as National Security Advisor in the Trump Administration—recalled that Trump made this request repeatedly, and Flynn subsequently contacted multiple people in an effort to obtain the emails.[265]

Barbara Ledeen and Peter Smith were among the people contacted by Flynn. Ledeen, a long-time Senate staffer who had previously sought the Clinton emails, provided updates to Flynn about her efforts throughout the summer of 2016.[266] Smith, an investment advisor who was active in Republican politics, also attempted to locate and obtain the deleted Clinton emails.[267]

Ledeen began her efforts to obtain the Clinton emails before Flynn's request, as early as December 2015.[268] On December 3, 2015, she emailed Smith a proposal to obtain the emails, stating, "Here is the proposal I briefly mentioned to you. The person I described to you would be happy to talk with you either in person or over the phone. The person can get the emails which 1. Were classified and 2. Were purloined by our enemies. That would demonstrate what needs to be demonstrated."[269]

Attached to the email was a 25-page proposal stating that the "Clinton email server was, in all likelihood, breached long ago," and that the Chinese, Russian, and Iranian intelligence services could "re-assemble the server's email content."[270] The proposal called for a three-phase approach. The first two phases consisted of open-source analysis. The third phase consisted of checking with certain intelligence sources "that have access through liaison work with various foreign services" to determine if any of those services had gotten to the server. The proposal noted, "Even if a single email was recovered and the providence [sic] of that email was a foreign service, it would be catastrophic to the Clinton campaign[.]" Smith forwarded the email to two colleagues and

---

[264] Flynn 4/25/18 302, at 5-6; Flynn 5/1/18 302, at 1-3.

[265] Flynn 5/1/18 302, at 1-3.

[266] Flynn 4/25/18 302, at 7; Flynn 5/4/18 302, at 1-2; Flynn 11/29/17 302, at 7-8.

[267] Flynn 11/29/17 302, at 7.

[268] Szobocsan 3/29/17 302, at 1.

[269] 12/3/15 Email, Ledeen to Smith.

[270] 12/3/15 Email, Ledeen to Smith (attachment).

U.S. Department of Justice

~~Attorney Work Product // May Contain Material Protected Under Fed. R. Crim. P. 6(e)~~

wrote, "we can discuss to whom it should be referred."[271] On December 16, 2015, Smith informed Ledeen that he declined to participate in her "initiative." According to one of Smith's business associates, Smith believed Ledeen's initiative was not viable at that time.[272]

Just weeks after Trump's July 2016 request to find the Clinton emails, however, Smith tried to locate and obtain the emails himself. He created a company, raised tens of thousands of dollars, and recruited security experts and business associates. Smith made claims to others involved in the effort (and those from whom he sought funding) that he was in contact with hackers with "ties and affiliations to Russia" who had access to the emails, and that his efforts were coordinated with the Trump Campaign.[273]

On August 28, 2016, Smith sent an email from an encrypted account with the subject "Sec. Clinton's unsecured private email server" to an undisclosed list of recipients, including Campaign co-chairman Sam Clovis. The email stated that Smith was "[j]ust finishing two days of sensitive meetings here in DC with involved groups to poke and probe on the above. It is clear that the Clinton's home-based, unprotected server was hacked with ease by both State-related players, and private mercenaries. Parties with varying interests, are circling to release ahead of the election."[274]

On September 2, 2016, Smith directed a business associate to establish KLS Research LLC in furtherance of his search for the deleted Clinton emails.[275] One of the purposes of KLS Research was to manage the funds Smith raised in support of his initiative.[276] KLS Research received over $30,000 during the presidential campaign, although Smith represented that he raised even more money.[277]

Smith recruited multiple people for his initiative, including security experts to search for and authenticate the emails.[278] In early September 2016, as part of his recruitment and fundraising effort, Smith circulated a document stating that his initiative was "in coordination" with the Trump Campaign, "to the extent permitted as an independent expenditure organization."[279] The document listed multiple individuals affiliated with the Trump Campaign, including Flynn, Clovis, Bannon,

[271] 12/3/15 Email, Smith to Szobocsan & Safron.

[272] Szobocsan 3/29/18 302, at 1.

[273] 8/31/16 Email, Smith to Smith.

[274] 8/28/16 Email, Smith to Smith.

[275] Incorporation papers of KLS Research LLC, 7/26/17 [Grand Jury] Szobocsan 3/29/18 302, at 2.

[276] Szobocsan 3/29/18 302, at 3.

[277] Financial Institution Record of Peter Smith and KLS Research LLC, 10/31/17 [redacted] [Grand Jury] 10/11/16 Email, Smith to [Personal Privacy]

[278] Tait 8/22/17 302, at 3; York 7/12/17 302, at 1-2; York 11/22/17 302, at 1.

[279] York 7/13/17 302 (attachment KLS Research, LLC, "Clinton Email Reconnaissance Initiative," Sept. 9, 2016).

U.S. Department of Justice

~~Attorney Work Product // May Contain Material Protected Under Fed. R. Crim. P. 6(e)~~

and Kellyanne Conway.[280] The investigation established that Smith communicated with at least Flynn and Clovis about his search for the deleted Clinton emails,[281] but the Office did not identify evidence that any of the listed individuals initiated or directed Smith's efforts.

In September 2016, Smith and Ledeen got back in touch with each other about their respective efforts. Ledeen wrote to Smith, "wondering if you had some more detailed reports or memos or other data you could share because we have come a long way in our efforts since we last visited. . . . We would need as much technical discussion as possible so we could marry it against the new data we have found and then could share it back to you 'your eyes only.'"[282]

Ledeen claimed to have obtained a trove of emails (from what she described as the "dark web") that purported to be the deleted Clinton emails. Ledeen wanted to authenticate the emails and solicited contributions to fund that effort. Erik Prince provided funding to hire a tech advisor to ascertain the authenticity of the emails. According to Prince, the tech advisor determined that the emails were not authentic.[283]

A backup of Smith's computer contained two files that had been downloaded from WikiLeaks and that were originally attached to emails received by John Podesta. The files on Smith's computer had creation dates of October 2, 2016, which was prior to the date of their release by WikiLeaks. Forensic examination, however, established that the creation date did not reflect when the files were downloaded to Smith's computer. (It appears the creation date was when WikiLeaks staged the document for release, as discussed in Volume I, Section III.B.3.c, *supra*.[284]) The investigation did not otherwise identify evidence that Smith obtained the files before their release by WikiLeaks.

Smith continued to send emails to an undisclosed recipient list about Clinton's deleted emails until shortly before the election. For example, on October 28, 2016, Smith wrote that there was a "tug-of-war going on within WikiLeaks over its planned releases in the next few days," and that WikiLeaks "has maintained that it will save its best revelations for last, under the theory this allows little time for response prior to the U.S. election November 8."[285] An attachment to the

---

[280] The same recruitment document listed Jerome Corsi under "Independent Groups/Organizations/Individuals," and described him as an "established author and writer from the right on President Obama and Sec. Clinton."

[281] Flynn 11/29/17 302, at 7-8; 10/15/16 Email, Smith to Flynn et al.; 8/28/16 Email, Smith to Smith (bcc: Clovis et al.).

[282] 9/16/16 Email, Ledeen to Smith.

[283] Prince 4/4/18 302, at 4-5.

[284] The forensic analysis of Smith's computer devices found that Smith used an older Apple operating system that would have preserved that October 2, 2016 creation date when it was downloaded (no matter what day it was in fact downloaded by Smith). *See* Volume I, Section III.B.3.c, *supra*. The Office tested this theory in March 2019 by downloading the two files found on Smith's computer from WikiLeaks's site using the same Apple operating system on Smith's computer; both files were successfully downloaded and retained the October 2, 2016 creation date. *See* SM-2284941, serial 62.

[285] 10/28/16 Email, Smith to Smith.

U.S. Department of Justice

~~Attorney Work Product // May Contain Material Protected Under Fed. R. Crim. P. 6(e)~~

email claimed that WikiLeaks would release "All 33k deleted Emails" by "November 1st." No emails obtained from Clinton's server were subsequently released.

Smith drafted multiple emails stating or intimating that he was in contact with Russian hackers. For example, in one such email, Smith claimed that, in August 2016, KLS Research had organized meetings with parties who had access to the deleted Clinton emails, including parties with "ties and affiliations to Russia."[286] The investigation did not identify evidence that any such meetings occurred. Associates and security experts who worked with Smith on the initiative did not believe that Smith was in contact with Russian hackers and were aware of no such connection.[287] The investigation did not establish that Smith was in contact with Russian hackers or that Smith, Ledeen, or other individuals in touch with the Trump Campaign ultimately obtained the deleted Clinton emails.

* * *

In sum, the investigation established that the GRU hacked into email accounts of persons affiliated with the Clinton Campaign, as well as the computers of the DNC and DCCC. The GRU then exfiltrated data related to the 2016 election from these accounts and computers, and disseminated that data through fictitious online personas (DCLeaks and Guccifer 2.0) and later through WikiLeaks. The investigation also established that the Trump Campaign displayed interest in the WikiLeaks releases, and that Harm to Ongoing Matter As explained in Volume I, Section V.B, *infra*, the evidence was sufficient to support computer-intrusion (and other) charges against GRU officers for their role in election-related hacking. Harm to Ongoing Matter

---

[286] 8/31/16 Email, Smith to Smith.

[287] Safron 3/20/18 302, at 3; Szobocsan 3/29/18 302, at 6.

IV. RUSSIAN GOVERNMENT LINKS TO AND CONTACTS WITH THE TRUMP CAMPAIGN

The Office identified multiple contacts—"links," in the words of the Appointment Order—between Trump Campaign officials and individuals with ties to the Russian government. The Office investigated whether those contacts constituted a third avenue of attempted Russian interference with or influence on the 2016 presidential election. In particular, the investigation examined whether these contacts involved or resulted in coordination or a conspiracy with the Trump Campaign and Russia, including with respect to Russia providing assistance to the Campaign in exchange for any sort of favorable treatment in the future. Based on the available information, the investigation did not establish such coordination.

This Section describes the principal links between the Trump Campaign and individuals with ties to the Russian government, including some contacts with Campaign officials or associates that have been publicly reported to involve Russian contacts. Each subsection begins with an overview of the Russian contact at issue and then describes in detail the relevant facts, which are generally presented in chronological order, beginning with the early months of the Campaign and extending through the post-election, transition period.

A. Campaign Period (September 2015 – November 8, 2016)

Russian-government-connected individuals and media entities began showing interest in Trump's campaign in the months after he announced his candidacy in June 2015.[288] Because Trump's status as a public figure at the time was attributable in large part to his prior business and entertainment dealings, this Office investigated whether a business contact with Russia-linked individuals and entities during the campaign period—the Trump Tower Moscow project, *see* Volume I, Section IV.A.1, *infra*—led to or involved coordination of election assistance.

Outreach from individuals with ties to Russia continued in the spring and summer of 2016, when Trump was moving toward—and eventually becoming—the Republican nominee for President. As set forth below, the Office also evaluated a series of links during this period: outreach to two of Trump's then-recently named foreign policy advisors, including a representation that Russia had "dirt" on Clinton in the form of thousands of emails (Volume I, Sections IV.A.2 & IV.A.3); dealings with a D.C.-based think tank that specializes in Russia and has connections with its government (Volume I, Section IV.A.4); a meeting at Trump Tower between the Campaign and a Russian lawyer promising dirt on candidate Clinton that was "part of Russia and its government's support for [Trump]" (Volume I, Section IV.A.5); events at the Republican National Convention (Volume I, Section IV.A.6); post-Convention contacts between Trump Campaign officials and Russia's ambassador to the United States (Volume I, Section IV.A.7); and contacts through campaign chairman Paul Manafort, who had previously worked for a Russian oligarch and a pro-Russian political party in Ukraine (Volume I, Section IV.A.8).

---

[288] For example, on August 18, 2015, on behalf of the editor-in-chief of the internet newspaper *Vzglyad*, Georgi Asatryan emailed campaign press secretary Hope Hicks asking for a phone or in-person candidate interview. 8/18/15 Email, Asatryan to Hicks. One day earlier, the publication's founder (and former Russian parliamentarian) Konstantin Rykov had registered two Russian websites—Trump2016.ru and DonaldTrump2016.ru. No interview took place.

U.S. Department of Justice

~~Attorney Work Product // May Contain Material Protected Under Fed. R. Crim. P. 6(e)~~

1. Trump Tower Moscow Project

The Trump Organization has pursued and completed projects outside the United States as part of its real estate portfolio. Some projects have involved the acquisition and ownership (through subsidiary corporate structures) of property. In other cases, the Trump Organization has executed licensing deals with real estate developers and management companies, often local to the country where the project was located.[289]

Between at least 2013 and 2016, the Trump Organization explored a similar licensing deal in Russia involving the construction of a Trump-branded property in Moscow. The project, commonly referred to as a "Trump Tower Moscow" or "Trump Moscow" project, anticipated a combination of commercial, hotel, and residential properties all within the same building. Between 2013 and June 2016, several employees of the Trump Organization, including then-president of the organization Donald J. Trump, pursued a Moscow deal with several Russian counterparties. From the fall of 2015 until the middle of 2016, Michael Cohen spearheaded the Trump Organization's pursuit of a Trump Tower Moscow project, including by reporting on the project's status to candidate Trump and other executives in the Trump Organization.[290]

a. *Trump Tower Moscow Venture with the Crocus Group (2013-2014)*

The Trump Organization and the Crocus Group, a Russian real estate conglomerate owned and controlled by Aras Agalarov, began discussing a Russia-based real estate project shortly after the conclusion of the 2013 Miss Universe pageant in Moscow.[291] Donald J. Trump Jr. served as the primary negotiator on behalf of the Trump Organization; Emin Agalarov (son of Aras Agalarov) and Irakli "Ike" Kaveladze represented the Crocus Group during negotiations,[292] with the occasional assistance of Robert Goldstone.[293]

In December 2013, Kaveladze and Trump Jr. negotiated and signed preliminary terms of

---

[289] *See, e.g., Interview of: Donald J. Trump, Jr, Senate Judiciary Committee*, 115th Cong. 151-52 (Sept. 7, 2017) (discussing licensing deals of specific projects).

[290] As noted in Volume I, Section III.D.1, *supra*, in November 2018, Cohen pleaded guilty to making false statements to Congress concerning, among other things, the duration of the Trump Tower Moscow project. *See* Information ¶ 7(a), *United States v. Michael Cohen*, 1:18-cr-850 (S.D.N.Y. Nov. 29, 2018), Doc. 2 ("*Cohen* Information").

[291] *See Interview of: Donald J. Trump, Jr, Senate Judiciary Committee,* 115th Cong. 13 (Sept. 7, 2017) ("Following the pageant the Trump Organization and Mr. Agalarov's company, Crocus Group, began preliminarily discussion [sic] potential real estate projects in Moscow."). As has been widely reported, the Miss Universe pageant—which Trump co-owned at the time—was held at the Agalarov-owned Crocus City Hall in Moscow in November 2013. Both groups were involved in organizing the pageant, and Aras Agalarov's son Emin was a musical performer at the event, which Trump attended.

[292] Kaveladze 11/16/17 302, at 2, 4-6; [Grand Jury] OSC-KAV_00385 (12/6/13 Email, Trump Jr. to Kaveladze & E. Agalarov).

[293] [Grand Jury]

U.S. Department of Justice

~~Attorney Work Product // May Contain Material Protected Under Fed. R. Crim. P. 6(e)~~

an agreement for the Trump Tower Moscow project.[294] On December 23, 2013, after discussions with Donald J. Trump, the Trump Organization agreed to accept an arrangement whereby the organization received a flat 3.5% commission on all sales, with no licensing fees or incentives.[295] The parties negotiated a letter of intent during January and February 2014.[296]

From January 2014 through November 2014, the Trump Organization and Crocus Group discussed development plans for the Moscow project. Some time before January 24, 2014, the Crocus Group sent the Trump Organization a proposal for a 800-unit, 194-meter building to be constructed at an Agalarov-owned site in Moscow called "Crocus City," which had also been the site of the Miss Universe pageant.[297] In February 2014, Ivanka Trump met with Emin Agalarov and toured the Crocus City site during a visit to Moscow.[298] From March 2014 through July 2014, the groups discussed "design standards" and other architectural elements.[299] For example, in July 2014, members of the Trump Organization sent Crocus Group counterparties questions about the "demographics of these prospective buyers" in the Crocus City area, the development of neighboring parcels in Crocus City, and concepts for redesigning portions of the building.[300] In August 2014, the Trump Organization requested specifications for a competing Marriott-branded tower being built in Crocus City.[301]

Beginning in September 2014, the Trump Organization stopped responding in a timely fashion to correspondence and proposals from the Crocus Group.[302] Communications between the two groups continued through November 2014 with decreasing frequency; what appears to be the last communication is dated November 24, 2014.[303] The project appears not to have developed past the planning stage, and no construction occurred.

---

[294] Grand Jury

[295] OSC-KAV_00452 (12/23/13 Email, Trump Jr. to Kaveladze & E. Agalarov).

[296] *See, e.g.*, OSC-KAV_01158 (Letter agreement signed by Trump Jr. & E. Agalarov); OSC-KAV_01147 (1/20/14 Email, Kaveladze to Trump Jr. et al.).

[297] *See, e.g.*, OSC-KAV_00972 (10/14/14 Email, McGee to Khoo et al.) (email from Crocus Group contractor about specifications); OSC-KAV_00540 (1/24/14 Email, McGee to Trump Jr. et al.).

[298] *See* OSC-KAV_00631 (2/5/14 Email, E. Agalarov to Ivanka Trump, Trump Jr. & Kaveladze); Goldstone Facebook post, 2/4/14 (8:01 a.m.) Investigative Technique

[299] *See, e.g.*, OSC-KAV_00791 (6/3/14 Email, Kaveladze to Trump Jr. et al.; OSC-KAV_00799 (6/10/14 Email, Trump Jr. to Kaveladze et al.); OSC-KAV_00817 (6/16/14 Email, Trump Jr. to Kaveladze et al.).

[300] OSC-KAV_00870 (7/17/14 Email, Khoo to McGee et al.).

[301] OSC-KAV_00855 (8/4/14 Email, Khoo to McGee et al.).

[302] OSC-KAV_00903 (9/29/14 Email, Tropea to McGee & Kaveladze (noting last response was on August 26, 2014)); OSC-KAV_00906 (9/29/14 Email, Kaveladze to Tropea & McGee (suggesting silence "proves my fear that those guys are bailing out of the project")); OSC-KAV_00972 (10/14/14 Email, McGee to Khoo et al.) (email from Crocus Group contractor about development specifications)).

[303] OSC-KAV_01140 (11/24/14 Email, Khoo to McGee et al.).

U.S. Department of Justice

~~Attorney Work Product // May Contain Material Protected Under Fed. R. Crim. P. 6~~(e)

b. *Communications with I.C. Expert Investment Company and Giorgi Rtskhiladze (Summer and Fall 2015)*

In the late summer of 2015, the Trump Organization received a new inquiry about pursuing a Trump Tower project in Moscow. In approximately September 2015, Felix Sater, a New York-based real estate advisor, contacted Michael Cohen, then-executive vice president of the Trump Organization and special counsel to Donald J. Trump.[304] Sater had previously worked with the Trump Organization and advised it on a number of domestic and international projects. Sater had explored the possibility of a Trump Tower project in Moscow while working with the Trump Organization and therefore knew of the organization's general interest in completing a deal there.[305] Sater had also served as an informal agent of the Trump Organization in Moscow previously and had accompanied Ivanka Trump and Donald Trump Jr. to Moscow in the mid-2000s.[306]

Sater contacted Cohen on behalf of I.C. Expert Investment Company (I.C. Expert), a Russian real-estate development corporation controlled by Andrei Vladimirovich Rozov.[307] Sater had known Rozov since approximately 2007 and, in 2014, had served as an agent on behalf of Rozov during Rozov's purchase of a building in New York City.[308] Sater later contacted Rozov and proposed that I.C. Expert pursue a Trump Tower Moscow project in which I.C. Expert would license the name and brand from the Trump Organization but construct the building on its own. Sater worked on the deal with Rozov and another employee of I.C. Expert.[309]

Cohen was the only Trump Organization representative to negotiate directly with I.C. Expert or its agents. In approximately September 2015, Cohen obtained approval to negotiate with I.C. Expert from candidate Trump, who was then president of the Trump Organization. Cohen provided updates directly to Trump about the project throughout 2015 and into 2016, assuring him the project was continuing.[310] Cohen also discussed the Trump Moscow project with Ivanka Trump as to design elements (such as possible architects to use for the project[311]) and Donald J. Trump Jr. (about his experience in Moscow and possible involvement in the project[312]) during the fall of 2015.

---

[304] Sater provided information to our Office in two 2017 interviews conducted under a proffer agreement. Grand Jury ▓▓▓▓▓▓▓▓

[305] Grand Jury ▓▓▓▓▓▓▓▓

[306] Sater 9/19/17 302, at 1-2, 5.

[307] Sater 9/19/17 302, at 3.

[308] Rozov 1/25/18 302, at 1.

[309] Rozov 1/25/18 302, at 1; *see also* 11/2/15 Email, Cohen to Rozov et al. (sending letter of intent).

[310] Cohen 9/12/18 302, at 1-2, 4-6.

[311] Cohen 9/12/18 302, at 5.

[312] Cohen 9/12/18 302, at 4-5.

U.S. Department of Justice

Attorney Work Product // May Contain Material Protected Under Fed. R. Crim. P. 6(e)

Also during the fall of 2015, Cohen communicated about the Trump Moscow proposal with Giorgi Rtskhiladze, a business executive who previously had been involved in a development deal with the Trump Organization in Batumi, Georgia.[313] Cohen stated that he spoke to Rtskhiladze in part because Rtskhiladze had pursued business ventures in Moscow, including a licensing deal with the Agalarov-owned Crocus Group.[314] On September 22, 2015, Cohen forwarded a preliminary design study for the Trump Moscow project to Rtskhiladze, adding "I look forward to your reply about this spectacular project in Moscow." Rtskhiladze forwarded Cohen's email to an associate and wrote, "[i]f we could organize the meeting in New York at the highest level of the Russian Government and Mr. Trump this project would definitely receive the worldwide attention."[315]

On September 24, 2015, Rtskhiladze sent Cohen an attachment that he described as a proposed "[l]etter to the Mayor of Moscow from Trump org," explaining that "[w]e need to send this letter to the Mayor of Moscow (second guy in Russia) he is aware of the potential project and will pledge his support."[316] In a second email to Cohen sent the same day, Rtskhiladze provided a translation of the letter, which described the Trump Moscow project as a "symbol of stronger economic, business and cultural relationships between New York and Moscow and therefore United States and the Russian Federation."[317] On September 27, 2015, Rtskhiladze sent another email to Cohen, proposing that the Trump Organization partner on the Trump Moscow project with "Global Development Group LLC," which he described as being controlled by Michail Posikhin, a Russian architect, and Simon Nizharadze.[318] Cohen told the Office that he ultimately declined the proposal and instead continued to work with I.C. Expert, the company represented by Felix Sater.[319]

c. Letter of Intent and Contacts to Russian Government (October 2015-January 2016)

i. Trump Signs the Letter of Intent on behalf of the Trump Organization

Between approximately October 13, 2015 and November 2, 2015, the Trump Organization (through its subsidiary Trump Acquisition, LLC) and I.C. Expert completed a letter of intent (LOI) for a Trump Moscow property. The LOI, signed by Trump for the Trump Organization and Rozov on behalf of I.C. Expert, was "intended to facilitate further discussions" in order to "attempt to

---

[313] Rtskhiladze was a U.S.-based executive of the Georgian company Silk Road Group. In approximately 2011, Silk Road Group and the Trump Organization entered into a licensing agreement to build a Trump-branded property in Batumi, Georgia. Rtskhiladze was also involved in discussions for a Trump-branded project in Astana, Kazakhstan. The Office twice interviewed Rtskhiladze, ████ Grand Jury

[314] Cohen 9/12/18 302, at 12; see also Rtskhiladze 5/10/18 302, at 1.

[315] 9/22/15 Email, Rtskhiladze to Nizharadze.

[316] 9/24/15 Email, Rtskhiladze to Cohen.

[317] 9/24/15 Email, Rtskhiladze to Cohen.

[318] 9/27/15 Email, Rtskhiladze to Cohen.

[319] Cohen 9/12/18 302, at 12.

U.S. Department of Justice

~~Attorney Work Product // May Contain Material Protected Under Fed. R. Crim. P. 6(e)~~

enter into a mutually acceptable agreement" related to the Trump-branded project in Moscow.[320] The LOI contemplated a development with residential, hotel, commercial, and office components, and called for "[a]pproximately 250 first class, luxury residential condominiums," as well as "[o]ne first class, luxury hotel consisting of approximately 15 floors and containing not fewer than 150 hotel rooms."[321] For the residential and commercial portions of the project, the Trump Organization would receive between 1% and 5% of all condominium sales,[322] plus 3% of all rental and other revenue.[323] For the project's hotel portion, the Trump Organization would receive a base fee of 3% of gross operating revenues for the first five years and 4% thereafter, plus a separate incentive fee of 20% of operating profit.[324] Under the LOI, the Trump Organization also would receive a $4 million "up-front fee" prior to groundbreaking.[325] Under these terms, the Trump Organization stood to earn substantial sums over the lifetime of the project, without assuming significant liabilities or financing commitments.[326]

On November 3, 2015, the day after the Trump Organization transmitted the LOI, Sater emailed Cohen suggesting that the Trump Moscow project could be used to increase candidate Trump's chances at being elected, writing:

> Buddy our boy can become President of the USA and we can engineer it. I will get all of Putins team to buy in on this, I will manage this process. . . . Michael, Putin gets on stage with Donald for a ribbon cutting for Trump Moscow, and Donald owns the republican nomination. And possibly beats Hillary and our boy is in. . . . We will manage this process better than anyone. You and I will get Donald and Vladimir on a stage together very shortly. That the game changer.[327]

Later that day, Sater followed up:

> Donald doesn't stare down, he negotiates and understands the economic issues and Putin only want to deal with a pragmatic leader, and a successful business man is a good candidate for someone who knows how to negotiate. "Business, politics, whatever it all is the same for someone who knows how to deal"

---

[320] 11/2/15 Email, Cohen to Rozov et al. (attachment) (hereinafter "LOI"); *see also* 10/13/15 Email, Sater to Cohen & Davis (attaching proposed letter of intent).

[321] LOI, p. 2.

[322] The LOI called for the Trump Organization to receive 5% of all gross sales up to $100 million; 4% of all gross sales from $100 million to $250 million; 3% of all gross sales from $250 million to $500 million; 2% of all gross sales from $500 million to $1 billion; and 1% of all gross sales over $1 billion. LOI, Schedule 2.

[323] LOI, Schedule 2.

[324] LOI, Schedule 1.

[325] LOI, Schedule 2.

[326] Cohen 9/12/18 302, at 3.

[327] 11/3/15 Email, Sater to Cohen (12:14 p.m.).

U.S. Department of Justice

~~Attorney Work Product // May Contain Material Protected Under Fed. R. Crim. P. 6(e)~~

I think I can get Putin to say that at the Trump Moscow press conference.
If he says it we own this election. Americas most difficult adversary agreeing that Donald is a good guy to negotiate. . . .
We can own this election.
Michael my next steps are very sensitive with Putins very very close people, we can pull this off.
Michael lets go. 2 boys from Brooklyn getting a USA president elected. This is good really good.[328]

According to Cohen, he did not consider the political import of the Trump Moscow project to the 2016 U.S. presidential election at the time. Cohen also did not recall candidate Trump or anyone affiliated with the Trump Campaign discussing the political implications of the Trump Moscow project with him. However, Cohen recalled conversations with Trump in which the candidate suggested that his campaign would be a significant "infomercial" for Trump-branded properties.[329]

ii. Post-LOI Contacts with Individuals in Russia

Given the size of the Trump Moscow project, Sater and Cohen believed the project required approval (whether express or implicit) from the Russian national government, including from the Presidential Administration of Russia.[330] Sater stated that he therefore began to contact the Presidential Administration through another Russian business contact.[331] In early negotiations with the Trump Organization, Sater had alluded to the need for government approval and his attempts to set up meetings with Russian officials. On October 12, 2015, for example, Sater wrote to Cohen that "all we need is Putin on board and we are golden," and that a "meeting with Putin and top deputy is tentatively set for the 14th [of October]."[332] Grand Jury ▮▮▮▮▮ this meeting was being coordinated by associates in Russia and that he had no direct interaction with the Russian government.[333]

Approximately a month later, after the LOI had been signed, Lana Erchova emailed Ivanka Trump on behalf of Erchova's then-husband Dmitry Klokov, to offer Klokov's assistance to the Trump Campaign.[334] Klokov was at that time Director of External Communications for PJSC Federal Grid Company of Unified Energy System, a large Russian electricity transmission

---

[328] 11/3/15 Email, Sater to Cohen (12:40 p.m.).

[329] Cohen 9/12/18 302, at 3-4; Cohen 8/7/18 302, at 15.

[330] Grand Jury ▮▮▮▮▮▮ Sater 12/15/17 302, at 2.

[331] Sater 12/15/17 302, at 3-4.

[332] 10/12/15 Email, Sater to Cohen (8:07 a.m.).

[333] Grand Jury ▮▮▮▮▮

[334] Ivanka Trump received an email from a woman who identified herself as "Lana E. Alexander," which said in part, "If you ask anyone who knows Russian to google my husband Dmitry Klokov, you'll see who he is close to and that he has done Putin's political campaigns." 11/16/15 Email, Erchova to I. Trump.

company, and had been previously employed as an aide and press secretary to Russia's energy minister. Ivanka Trump forwarded the email to Cohen.[335] He told the Office that, after receiving this inquiry, he had conducted an internet search for Klokov's name and concluded (incorrectly) that Klokov was a former Olympic weightlifter.[336]

Between November 18 and 19, 2015, Klokov and Cohen had at least one telephone call and exchanged several emails. Describing himself in emails to Cohen as a "trusted person" who could offer the Campaign "political synergy" and "synergy on a government level," Klokov recommended that Cohen travel to Russia to speak with him and an unidentified intermediary. Klokov said that those conversations could facilitate a later meeting in Russia between the candidate and an individual Klokov described as "our person of interest."[337] In an email to the Office, Erchova later identified the "person of interest" as Russian President Vladimir Putin.[338]

In the telephone call and follow-on emails with Klokov, Cohen discussed his desire to use a near-term trip to Russia to do site surveys and talk over the Trump Moscow project with local developers. Cohen registered his willingness also to meet with Klokov and the unidentified intermediary, but was emphatic that all meetings in Russia involving him or candidate Trump—including a possible meeting between candidate Trump and Putin—would need to be "in conjunction with the development and an official visit" with the Trump Organization receiving a formal invitation to visit.[339] (Klokov had written previously that "the visit [by candidate Trump to Russia] has to be informal.")[340]

Klokov had also previously recommended to Cohen that he separate their negotiations over a possible meeting between Trump and "the person of interest" from any existing business track.[341] Re-emphasizing that his outreach was not done on behalf of any business, Klokov added in second email to Cohen that, if publicized well, such a meeting could have "phenomenal" impact "in a business dimension" and that the "person of interest['s]" "most important support" could have significant ramifications for the "level of projects and their capacity." Klokov concluded by telling

---

[335] 11/16/15 Email, I. Trump to Cohen.

[336] Cohen 8/7/18 302, at 17. During his interviews with the Office, Cohen still appeared to believe that the Klokov he spoke with was that Olympian. The investigation, however, established that the email address used to communicate with Cohen belongs to a different Dmitry Klokov, as described above.

[337] 11/18/15 Email, Klokov to Cohen (6:51 a.m.).

[338] In July 2018, the Office received an unsolicited email purporting to be from Erchova, in which she wrote that "[a]t the end of 2015 and beginning of 2016 I was asked by my ex-husband to contact Ivanka Trump . . . and offer cooperation to Trump's team on behalf of the Russian officials." 7/27/18 Email, Erchova to Special Counsel's Office. The email claimed that the officials wanted to offer candidate Trump "land in Crimea among other things and unofficial meeting with Putin." *Id.* In order to vet the email's claims, the Office responded requesting more details. The Office did not receive any reply.

[339] 11/18/15 Email, Cohen to Klokov (7:15 a.m.).

[340] 11/18/15 Email, Klokov to Cohen (6:51 a.m.).

[341] 11/18/15 Email, Klokov to Cohen (6:51 a.m.) ("I would suggest separating your negotiations and our proposal to meet. I assure you, after the meeting level of projects and their capacity can be completely different, having the most important support.").

U.S. Department of Justice

~~Attorney Work Product // May Contain Material Protected Under Fed. R. Crim. P. 6(e)~~

Cohen that there was "no bigger warranty in any project than [the] consent of the person of interest."[342] Cohen rejected the proposal, saying that "[c]urrently our LOI developer is in talks with VP's Chief of Staff and arranging a formal invite for the two to meet."[343] This email appears to be their final exchange, and the investigation did not identify evidence that Cohen brought Klokov's initial offer of assistance to the Campaign's attention or that anyone associated with the Trump Organization or the Campaign dealt with Klokov at a later date. Cohen explained that he did not pursue the proposed meeting because he was already working on the Moscow Project with Sater, who Cohen understood to have his own connections to the Russian government.[344]

By late December 2015, however, Cohen was complaining that Sater had not been able to use those connections to set up the promised meeting with Russian government officials. Cohen told Sater that he was "setting up the meeting myself."[345] On January 11, 2016, Cohen emailed the office of Dmitry Peskov, the Russian government's press secretary, indicating that he desired contact with Sergei Ivanov, Putin's chief of staff. Cohen erroneously used the email address "Pr_peskova@prpress.**gof**.ru" instead of "Pr_peskova@prpress.**gov**.ru," so the email apparently did not go through.[346] On January 14, 2016, Cohen emailed a different address (info@prpress.gov.ru) with the following message:

> Dear Mr. Peskov,
> Over the past few months, I have been working with a company based in Russia regarding the development of a Trump Tower-Moscow project in Moscow City.
> Without getting into lengthy specifics, the communication between our two sides has stalled. As this project is too important, I am hereby requesting your assistance.
> I respectfully request someone, preferably you; contact me so that I might discuss the specifics as well as arranging meetings with the appropriate individuals.
> I thank you in advance for your assistance and look forward to hearing from you soon.[347]

Two days later, Cohen sent an email to Pr_peskova@prpress.**gov**.ru, repeating his request to speak with Sergei Ivanov.[348]

Cohen testified to Congress, and initially told the Office, that he did not recall receiving a response to this email inquiry and that he decided to terminate any further work on the Trump Moscow project as of January 2016. Cohen later admitted that these statements were false. In

---

[342] 11/19/15 Email, Klokov to Cohen (7:40 a.m.).

[343] 11/19/15 Email, Cohen to Klokov (12:56 p.m.).

[344] Cohen 9/18/18 302, at 12.

[345] FS00004 (12/30/15 Text Message, Cohen to Sater (6:17 p.m.)).

[346] 1/11/16 Email, Cohen to pr_peskova@prpress.gof.ru (9:12 a.m.).

[347] 1/14/16 Email, Cohen to info@prpress.gov.ru (9:21 a.m.).

[348] 1/16/16 Email, Cohen to pr_peskova@prpress.gov.ru (10:28 a.m.).

U.S. Department of Justice

~~Attorney Work Product // May Contain Material Protected Under Fed. R. Crim. P. 6(e)~~

fact, Cohen had received (and recalled receiving) a response to his inquiry, and he continued to work on and update candidate Trump on the project through as late as June 2016.[349]

On January 20, 2016, Cohen received an email from Elena Poliakova, Peskov's personal assistant. Writing from her personal email account, Poliakova stated that she had been trying to reach Cohen and asked that he call her on the personal number that she provided.[350] Shortly after receiving Poliakova's email, Cohen called and spoke to her for 20 minutes.[351] Cohen described to Poliakova his position at the Trump Organization and outlined the proposed Trump Moscow project, including information about the Russian counterparty with which the Trump Organization had partnered. Cohen requested assistance in moving the project forward, both in securing land to build the project and with financing. According to Cohen, Poliakova asked detailed questions and took notes, stating that she would need to follow up with others in Russia.[352]

Cohen could not recall any direct follow-up from Poliakova or from any other representative of the Russian government, nor did the Office identify any evidence of direct follow-up. However, the day after Cohen's call with Poliakova, Sater texted Cohen, asking him to "[c]all me when you have a few minutes to chat . . . It's about Putin they called today."[353] Sater then sent a draft invitation for Cohen to visit Moscow to discuss the Trump Moscow project,[354] along with a note to "[t]ell me if the letter is good as amended by me or make whatever changes you want and send it back to me."[355] After a further round of edits, on January 25, 2016, Sater sent Cohen an invitation—signed by Andrey Ryabinskiy of the company MHJ—to travel to "Moscow for a working visit" about the "prospects of development and the construction business in Russia," "the various land plots available suited for construction of this enormous Tower," and "the opportunity to co-ordinate a follow up visit to Moscow by Mr. Donald Trump."[356] According

---

[349] *Cohen* Information ¶¶ 4, 7. Cohen's interactions with President Trump and the President's lawyers when preparing his congressional testimony are discussed further in Volume II. *See* Vol. II, Section II.K.3, *infra*.

[350] 1/20/16 Email, Poliakova to Cohen (5:57 a.m.) ("Mr. Cohen[,] I can't get through to both your phones. Pls, call me.").

[351] Telephone records show a 20-minute call on January 20, 2016 between Cohen and the number Poliakova provided in her email. Call Records of Michael Cohen ▚Grand Jury▚ After the call, Cohen saved Poliakova's contact information in his Trump Organization Outlook contact list. 1/20/16 Cohen Microsoft Outlook Entry (6:22 a.m.).

[352] Cohen 9/12/18 302, at 2-3.

[353] FS00011 (1/21/16 Text Messages, Sater to Cohen).

[354] The invitation purported to be from Genbank, a Russian bank that was, according to Sater, working at the behest of a larger bank, VTB, and would consider providing financing. FS00008 (12/31/15 Text Messages, Sater & Cohen). Additional information about Genbank can be found *infra*.

[355] FS00011 (1/21/16 Text Message, Sater to Cohen (7:44 p.m.)); 1/21/16 Email, Sater to Cohen (6:49 p.m.).

[356] 1/25/16 Email, Sater to Cohen (12:01 p.m.) (attachment).

U.S. Department of Justice

~~Attorney Work Product // May Contain Material Protected Under Fed. R. Crim. P. 6(e)~~

to Cohen, he elected not to travel at the time because of concerns about the lack of concrete proposals about land plots that could be considered as options for the project.[357]

d. Discussions about Russia Travel by Michael Cohen or Candidate Trump (December 2015-June 2016)

i. Sater's Overtures to Cohen to Travel to Russia

The late January communication was neither the first nor the last time that Cohen contemplated visiting Russia in pursuit of the Trump Moscow project. Beginning in late 2015, Sater repeatedly tried to arrange for Cohen and candidate Trump, as representatives of the Trump Organization, to travel to Russia to meet with Russian government officials and possible financing partners. In December 2015, Sater sent Cohen a number of emails about logistics for traveling to Russia for meetings.[358] On December 19, 2015, Sater wrote:

> Please call me I have Evgeney [Dvoskin] on the other line.[[359]] He needs a copy of your and Donald's passports they need a scan of every page of the passports. Invitations & Visas will be issued this week by VTB Bank to discuss financing for Trump Tower Moscow. Politically neither Putins office nor Ministry of Foreign Affairs cannot issue invite, so they are inviting commercially/ business. VTB is Russia's 2 biggest bank and VTB Bank CEO Andrey Kostin, will be at all meetings with Putin so that it is a business meeting not political. We will be invited to Russian consulate this week to receive invite & have visa issued.[360]

In response, Cohen texted Sater an image of his own passport.[361] Cohen told the Office that at one point he requested a copy of candidate Trump's passport from Rhona Graff, Trump's executive assistant at the Trump Organization, and that Graff later brought Trump's passport to Cohen's

---

[357] Cohen 9/12/18 302, at 6-7.

[358] See, e.g., 12/1/15 Email, Sater to Cohen (12:41 p.m.) ("Please scan and send me a copy of your passport for the Russian Ministry of Foreign Affairs.").

[359] Toll records show that Sater was speaking to Evgeny Dvoskin. Call Records of Felix Sater [Grand Jury] Dvoskin is an executive of Genbank, a large bank with lending focused in Crimea, Ukraine. At the time that Sater provided this financing letter to Cohen, Genbank was subject to U.S. government sanctions, see Russia/Ukraine-related Sanctions and Identifications, Office of Foreign Assets Control (Dec. 22, 2015), available at https://www.treasury.gov/resource-center/sanctions/OFAC-Enforcement/Pages/20151222.aspx. Dvoskin, who had been deported from the United States in 2000 for criminal activity, was under indictment in the United States for stock fraud under the aliases Eugene Slusker and Gene Shustar. See United States v. Rizzo, et al., 2:03-cr-63 (E.D.N.Y. Feb. 6, 2003).

[360] 12/19/15 Email, Sater to Cohen (10:50 a.m.); FS00002 (12/19/15 Text Messages, Sater to Cohen, (10:53 a.m.).

[361] FS00004 (12/19/15 Text Message, Cohen to Sater); ERT_0198-256 (12/19/15 Text Messages, Cohen & Sater).

U.S. Department of Justice

~~Attorney Work Product // May Contain Material Protected Under Fed. R. Crim. P. 6(e)~~

office.[362] The investigation did not, however, establish that the passport was forwarded to Sater.[363]

Into the spring of 2016, Sater and Cohen continued to discuss a trip to Moscow in connection with the Trump Moscow project. On April 20, 2016, Sater wrote Cohen, "[t]he People wanted to know when you are coming?"[364] On May 4, 2016, Sater followed up:

> I had a chat with Moscow. ASSUMING the trip does happen the question is before or after the convention. I said I believe, but don't know for sure, that's it's probably after the convention. Obviously the pre-meeting trip (you only) can happen anytime you want but the 2 big guys where [sic] the question. I said I would confirm and revert. . . . Let me know about If I was right by saying I believe after Cleveland and also when you want to speak to them and possibly fly over.[365]

Cohen responded, "My trip before Cleveland. Trump once he becomes the nominee after the convention."[366]

The day after this exchange, Sater tied Cohen's travel to Russia to the St. Petersburg International Economic Forum ("Forum"), an annual event attended by prominent Russian politicians and businessmen. Sater told the Office that he was informed by a business associate that Peskov wanted to invite Cohen to the Forum.[367] On May 5, 2016, Sater wrote to Cohen:

> Peskov would like to invite you as his guest to the St. Petersburg Forum which is Russia's Davos it's June 16-19. He wants to meet there with you and possibly introduce you to either Putin or Medvedev, as they are not sure if 1 or both will be there.
> This is perfect. The entire business class of Russia will be there as well.
> He said anything you want to discuss including dates and subjects are on the table to discuss[.][368]

The following day, Sater asked Cohen to confirm those dates would work for him to travel; Cohen wrote back, "[w]orks for me."[369]

---

[362] Cohen 9/12/18 302, at 5.

[363] On December 21, 2015, Sater sent Cohen a text message that read, "They need a copy of DJT passport," to which Cohen responded, "After I return from Moscow with you with a date for him." FS00004 (12/21/15 Text Messages, Cohen & Sater).

[364] FS00014 (4/20/16 Text Message, Sater to Cohen (9:06 p.m.)).

[365] FS00015 (5/4/16 Text Message, Sater to Cohen (7:38 p.m.)).

[366] FS00015 (5/4/16 Text Message, Cohen to Sater (8:03 p.m.)).

[367] Sater 12/15/17 302, at 4.

[368] FS00016 (5/5/16 Text Messages, Sater to Cohen (6:26 & 6:27 a.m.)).

[369] FS00016 (5/6/16 Text Messages, Cohen & Sater).

U.S. Department of Justice

~~Attorney Work Product // May Contain Material Protected Under Fed. R. Crim. P. 6(e)~~

On June 9, 2016, Sater sent Cohen a notice that he (Sater) was completing the badges for the Forum, adding, "Putin is there on the 17th very strong chance you will meet him as well."[370] On June 13, 2016, Sater forwarded Cohen an invitation to the Forum signed by the Director of the Roscongress Foundation, the Russian entity organizing the Forum.[371] Sater also sent Cohen a Russian visa application and asked him to send two passport photos.[372] According to Cohen, the invitation gave no indication that Peskov had been involved in inviting him. Cohen was concerned that Russian officials were not actually involved or were not interested in meeting with him (as Sater had alleged), and so he decided not to go to the Forum.[373] On June 14, 2016, Cohen met Sater in the lobby of the Trump Tower in New York and informed him that he would not be traveling at that time.[374]

ii. Candidate Trump's Opportunities to Travel to Russia

The investigation identified evidence that, during the period the Trump Moscow project was under consideration, the possibility of candidate Trump visiting Russia arose in two contexts.

First, in interviews with the Office, Cohen stated that he discussed the subject of traveling to Russia with Trump twice: once in late 2015; and again in spring 2016.[375] According to Cohen, Trump indicated a willingness to travel if it would assist the project significantly. On one occasion, Trump told Cohen to speak with then-campaign manager Corey Lewandowski to coordinate the candidate's schedule. Cohen recalled that he spoke with Lewandowski, who suggested that they speak again when Cohen had actual dates to evaluate. Cohen indicated, however, that he knew that travel prior to the Republican National Convention would be impossible given the candidate's preexisting commitments to the Campaign.[376]

Second, like Cohen, Trump received and turned down an invitation to the St. Petersburg International Economic Forum. In late December 2015, Mira Duma—a contact of Ivanka Trump's from the fashion industry—first passed along invitations for Ivanka Trump and candidate Trump from Sergei Prikhodko, a Deputy Prime Minister of the Russian Federation.[377] On January 14, 2016, Rhona Graff sent an email to Duma stating that Trump was "honored to be asked to participate in the highly prestigious" Forum event, but that he would "have to decline" the invitation given his "very grueling and full travel schedule" as a presidential candidate.[378] Graff

---

[370] FS00018 (6/9/16 Text Messages, Sater & Cohen).

[371] 6/13/16 Email, Sater to Cohen (2:10 p.m.).

[372] FS00018 (6/13/16 Text Message, Sater to Cohen (2:20 p.m.)); 6/13/16 Email, Sater to Cohen.

[373] Cohen 9/12/18 302, at 6-8.

[374] FS00019 (6/14/16 Text Messages, Cohen & Sater (12:06 and 2:50 p.m.)).

[375] Cohen 9/12/18 302, at 2.

[376] Cohen 9/12/18 302, at 7.

[377] 12/21/15 Email, Mira to Ivanka Trump (6:57 a.m.) (attachments); TRUMPORG_16_000057 (1/7/16 Email, I. Trump to Graff (9:18 a.m.)).

[378] 1/14/16 Email, Graff to Mira.

asked Duma whether she recommended that Graff "send a formal note to the Deputy Prime Minister" declining his invitation; Duma replied that a formal note would be "great."[379]

It does not appear that Graff prepared that note immediately. According to written answers from President Trump,[380] Graff received an email from Deputy Prime Minister Prikhodko on March 17, 2016, again inviting Trump to participate in the 2016 Forum in St. Petersburg.[381] Two weeks later, on March 31, 2016, Graff prepared for Trump's signature a two-paragraph letter declining the invitation.[382] The letter stated that Trump's "schedule has become extremely demanding" because of the presidential campaign, that he "already ha[d] several commitments in the United States" for the time of the Forum, but that he otherwise "would have gladly given every consideration to attending such an important event."[383] Graff forwarded the letter to another executive assistant at the Trump Organization with instructions to print the document on letterhead for Trump to sign.[384]

At approximately the same time that the letter was being prepared, Robert Foresman—a New York-based investment banker—began reaching out to Graff to secure an in-person meeting with candidate Trump. According to Foresman, he had been asked by Anton Kobyakov, a Russian presidential aide involved with the Roscongress Foundation, to see if Trump could speak at the Forum.[385] Foresman first emailed Graff on March 31, 2016, following a phone introduction brokered through Trump business associate Mark Burnett (who produced the television show *The Apprentice*). In his email, Foresman referenced his long-standing personal and professional expertise in Russia and Ukraine, his work setting up an early "private channel" between Vladimir Putin and former U.S. President George W. Bush, and an "approach" he had received from "senior Kremlin officials" about the candidate. Foresman asked Graff for a meeting with the candidate, Corey Lewandowski, or "another relevant person" to discuss this and other "concrete things" Foresman felt uncomfortable discussing over "unsecure email."[386] On April 4, 2016, Graff forwarded Foresman's meeting request to Jessica Macchia, another executive assistant to Trump.[387]

---

[379] 1/15/16 Email, Mira to Graff.

[380] As explained in Volume II and Appendix C, on September 17, 2018, the Office sent written questions to the President's counsel. On November 20, 2018, the President provided written answers to those questions through counsel.

[381] Written Responses of Donald J. Trump (Nov. 20, 2018), at 17 (Response to Question IV, Part (e)) ("[D]ocuments show that Ms. Graff prepared for my signature a brief response declining the invitation.").

[382] Written Responses of Donald J. Trump (Nov. 20, 2018), at 17 (Response to Question IV, Part (e)); *see also* TRUMPORG_16_000134 (unsigned letter dated March 31, 2016).

[383] TRUMPORG_16_000134 (unsigned letter).

[384] TRUMPORG_16_000133 (3/31/16 Email, Graff to Macchia).

[385] Foresman 10/17/18 302, at 3-4.

[386] *See* TRUMPORG_16_00136 (3/31/16 Email, Foresman to Graff); *see also* Foresman 10/17/18 302, at 3-4.

[387] *See* TRUMPORG_16_00136 (4/4/16 Email, Graff to Macchia).

U.S. Department of Justice

~~Attorney Work Product // May Contain Material Protected Under Fed. R. Crim. P. 6(e)~~

With no response forthcoming, Foresman twice sent reminders to Graff—first on April 26 and again on April 30, 2016.[388] Graff sent an apology to Foresman and forwarded his April 26 email (as well as his initial March 2016 email) to Lewandowski.[389] On May 2, 2016, Graff forwarded Foresman's April 30 email—which suggested an alternative meeting with Donald Trump Jr. or Eric Trump so that Foresman could convey to them information that "should be conveyed to [the candidate] personally or [to] someone [the candidate] absolutely trusts"—to policy advisor Stephen Miller.[390]

No communications or other evidence obtained by the Office indicate that the Trump Campaign learned that Foresman was reaching out to invite the candidate to the Forum or that the Campaign otherwise followed up with Foresman until after the election, when he interacted with the Transition Team as he pursued a possible position in the incoming Administration.[391] When interviewed by the Office, Foresman denied that the specific "approach" from "senior Kremlin officials" noted in his March 31, 2016 email was anything other than Kobyakov's invitation to Roscongress. According to Foresman, the "concrete things" he referenced in the same email were a combination of the invitation itself, Foresman's personal perspectives on the invitation and Russia policy in general, and details of a Ukraine plan supported by a U.S. think tank (EastWest Institute). Foresman told the Office that Kobyakov had extended similar invitations through him to another Republican presidential candidate and one other politician. Foresman also said that Kobyakov had asked Foresman to invite Trump to speak after that other presidential candidate withdrew from the race and the other politician's participation did not work out.[392] Finally, Foresman claimed to have no plans to establish a back channel involving Trump, stating the reference to his involvement in the Bush-Putin back channel was meant to burnish his credentials to the Campaign. Foresman commented that he had not recognized any of the experts announced as Trump's foreign policy team in March 2016, and wanted to secure an in-person meeting with the candidate to share his professional background and policy views, including that Trump should decline Kobyakov's invitation to speak at the Forum.[393]

2. George Papadopoulos

George Papadopoulos was a foreign policy advisor to the Trump Campaign from March

---

[388] *See* TRUMPORG_16_00137 (4/26/16 Email, Foresman to Graff); TRUMPORG_16_00141 (4/30/16 Email, Foresman to Graff).

[389] *See* TRUMPORG_16_00139 (4/27/16 Email, Graff to Foresman); TRUMPORG_16_00137 (4/27/16 Email, Graff to Lewandowski).

[390] TRUMPORG_16_00142 (5/2/16 Email, Graff to S. Miller); *see also* TRUMPORG_16_00143 (5/2/16 Email, Graff to S. Miller) (forwarding March 2016 email from Foresman).

[391] Foresman's contacts during the transition period are discussed further in Volume I, Section IV.B.3, *infra*.

[392] Foresman 10/17/18 302, at 4.

[393] Foresman 10/17/18 302, at 8-9.

U.S. Department of Justice

~~Attorney-Work-Product // May Contain Material Protected Under Fed. R. Crim. P. 6(e)~~

2016 to early October 2016.[394] In late April 2016, Papadopoulos was told by London-based professor Joseph Mifsud, immediately after Mifsud's return from a trip to Moscow, that the Russian government had obtained "dirt" on candidate Clinton in the form of thousands of emails. One week later, on May 6, 2016, Papadopoulos suggested to a representative of a foreign government that the Trump Campaign had received indications from the Russian government that it could assist the Campaign through the anonymous release of information that would be damaging to candidate Clinton.

Papadopoulos shared information about Russian "dirt" with people outside of the Campaign, and the Office investigated whether he also provided it to a Campaign official. Papadopoulos and the Campaign officials with whom he interacted told the Office that they did not recall that Papadopoulos passed them the information. Throughout the relevant period of time and for several months thereafter, Papadopoulos worked with Mifsud and two Russian nationals to arrange a meeting between the Campaign and the Russian government. That meeting never came to pass.

a. Origins of Campaign Work

In March 2016, Papadopoulos became a foreign policy advisor to the Trump Campaign.[395] As early as the summer of 2015, he had sought a role as a policy advisor to the Campaign but, in a September 30, 2015 email, he was told that the Campaign was not hiring policy advisors.[396] In late 2015, Papadopoulos obtained a paid position on the campaign of Republican presidential candidate Ben Carson.[397]

Although Carson remained in the presidential race until early March 2016, Papadopoulos had stopped actively working for his campaign by early February 2016.[398] At that time, Papadopoulos reached out to a contact at the London Centre of International Law Practice (LCILP), which billed itself as a "unique institution . . . comprising high-level professional international law practitioners, dedicated to the advancement of global legal knowledge and the practice of international law."[399] Papadopoulos said that he had finished his role with the Carson

---

[394] Papadopoulos met with our Office for debriefings on several occasions in the summer and fall of 2017, after he was arrested and charged in a sealed criminal complaint with making false statements in a January 2017 FBI interview about, *inter alia*, the timing, extent, and nature of his interactions and communications with Joseph Mifsud and two Russian nationals: Olga Polonskaya and Ivan Timofeev. Papadopoulos later pleaded guilty, pursuant to a plea agreement, to an information charging him with making false statements to the FBI, in violation of 18 U.S.C. § 1001(a).

[395] *A Transcript of Donald Trump's Meeting with the Washington Post Editorial Board*, Washington Post (Mar. 21, 2016).

[396] 7/15/15 LinkedIn Message, Papadopoulos to Lewandowski (6:57 a.m.); 9/30/15 Email, Glassner to Papadopoulos (7:42:21 a.m.).

[397] Papadopoulos 8/10/17 302, at 2.

[398] Papadopoulos 8/10/17 302, at 2; 2/4/16 Email, Papadopoulos to Idris.

[399] London Centre of International Law Practice, at https://www.lcilp.org/ (via web.archive.org).

campaign and asked if LCILP was hiring.[400] In early February, Papadopoulos agreed to join LCILP and arrived in London to begin work.[401]

As he was taking his position at LCILP, Papadopoulos contacted Trump campaign manager Corey Lewandowski via LinkedIn and emailed campaign official Michael Glassner about his interest in joining the Trump Campaign.[402] On March 2, 2016, Papadopoulos sent Glassner another message reiterating his interest.[403] Glassner passed along word of Papadopoulos's interest to another campaign official, Joy Lutes, who notified Papadopoulos by email that she had been told by Glassner to introduce Papadopoulos to Sam Clovis, the Trump Campaign's national co-chair and chief policy advisor.[404]

At the time of Papadopoulos's March 2 email, the media was criticizing the Trump Campaign for lack of experienced foreign policy or national security advisors within its ranks.[405] To address that issue, senior Campaign officials asked Clovis to put a foreign policy team together on short notice.[406] After receiving Papadopoulos's name from Lutes, Clovis performed a Google search on Papadopoulos, learned that he had worked at the Hudson Institute, and believed that he had credibility on energy issues.[407] On March 3, 2016, Clovis arranged to speak with Papadopoulos by phone to discuss Papadopoulos joining the Campaign as a foreign policy advisor, and on March 6, 2016, the two spoke.[408] Papadopoulos recalled that Russia was mentioned as a topic, and he understood from the conversation that Russia would be an important aspect of the Campaign's foreign policy.[409] At the end of the conversation, Clovis offered Papadopoulos a role as a foreign policy advisor to the Campaign, and Papadopoulos accepted the offer.[410]

b. Initial Russia-Related Contacts

Approximately a week after signing on as a foreign policy advisor, Papadopoulos traveled

---

[400] 2/4/16 Email, Papadopoulos to Idris.

[401] 2/5/16 Email, Idris to Papadopoulos (6:11:25 p.m.); 2/6/16 Email, Idris to Papadopoulos (5:34:15 p.m.).

[402] 2/4/16 LinkedIn Message, Papadopoulos to Lewandowski (1:28 p.m.); 2/4/16 Email, Papadopoulos to Glassner (2:10:36 p.m.).

[403] 3/2/16 Email, Papadopoulos to Glassner (11:17:23 a.m.).

[404] 3/2/16 Email, Lutes to Papadopoulos (10:08:15 p.m.).

[405] Clovis 10/3/17 302 (1 of 2), at 4.

[406] Clovis 10/3/17 302 (1 of 2), at 4.

[407] Grand Jury ; 3/3/16 Email, Lutes to Clovis & Papadopoulos (6:05:47 p.m.).

[408] 3/6/16 Email, Papadopoulos to Clovis (4:24:21 p.m.).

[409] Statement of Offense ¶ 4, *United States v. George Papadopoulos*, 1:17-cr-182 (D.D.C. Oct. 5, 2017), Doc. 19 ("*Papadopoulos* Statement of Offense").

[410] Papadopoulos 8/10/17 302, at 2.

U.S. Department of Justice

~~Attorney Work Product // May Contain Material Protected Under Fed. R. Crim. P. 6(e)~~

to Rome, Italy, as part of his duties with LCILP.[411] The purpose of the trip was to meet officials affiliated with Link Campus University, a for-profit institution headed by a former Italian government official.[412] During the visit, Papadopoulos was introduced to Joseph Mifsud.

Mifsud is a Maltese national who worked as a professor at the London Academy of Diplomacy in London, England.[413] Although Mifsud worked out of London and was also affiliated with LCILP, the encounter in Rome was the first time that Papadopoulos met him.[414] Mifsud maintained various Russian contacts while living in London, as described further below. Among his contacts was ▓▓▓▓▓▓▓▓,[415] a one-time employee of the IRA, the entity that carried out the Russian social media campaign (see Volume I, Section II, supra). In January and February 2016, Mifsud and ▓▓▓▓ discussed ▓▓▓▓▓▓▓▓ possibly meeting in Russia. The investigation did not identify evidence of them meeting. Later, in the spring of 2016, ▓▓▓▓ was also in contact ▓▓▓▓▓▓▓▓▓ that was linked to an employee of the Russian Ministry of Defense, and that account had overlapping contacts with a group of Russian military-controlled Facebook accounts that included accounts used to promote the DCLeaks releases in the course of the GRU's hack-and-release operations (see Volume I, Section III.B.1, supra).

According to Papadopoulos, Mifsud at first seemed uninterested in Papadopoulos when they met in Rome.[416] After Papadopoulos informed Mifsud about his role in the Trump Campaign, however, Mifsud appeared to take greater interest in Papadopoulos.[417] The two discussed Mifsud's European and Russian contacts and had a general discussion about Russia; Mifsud also offered to introduce Papadopoulos to European leaders and others with contacts to the Russian government.[418] Papadopoulos told the Office that Mifsud's claim of substantial connections with Russian government officials interested Papadopoulos, who thought that such connections could increase his importance as a policy advisor to the Trump Campaign.[419]

---

[411] Papadopoulos 8/10/17 302, at 2-3; *Papadopoulos* Statement of Offense ¶ 5.

[412] Papadopoulos 8/10/17 302, at 2-3; Stephanie Kirchgaessner et al., *Joseph Mifsud: more questions than answers about mystery professor linked to Russia*, The Guardian (Oct. 31, 2017) ("Link Campus University . . . is headed by a former Italian interior minister named Vincenzo Scotti.").

[413] *Papadopoulos* Statement of Offense ¶ 5.

[414] Papadopoulos 8/10/17 302, at 3.

[415] *See, e.g.,* **Investigative Technique**
Harm to Ongoing Matter
▓▓▓▓▓▓▓▓▓▓▓▓▓▓▓▓▓▓▓▓▓▓▓▓▓▓▓▓

[416] *Papadopoulos* Statement of Offense ¶ 5.

[417] *Papadopoulos* Statement of Offense ¶ 5.

[418] Papadopoulos 8/10/17 302, at 3; Papadopoulos 8/11/17 302, at 2.

[419] *Papadopoulos* Statement of Offense ¶ 5.

U.S. Department of Justice

~~Attorney Work Product // May Contain Material Protected Under Fed. R. Crim. P. 6(e)~~

On March 17, 2016, Papadopoulos returned to London.[420] Four days later, candidate Trump publicly named him as a member of the foreign policy and national security advisory team chaired by Senator Jeff Sessions, describing Papadopoulos as "an oil and energy consultant" and an "[e]xcellent guy."[421]

On March 24, 2016, Papadopoulos met with Mifsud in London.[422] Mifsud was accompanied by a Russian female named Olga Polonskaya. Mifsud introduced Polonskaya as a former student of his who had connections to Vladimir Putin.[423] Papadopoulos understood at the time that Polonskaya may have been Putin's niece but later learned that this was not true.[424] During the meeting, Polonskaya offered to help Papadopoulos establish contacts in Russia and stated that the Russian ambassador in London was a friend of hers.[425] Based on this interaction, Papadopoulos expected Mifsud and Polonskaya to introduce him to the Russian ambassador in London, but that did not occur.[426]

Following his meeting with Mifsud, Papadopoulos sent an email to members of the Trump Campaign's foreign policy advisory team. The subject line of the message was "Meeting with Russian leadership--including Putin."[427] The message stated in pertinent part:

> I just finished a very productive lunch with a good friend of mine, Joseph Mifsud, the director of the London Academy of Diplomacy--who introduced me to both Putin's niece and the Russian Ambassador in London--who also acts as the Deputy Foreign Minister.[428]
>
> The topic of the lunch was to arrange a meeting between us and the Russian leadership to discuss U.S.-Russia ties under President Trump. They are keen to host us in a "neutral" city, or directly in Moscow. They said the leadership, including Putin, is ready to meet with us and Mr. Trump should there be interest. Waiting for everyone's thoughts on moving forward with this very important issue.[429]

---

[420] Papadopoulos 8/10/17 302, at 2.

[421] Phillip Rucker & Robert Costa, *Trump Questions Need for NATO, Outlines Noninterventionist Foreign Policy*, Washington Post (Mar. 21, 2016).

[422] Papadopoulos 8/10/17 302, at 3; 3/24/16 Text Messages, Mifsud & Papadopoulos.

[423] Papadopoulos 8/10/17 302, at 3.

[424] Papadopoulos 8/10/17 302, at 3; Papadopoulos 2/10/17 302, at 2-3; Papadopoulos Internet Search History (3/24/16) (revealing late-morning and early-afternoon searches on March 24, 2016 for "putin's niece," "olga putin," and "russian president niece olga," among other terms).

[425] Papadopoulos 8/10/17 302, at 3.

[426] *Papadopoulos* Statement of Offense ¶ 8 n.1.

[427] 3/24/16 Email, Papadopoulos to Page et al. (8:48:21 a.m.).

[428] Papadopoulos's statements to the Campaign were false. As noted above, the woman he met was not Putin's niece, he had not met the Russian Ambassador in London, and the Ambassador did not also serve as Russia's Deputy Foreign Minister.

[429] 3/24/16 Email, Papadopoulos to Page et al. (8:48:21 a.m.).

U.S. Department of Justice

~~Attorney Work Product // May Contain Material Protected Under Fed. R. Crim. P. 6(e)~~

Papadopoulos's message came at a time when Clovis perceived a shift in the Campaign's approach toward Russia—from one of engaging with Russia through the NATO framework and taking a strong stance on Russian aggression in Ukraine, ███[430]

Clovis's response to Papadopoulos, however, did not reflect that shift. Replying to Papadopoulos and the other members of the foreign policy advisory team copied on the initial email, Clovis wrote:

> This is most informative. Let me work it through the campaign. No commitments until we see how this plays out. My thought is that we probably should not go forward with any meetings with the Russians until we have had occasion to sit with our NATO allies, especially France, Germany and Great Britain. We need to reassure our allies that we are not going to advance anything with Russia until we have everyone on the same page.
>
> More thoughts later today. Great work.[431]

c. March 31 Foreign Policy Team Meeting

The Campaign held a meeting of the foreign policy advisory team with Senator Sessions and candidate Trump approximately one week later, on March 31, 2016, in Washington, D.C.[432] The meeting—which was intended to generate press coverage for the Campaign[433]—took place at the Trump International Hotel.[434] Papadopoulos flew to Washington for the event. At the meeting, Senator Sessions sat at one end of an oval table, while Trump sat at the other. As reflected in the photograph below (which was posted to Trump's Instagram account), Papadopoulos sat between the two, two seats to Sessions's left:

---

[430] ██ Grand Jury ██

[431] 3/24/16 Email, Clovis to Papadopoulos et al. (8:55:04 a.m.).

[432] Papadopoulos 8/10/17 302, at 4; Papadopoulos 8/11/17 302, at 3.

[433] Sessions 1/17/18 302, at 16-17.

[434] Papadopoulos 8/10/17 302, at 4.

U.S. Department of Justice

~~Attorney Work Product // May Contain Material Protected Under Fed. R. Crim. P. 6(e)~~

March 31, 2016 Meeting of Foreign Policy Team, with Papadopoulos (Fourth from Right of Candidate Trump)

During the meeting, each of the newly announced foreign policy advisors introduced themselves and briefly described their areas of experience or expertise.[435] Papadopoulos spoke about his previous work in the energy sector and then brought up a potential meeting with Russian officials.[436] Specifically, Papadopoulos told the group that he had learned through his contacts in London that Putin wanted to meet with candidate Trump and that these connections could help arrange that meeting.[437]

Trump and Sessions both reacted to Papadopoulos's statement. Papadopoulos and Campaign advisor J.D. Gordon—who told investigators in an interview that he had a "crystal clear" recollection of the meeting—have stated that Trump was interested in and receptive to the idea of a meeting with Putin.[438] Papadopoulos understood Sessions to be similarly supportive of his efforts to arrange a meeting.[439] Gordon and two other attendees, however, recall that Sessions generally opposed the proposal, though they differ in their accounts of the concerns he voiced or the strength of the opposition he expressed.[440]

d. George Papadopoulos Learns That Russia Has "Dirt" in the Form of Clinton Emails

Whatever Sessions's precise words at the March 31 meeting, Papadopoulos did not understand Sessions or anyone else in the Trump Campaign to have directed that he refrain from

---

[435] Papadopoulos 8/10/17 302, at 4.

[436] Papadopoulos 8/10/17 302, at 4.

[437] *Papadopoulos* Statement of Offense ¶ 9; *see* Gordon 8/29/17 302, at 14; Carafano 9/12/17 302, at 2; Hoskins 9/14/17 302, at 1.

[438] Papadopoulos 8/10/17 302, at 4-5; Gordon 9/7/17 302, at 4-5.

[439] Papadopoulos 8/10/17 302, at 5; Papadopoulos 8/11/17 302, at 3.

[440] Sessions 1/17/18 302, at 17; Gordon 9/7/17 302, at 5; Hoskins 9/14/17 302, at 1; Carafano 9/12/17 302, at 2.

making further efforts to arrange a meeting between the Campaign and the Russian government. To the contrary, Papadopoulos told the Office that he understood the Campaign to be supportive of his efforts to arrange such a meeting.[441]   Accordingly, when he returned to London, Papadopoulos resumed those efforts.[442]

Throughout April 2016, Papadopoulos continued to correspond with, meet with, and seek Russia contacts through Mifsud and, at times, Polonskaya.[443] For example, within a week of her initial March 24 meeting with him, Polonskaya attempted to send Papadopoulos a text message—which email exchanges show to have been drafted or edited by Mifsud—addressing Papadopoulos's "wish to engage with the Russian Federation."[444] When Papadopoulos learned from Mifsud that Polonskaya had tried to message him, he sent her an email seeking another meeting.[445] Polonskaya responded the next day that she was "back in St. Petersburg" but "would be very pleased to support [Papadopoulos's] initiatives between our two countries" and "to meet [him] again."[446] Papadopoulos stated in reply that he thought "a good step" would be to introduce him to "the Russian Ambassador in London," and that he would like to talk to the ambassador, "or anyone else you recommend, about a potential foreign policy trip to Russia."[447]

Mifsud, who had been copied on the email exchanges, replied on the morning of April 11, 2016. He wrote, "This is already been agreed. I am flying to Moscow on the 18th for a Valdai meeting, plus other meetings at the Duma. We will talk tomorrow."[448] The two bodies referenced by Mifsud are part of or associated with the Russian government: the Duma is a Russian legislative assembly,[449] while "Valdai" refers to the Valdai Discussion Club, a Moscow-based group that "is close to Russia's foreign-policy establishment."[450] Papadopoulos thanked Mifsud and said that he would see him "tomorrow."[451] For her part, Polonskaya responded that she had "already alerted my personal links to our conversation and your request," that "we are all very excited the possibility of a good relationship with Mr. Trump," and that "[t]he Russian Federation would love to welcome him once his candidature would be officially announced."[452]

---

[441] Papadopoulos 8/10/17 302, at 4-5; Papadopoulos 8/11/17 302, at 3; Papadopoulos 9/20/17 302, at 2.

[442] *Papadopoulos* Statement of Offense ¶ 10.

[443] *Papadopoulos* Statement of Offense ¶¶ 10-15.

[444] 3/29/16 Emails, Mifsud to Polonskaya (3:39 a.m. and 5:36 a.m.).

[445] 4/10/16 Email, Papadopoulos to Polonskaya (2:45:59 p.m.).

[446] 4/11/16 Email, Polonskaya to Papadopoulos (3:11:24 a.m.).

[447] 4/11/16 Email, Papadopoulos to Polonskaya (9:21:56 a.m.).

[448] 4/11/16 Email, Mifsud to Papadopoulos (11:43:53).

[449] *Papadopoulos* Statement of Offense ¶ 10(c).

[450] Anton Troianovski, *Putin Ally Warns of Arms Race as Russia Considers Response to U.S. Nuclear Stance*, Washington Post (Feb. 10, 2018).

[451] 4/11/16 Email, Papadopoulos to Mifsud (11:51:53 a.m.).

[452] 4/12/16 Email, Polonskaya to Papadopoulos (4:47:06 a.m.).

U.S. Department of Justice

~~Attorney Work Product // May Contain Material Protected Under Fed. R. Crim. P. 6(e)~~

Papadopoulos's and Mifsud's mentions of seeing each other "tomorrow" referenced a meeting that the two had scheduled for the next morning, April 12, 2016, at the Andaz Hotel in London. Papadopoulos acknowledged the meeting during interviews with the Office,[453] and records from Papadopoulos's UK cellphone and his internet-search history all indicate that the meeting took place.[454]

Following the meeting, Mifsud traveled as planned to Moscow.[455] On April 18, 2016, while in Russia, Mifsud introduced Papadopoulos over email to Ivan Timofeev, a member of the Russian International Affairs Council (RIAC).[456] Mifsud had described Timofeev as having connections with the Russian Ministry of Foreign Affairs (MFA),[457] the executive entity in Russia responsible for Russian foreign relations.[458] Over the next several weeks, Papadopoulos and Timofeev had multiple conversations over Skype and email about setting "the groundwork" for a "potential" meeting between the Campaign and Russian government officials.[459] Papadopoulos told the Office that, on one Skype call, he believed that his conversation with Timofeev was being monitored or supervised by an unknown third party, because Timofeev spoke in an official manner and Papadopoulos heard odd noises on the line.[460] Timofeev also told Papadopoulos in an April 25, 2016 email that he had just spoken "to Igor Ivanov[,] the President of RIAC and former Foreign Minister of Russia," and conveyed Ivanov's advice about how best to arrange a "Moscow visit."[461]

After a stop in Rome, Mifsud returned to England on April 25, 2016.[462] The next day, Papadopoulos met Mifsud for breakfast at the Andaz Hotel (the same location as their last

---

[453] Papadopoulos 9/19/17 302, at 7.

[454] 4/12/16 Email, Mifsud to Papadopoulos (5:44:39 a.m.) (forwarding Libya-related document); 4/12/16 Email, Mifsud to Papadopoulos & Obaid (10:28:20 a.m.); Papadopoulos Internet Search History (Apr. 11, 2016 10:56:49 p.m.) (search for "andaz hotel liverpool street"); 4/12/16 Text Messages, Mifsud & Papadopoulos.

[455] See, e.g., 4/18/16 Email, Mifsud to Papadopoulos (8:04:54 a.m.).

[456] Papadopoulos 8/10/17 302, at 5.

[457] *Papadopoulos* Statement of Offense ¶ 11.

[458] During the campaign period, Papadopoulos connected over LinkedIn with several MFA-affiliated individuals in addition to Timofeev. On April 25, 2016, he connected with Dmitry Andreyko, publicly identified as a First Secretary at the Russian Embassy in Ireland. In July 2016, he connected with Yuriy Melnik, the spokesperson for the Russian Embassy in Washington and with Alexey Krasilnikov, publicly identified as a counselor with the MFA. And on September 16, 2016, he connected with Sergei Nalobin, also identified as an MFA official. *See* Papadopoulos LinkedIn Connections ▮▮

[459] *Papadopoulos* Statement of Offense ¶ 11.

[460] Papadopoulos 8/10/17 302, at 5; Papadopoulos 9/19/17 302, at 10.

[461] 4/25/16 Email, Timofeev to Papadopoulos (8:16:35 a.m.).

[462] 4/22/16 Email, Mifsud to Papadopoulos (12:41:01 a.m.).

meeting).[463] During that meeting, Mifsud told Papadopoulos that he had met with high-level Russian government officials during his recent trip to Moscow. Mifsud also said that, on the trip, he learned that the Russians had obtained "dirt" on candidate Hillary Clinton. As Papadopoulos later stated to the FBI, Mifsud said that the "dirt" was in the form of "emails of Clinton," and that they "have thousands of emails."[464] On May 6, 2016, 10 days after that meeting with Mifsud, Papadopoulos suggested to a representative of a foreign government that the Trump Campaign had received indications from the Russian government that it could assist the Campaign through the anonymous release of information that would be damaging to Hillary Clinton.[465]

e. Russia-Related Communications With The Campaign

While he was discussing with his foreign contacts a potential meeting of campaign officials with Russian government officials, Papadopoulos kept campaign officials apprised of his efforts. On April 25, 2016, the day before Mifsud told Papadopoulos about the emails, Papadopoulos wrote to senior policy advisor Stephen Miller that "[t]he Russian government has an open invitation by Putin for Mr. Trump to meet him when he is ready," and that "[t]he advantage of being in London is that these governments tend to speak a bit more openly in 'neutral' cities."[466] On April 27, 2016, after his meeting with Mifsud, Papadopoulos wrote a second message to Miller stating that "some interesting messages [were] coming in from Moscow about a trip when the time is right."[467] The same day, Papadopoulos sent a similar email to campaign manager Corey Lewandowski, telling Lewandowski that Papadopoulos had "been receiving a lot of calls over the last month about Putin wanting to host [Trump] and the team when the time is right."[468]

Papadopoulos's Russia-related communications with Campaign officials continued throughout the spring and summer of 2016. On May 4, 2016, he forwarded to Lewandowski an email from Timofeev raising the possibility of a meeting in Moscow, asking Lewandowski whether that was "something we want to move forward with."[469] The next day, Papadopoulos forwarded the same Timofeev email to Sam Clovis, adding to the top of the email "Russia update."[470] He included the same email in a May 21, 2016 message to senior Campaign official Paul Manafort, under the subject line "Request from Russia to meet Mr. Trump," stating that "Russia has been eager to meet Mr. Trump for quite sometime and have been reaching out to me

---

[463] *Papadopoulos* Statement of Offense ¶ 14; 4/25/16 Text Messages, Mifsud & Papadopoulos.

[464] *Papadopoulos* Statement of Offense ¶ 14.

[465] This information is contained in the FBI case-opening document and related materials. ~~The information is law-enforcement sensitive (LES) and must be treated accordingly in any external dissemination.~~ The foreign government conveyed this information to the U.S. government on July 26, 2016, a few days after WikiLeaks's release of Clinton-related emails. The FBI opened its investigation of potential coordination between Russia and the Trump Campaign a few days later based on the information.

[466] 4/25/16 Email, Papadopoulos to S. Miller (8:12:44 p.m.).

[467] 4/27/16 Email, Papadopoulos to S. Miller (6:55:58 p.m.).

[468] 4/27/16 Email, Papadopoulos to Lewandowski (7:15:14 p.m.).

[469] 5/4/16 Email, Papadopoulos to Lewandowski (8:14:49 a.m.).

[470] 5/5/16 Email, Papadopoulos to Clovis (7:15:21 p.m.).

to discuss."[471] Manafort forwarded the message to another Campaign official, without including Papadopoulos, and stated: "Let[']s discuss. We need someone to communicate that [Trump] is not doing these trips. It should be someone low level in the Campaign so as not to send any signal."[472]

On June 1, 2016, Papadopoulos replied to an earlier email chain with Lewandowski about a Russia visit, asking if Lewandowski "want[ed] to have a call about this topic" and whether "we were following up with it."[473] After Lewandowski told Papadopoulos to "connect with" Clovis because he was "running point," Papadopoulos emailed Clovis that "the Russian MFA" was asking him "if Mr. Trump is interested in visiting Russia at some point."[474] Papadopoulos wrote in an email that he "[w]anted to pass this info along to you for you to decide what's best to do with it and what message I should send (or to ignore)."[475]

After several email and Skype exchanges with Timofeev,[476] Papadopoulos sent one more email to Lewandowski on June 19, 2016, Lewandowski's last day as campaign manager.[477] The email stated that "[t]he Russian ministry of foreign affairs" had contacted him and asked whether, if Mr. Trump could not travel to Russia, a campaign representative such as Papadopoulos could attend meetings.[478] Papadopoulos told Lewandowski that he was "willing to make the trip off the record if it's in the interest of Mr. Trump and the campaign to meet specific people."[479]

Following Lewandowski's departure from the Campaign, Papadopoulos communicated with Clovis and Walid Phares, another member of the foreign policy advisory team, about an off-the-record meeting between the Campaign and Russian government officials or with Papadopoulos's other Russia connections, Mifsud and Timofeev.[480] Papadopoulos also interacted

---

[471] 5/21/16 Email, Papadopoulos to Manafort (2:30:14 p.m.).

[472] *Papadopoulos* Statement of Offense ¶ 19 n.2.

[473] 6/1/16 Email, Papadopoulos to Lewandowski (3:08:18 p.m.).

[474] 6/1/16 Email, Lewandowski to Papadopoulos (3:20:03 p.m.); 6/1/16 Email, Papadopoulos to Clovis (3:29:14 p.m.).

[475] 6/1/16 Email, Papadopoulos to Clovis (3:29:14 p.m.). Papadopoulos's email coincided in time with another message to Clovis suggesting a Trump-Putin meeting. First, on May 15, 2016, David Klein— a distant relative of then-Trump Organization lawyer Jason Greenblatt—emailed Clovis about a potential Campaign meeting with Berel Lazar, the Chief Rabbi of Russia. The email stated that Klein had contacted Lazar in February about a possible Trump-Putin meeting and that Lazar was "a very close confidante of Putin." DJTFP00011547 (5/15/16 Email, Klein to Clovis (5:45:24 p.m.)). The investigation did not find evidence that Clovis responded to Klein's email or that any further contacts of significance came out of Klein's subsequent meeting with Greenblatt and Rabbi Lazar at Trump Tower. Klein 8/30/18 302, at 2.

[476] *Papadopoulos* Statement of Offense ¶ 21(a).

[477] Grand Jury

[478] 6/19/16 Email, Papadopoulos to Lewandowski (1:11:11 p.m.).

[479] 6/19/16 Email, Papadopoulos to Lewandowski (1:11:11 p.m.).

[480] *Papadopoulos* Statement of Offense ¶ 21; 7/14/16 Email, Papadopoulos to Timofeev (11:57:24 p.m.); 7/15/16 Email, Papadopoulos to Mifsud; 7/27/16 Email, Papadopoulos to Mifsud (2:14:18 p.m.).

U.S. Department of Justice

~~Attorney Work Product // May Contain Material Protected Under Fed. R. Crim. P. 6(e)~~

directly with Clovis and Phares in connection with the summit of the Transatlantic Parliamentary Group on Counterterrorism (TAG), a group for which Phares was co-secretary general.[481] On July 16, 2016, Papadopoulos attended the TAG summit in Washington, D.C., where he sat next to Clovis (as reflected in the photograph below).[482]

George Papadopoulos (far right) and Sam Clovis (second from right)

Although Clovis claimed to have no recollection of attending the TAG summit,[483] Papadopoulos remembered discussing Russia and a foreign policy trip with Clovis and Phares during the event.[484] Papadopoulos's recollection is consistent with emails sent before and after the TAG summit. The pre-summit messages included a July 11, 2016 email in which Phares suggested meeting Papadopoulos the day after the summit to chat,[485] and a July 12 message in the same chain in which Phares advised Papadopoulos that other summit attendees "are very nervous about Russia. So be aware."[486] Ten days after the summit, Papadopoulos sent an email to Mifsud listing Phares and Clovis as other "participants" in a potential meeting at the London Academy of Diplomacy.[487]

Finally, Papadopoulos's recollection is also consistent with handwritten notes from a

---

[481] Papadopoulos 9/19/17 302, at 16-17; *9th TAG Summit in Washington DC*, Transatlantic Parliament Group on Counter Terrorism.

[482] *9th TAG Summit in Washington DC*, Transatlantic Parliament Group on Counter Terrorism.

[483] Grand Jury

[484] Papadopoulos 9/19/17 302, at 16-17.

[485] 7/11/16 Email, Phares to Papadopoulos.

[486] 7/12/16 Email, Phares to Papadopoulos (14:52:29).

[487] 7/27/16 Email, Papadopoulos to Mifsud (14:14:18).

U.S. Department of Justice

Attorney Work Product // May Contain Material Protected Under Fed. R. Crim. P. 6(e)

journal that he kept at the time.[488] Those notes, which are reprinted in part below, appear to refer to potential September 2016 meetings in London with representatives of the "office of Putin," and suggest that Phares, Clovis, and Papadopoulos ("Walid/Sam me") would attend without the official backing of the Campaign ("no official letter/no message from Trump").[489]

September: Have an exploratory meeting to or lose. In September – if allowed they will blast Mr. Trump. We want the meeting in London/England Walid/Sam me No official letter/no message from Trump They are talking to us. -It is a lot of risk. -Office of Putin. -Explore: we are a campaign. off Israel! EGYPT Willingness to meet the FM sp with Walid/Sam -FM coming -Useful to have a session with him.	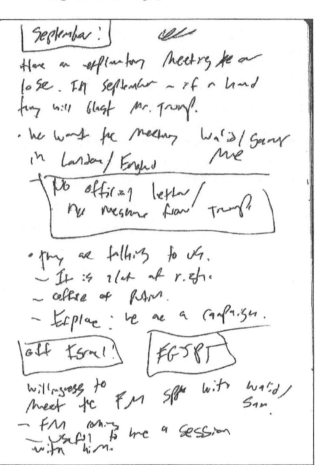

Later communications indicate that Clovis determined that he (Clovis) could not travel. On August 15, 2016, Papadopoulos emailed Clovis that he had received requests from multiple foreign governments, "even Russia[]," for "closed door workshops/consultations abroad," and asked whether there was still interest for Clovis, Phares, and Papadopoulos "to go on that trip."[490] Clovis copied Phares on his response, which said that he could not "travel before the election" but that he "would encourage [Papadopoulos] and Walid to make the trips, if it is feasible."[491]

---

[488] Papadopoulos 9/20/17 302, at 3.

[489] Papadopoulos declined to assist in deciphering his notes, telling investigators that he could not read his own handwriting from the journal. Papadopoulos 9/19/17 302, at 21. The notes, however, appear to read as listed in the column to the left of the image above.

[490] 8/15/16 Email, Papadopoulos to Clovis (11:59:07 a.m.).

[491] 8/15/16 Email, Clovis to Papadopoulos (12:01:45 p.m.).

U.S. Department of Justice

~~Attorney Work Product // May Contain Material Protected Under Fed. R. Crim. P. 6(e)~~

Papadopoulos was dismissed from the Trump Campaign in early October 2016, after an interview he gave to the Russian news agency *Interfax* generated adverse publicity.[492]

f. Trump Campaign Knowledge of "Dirt"

Papadopoulos admitted telling at least one individual outside of the Campaign—specifically, the then-Greek foreign minister—about Russia's obtaining Clinton-related emails.[493] In addition, a different foreign government informed the FBI that, 10 days after meeting with Mifsud in late April 2016, Papadopoulos suggested that the Trump Campaign had received indications from the Russian government that it could assist the Campaign through the anonymous release of information that would be damaging to Hillary Clinton.[494] (This conversation occurred after the GRU spearphished Clinton Campaign chairman John Podesta and stole his emails, and the GRU hacked into the DCCC and DNC, *see* Volume I, Sections III.A & III.B, *supra*.) Such disclosures raised questions about whether Papadopoulos informed any Trump Campaign official about the emails.

When interviewed, Papadopoulos and the Campaign officials who interacted with him told the Office that they could not recall Papadopoulos's sharing the information that Russia had obtained "dirt" on candidate Clinton in the form of emails or that Russia could assist the Campaign through the anonymous release of information about Clinton. Papadopoulos stated that he could not clearly recall having told anyone on the Campaign and wavered about whether he accurately remembered an incident in which Clovis had been upset after hearing Papadopoulos tell Clovis that Papadopoulos thought "they have her emails."[495] The Campaign officials who interacted or corresponded with Papadopoulos have similarly stated, with varying degrees of certainty, that he did not tell them. Senior policy advisor Stephen Miller, for example, did not remember hearing anything from Papadopoulos or Clovis about Russia having emails of or dirt on candidate Clinton.[496] Clovis stated that he did not recall anyone, including Papadopoulos, having given him non-public information that a foreign government might be in possession of material damaging to Hillary Clinton.[497] Grand Jury

[98] Grand Jury

---

[492] *George Papadopoulos: Sanctions Have Done Little More Than to Turn Russia Towards China*, Interfax (Sept. 30, 2016).

[493] Papadopoulos 9/19/17 302, at 14-15; Def. Sent. Mem., *United States v. George Papadopoulos*, 1:17-cr-182 (D.D.C. Aug. 31, 2018), Doc. 45.

[494] *See* footnote 465 of Volume I, Section IV.A.2.d, *supra*.

[495] Papadopoulos 8/10/17 302, at 5; Papadopoulos 8/11/17 302, at 5; Papadopoulos 9/20/17 302, at 2.

[496] S. Miller 12/14/17 302, at 10.

[497] Grand Jury

[498] Grand Jury

U.S. Department of Justice

~~Attorney Work Product // May Contain Material Protected Under Fed. R. Crim. P. 6(e)~~

.[499] No documentary evidence, and nothing in the email accounts or other communications facilities reviewed by the Office, shows that Papadopoulos shared this information with the Campaign.

g. Additional George Papadopoulos Contact

The Office investigated another Russia-related contact with Papadopoulos. The Office was not fully able to explore the contact because the individual at issue—Sergei Millian—remained out of the country since the inception of our investigation and declined to meet with members of the Office despite our repeated efforts to obtain an interview.

Papadopoulos first connected with Millian via LinkedIn on July 15, 2016, shortly after Papadopoulos had attended the TAG Summit with Clovis.[500] Millian, an American citizen who is a native of Belarus, introduced himself "as president of [the] New York-based Russian American Chamber of Commerce," and claimed that through that position he had "insider knowledge and direct access to the top hierarchy in Russian politics."[501] Papadopoulos asked Timofeev whether he had heard of Millian.[502] Although Timofeev said no,[503] Papadopoulos met Millian in New York City.[504] The meetings took place on July 30 and August 1, 2016.[505] Afterwards, Millian invited Papadopoulos to attend—and potentially speak at—two international energy conferences, including one that was to be held in Moscow in September 2016.[506] Papadopoulos ultimately did not attend either conference.

On July 31, 2016, following his first in-person meeting with Millian, Papadopoulos emailed Trump Campaign official Bo Denysyk to say that he had been contacted "by some leaders of Russian-American voters here in the US about their interest in voting for Mr. Trump," and to ask whether he should "put you in touch with their group (US-Russia chamber of commerce)."[507] Denysyk thanked Papadopoulos "for taking the initiative," but asked him to "hold off with

---

[499] [Grand Jury]

[500] 7/15/16 LinkedIn Message, Millian to Papadopoulos.

[501] 7/15/16 LinkedIn Message, Millian to Papadopoulos.

[502] 7/22/16 Facebook Message, Papadopoulos to Timofeev (7:40:23 p.m.); 7/26/16 Facebook Message, Papadopoulos to Timofeev (3:08:57 p.m.).

[503] 7/23/16 Facebook Message, Timofeev to Papadopoulos (4:31:37 a.m.); 7/26/16 Facebook Message, Timofeev to Papadopoulos (3:37:16 p.m.).

[504] 7/16/16 Text Messages, Papadopoulos & Millian (7:55:43 p.m.).

[505] 7/30/16 Text Messages, Papadopoulos & Millian (5:38 & 6:05 p.m.); 7/31/16 Text Messages, Millian & Papadopoulos (3:48 & 4:18 p.m.); 8/1/16 Text Message, Millian to Papadopoulos (8:19 p.m.).

[506] 8/2/16 Text Messages, Millian & Papadopoulos (3:04 & 3:05 p.m.); 8/3/16 Facebook Messages, Papadopoulos & Millian (4:07:37 a.m. & 1:11:58 p.m.).

[507] 7/31/16 Email, Papadopoulos to Denysyk (12:29:59 p.m.).

U.S. Department of Justice

~~Attorney Work Product // May Contain Material Protected Under Fed. R. Crim. P. 6(e)~~

outreach to Russian-Americans" because "too many articles" had already portrayed the Campaign, then-campaign chairman Paul Manafort, and candidate Trump as "being pro-Russian."[508]

On August 23, 2016, Millian sent a Facebook message to Papadopoulos promising that he would "share with you a disruptive technology that might be instrumental in your political work for the campaign."[509] Papadopoulos claimed to have no recollection of this matter.[510]

On November 9, 2016, shortly after the election, Papadopoulos arranged to meet Millian in Chicago to discuss business opportunities, including potential work with Russian "billionaires who are not under sanctions."[511] The meeting took place on November 14, 2016, at the Trump Hotel and Tower in Chicago.[512] According to Papadopoulos, the two men discussed partnering on business deals, but Papadopoulos perceived that Millian's attitude toward him changed when Papadopoulos stated that he was only pursuing private-sector opportunities and was not interested in a job in the Administration.[513] The two remained in contact, however, and had extended online discussions about possible business opportunities in Russia.[514] The two also arranged to meet at a Washington, D.C. bar when both attended Trump's inauguration in late January 2017.[515]

3. Carter Page

Carter Page worked for the Trump Campaign from January 2016 to September 2016. He was formally and publicly announced as a foreign policy advisor by the candidate in March 2016.[516] Page had lived and worked in Russia, and he had been approached by Russian intelligence officers several years before he volunteered for the Trump Campaign. During his time with the Campaign, Page advocated pro-Russia foreign policy positions and traveled to Moscow in his personal capacity. Russian intelligence officials had formed relationships with Page in 2008 and 2013 and Russian officials may have focused on Page in 2016 because of his affiliation with the Campaign. However, the investigation did not establish that Page coordinated with the Russian government in its efforts to interfere with the 2016 presidential election.

---

[508] 7/31/16 Email, Denysyk to Papadopoulos (21:54:52).

[509] 8/23/16 Facebook Message, Millian to Papadopoulos (2:55:36 a.m.).

[510] Papadopoulos 9/20/17 302, at 2.

[511] 11/10/16 Facebook Message, Millian to Papadopoulos (9:35:05 p.m.).

[512] 11/14/16 Facebook Message, Millian to Papadopoulos (1:32:11 a.m.).

[513] Papadopoulos 9/19/17 302, at 19.

[514] E.g., 11/29/16 Facebook Messages, Papadopoulos & Millian (5:09 - 5:11 p.m.); 12/7/16 Facebook Message, Millian to Papadopoulos (5:10:54 p.m.).

[515] 1/20/17 Facebook Messages, Papadopoulos & Millian (4:37-4:39 a.m.).

[516] Page was interviewed by the FBI during five meetings in March 2017, before the Special Counsel's appointment. Grand Jury

95

U.S. Department of Justice

~~Attorney Work Product // May Contain Material Protected Under Fed. R. Crim. P. 6(e)~~

a. Background

Before he began working for the Campaign in January 2016, Page had substantial prior experience studying Russian policy issues and living and working in Moscow. From 2004 to 2007, Page was the deputy branch manager of Merrill Lynch's Moscow office.[517] There, he worked on transactions involving the Russian energy company Gazprom and came to know Gazprom's deputy chief financial officer, Sergey Yatsenko.[518]

In 2008, Page founded Global Energy Capital LLC (GEC), an investment management and advisory firm focused on the energy sector in emerging markets.[519] Grand Jury [520] The company otherwise had no sources of income, and Page was forced to draw down his life savings to support himself and pursue his business venture.[521] Page asked Yatsenko to work with him at GEC as a senior advisor on a contingency basis, Grand Jury [522]

In 2008, Page met Alexander Bulatov, a Russian government official who worked at the Russian Consulate in New York.[523] Page later learned that Bulatov was a Russian intelligence officer, Grand Jury [524]

In 2013, Victor Podobnyy, another Russian intelligence officer working covertly in the United States under diplomatic cover, formed a relationship with Page.[525] Podobnyy met Page at an energy symposium in New York City and began exchanging emails with him.[526] Podobnyy and Page also met in person on multiple occasions, during which Page offered his outlook on the future of the energy industry and provided documents to Podobnyy about the energy business.[527] In a recorded conversation on April 8, 2013, Podobnyy told another intelligence officer that Page was interested in business opportunities in Russia.[528] In Podobnyy's words, Page "got hooked on

---

[517] *Testimony of Carter Page, Hearing Before the U.S. House of Representatives, Permanent Select Committee on Intelligence*, 115th Cong. 40 (Nov. 2, 2017) (exhibit).

[518] Page 3/30/17 302, at 10.

[519] Grand Jury

[520] Grand Jury

[521] Grand Jury

[522] Page 3/30/17 302, at 10; Grand Jury

[523] Grand Jury

[524] Grand Jury

[525] Grand Jury Complaint ¶¶ 22, 24, 32, *United States v. Buryakov*, 1:15-mj-215 (S.D.N.Y. Jan. 23, 2015), Doc. 1 ("*Buryakov* Complaint").

[526] *Buryakov* Complaint ¶ 34.

[527] *Buryakov* Complaint ¶ 34.

[528] *Buryakov* Complaint ¶ 32.

U.S. Department of Justice

~~Attorney Work Product // May Contain Material Protected Under Fed. R. Crim. P. 6(e)~~

Gazprom thinking that if they have a project, he could . . . rise up. Maybe he can. . . . [I]t's obvious that he wants to earn lots of money."[529] Podobnyy said that he had led Page on by "feed[ing] him empty promises" that Podobnyy would use his Russian business connections to help Page.[530] Podobnyy told the other intelligence officer that his method of recruiting foreign sources was to promise them favors and then discard them once he obtained relevant information from them.[531]

In 2015, Podobnyy and two other Russian intelligence officers were charged with conspiracy to act as an unregistered agent of a foreign government.[532] The criminal complaint detailed Podobnyy's interactions with and conversations about Page, who was identified only as "Male-1."[533] Based on the criminal complaint's description of the interactions, Page was aware that he was the individual described as "Male-1."[534] Page later spoke with a Russian government official at the United Nations General Assembly and identified himself so that the official would understand he was "Male-1" from the Podobnyy complaint.[535] Page told the official that he "didn't do anything" Grand Jury .[536]

In interviews with the FBI before the Office's opening, Page acknowledged that he understood that the individuals he had associated with were members of the Russian intelligence services, but he stated that he had only provided immaterial non-public information to them and that he did not view this relationship as a backchannel.[537] Page told investigating agents that "the more immaterial non-public information I give them, the better for this country."[538]

b. Origins of and Early Campaign Work

In January 2016, Page began volunteering on an informal, unpaid basis for the Trump Campaign after Ed Cox, a state Republican Party official, introduced Page to Trump Campaign officials.[539] Page told the Office that his goal in working on the Campaign was to help candidate Trump improve relations with Russia.[540] To that end, Page emailed Campaign officials offering his thoughts on U.S.-Russia relations, prepared talking points and briefing memos on Russia, and

---

[529] *Buryakov* Complaint.

[530] *Buryakov* Complaint.

[531] *Buryakov* Complaint.

[532] *See Buryakov* Complaint; *see also* Indictment, *United States v. Buryakov*, 1:15-cr-73 (S.D.N.Y. Feb. 9, 2015), Doc. 10; Grand Jury

[533] *Buryakov* Complaint ¶¶ 32-34; Grand Jury

[534] Grand Jury

[535] Page 3/16/17 302, at 4; Grand Jury

[536] Page 3/16/17 302, at 4; Grand Jury

[537] Page 3/30/17 302, at 6; Page 3/31/17 302, at 1.

[538] Page 3/31/17 302, at 1.

[539] Page 3/16/17 302, at 1; Grand Jury

[540] Page 3/10/17 302, at 2.

U.S. Department of Justice

~~Attorney Work Product // May Contain Material Protected Under Fed. R. Crim. P. 6(e)~~

proposed that candidate Trump meet with President Vladimir Putin in Moscow.[541]

In communications with Campaign officials, Page also repeatedly touted his high-level contacts in Russia and his ability to forge connections between candidate Trump and senior Russian governmental officials. For example, on January 30, 2016, Page sent an email to senior Campaign officials stating that he had "spent the past week in Europe and ha[d] been in discussions with some individuals with close ties to the Kremlin" who recognized that Trump could have a "game-changing effect . . . in bringing the end of the new Cold War."[542] The email stated that "[t]hrough [his] discussions with these high level contacts," Page believed that "a direct meeting in Moscow between Mr[.] Trump and Putin could be arranged."[543] Page closed the email by criticizing U.S. sanctions on Russia.[544] Grand Jury

[545]

On March 21, 2016, candidate Trump formally and publicly identified Page as a member of his foreign policy team to advise on Russia and the energy sector.[546] Over the next several months, Page continued providing policy-related work product to Campaign officials. For example, in April 2016, Page provided feedback on an outline for a foreign policy speech that the candidate gave at the Mayflower Hotel,[547] *see* Volume I, Section IV.A.4, *infra*. In May 2016, Page prepared an outline of an energy policy speech for the Campaign and then traveled to Bismarck, North Dakota, to watch the candidate deliver the speech.[548] Chief policy advisor Sam Clovis expressed appreciation for Page's work and praised his work to other Campaign officials.[549]

c. Carter Page's July 2016 Trip To Moscow

Page's affiliation with the Trump Campaign took on a higher profile and drew the attention of Russian officials after the candidate named him a foreign policy advisor. As a result, in late April 2016, Page was invited to give a speech at the July 2016 commencement ceremony at the

---

[541] *See, e.g.*, 1/30/16 Email, Page to Glassner et al.; 3/17/16 Email, Page to Clovis (attaching a "President's Daily Brief" prepared by Page that discussed the "severe degradation of U.S.-Russia relations following Washington's meddling" in Ukraine); Grand Jury

[542] 1/30/16 Email, Page to Glassner et al.

[543] 1/30/16 Email, Page to Glassner et al.

[544] 1/30/16 Email, Page to Glassner et al.

[545] Grand Jury

[546] *A Transcript of Donald Trump's Meeting with the Washington Post Editorial Board*, Washington Post (Mar. 21, 2016); Grand Jury

[547] Grand Jury

[548] Grand Jury

[549] *See, e.g.*, 3/28/16 Email, Clovis to Lewandowski et al. (forwarding notes prepared by Page and stating, "I wanted to let you know the type of work some of our advisors are capable of.").

New Economic School (NES) in Moscow.[550] The NES commencement ceremony generally featured high-profile speakers; for example, President Barack Obama delivered a commencement address at the school in 2009.[551] NES officials told the Office that the interest in inviting Page to speak at NES was based entirely on his status as a Trump Campaign advisor who served as the candidate's Russia expert.[552] Andrej Krickovic, an associate of Page's and assistant professor at the Higher School of Economics in Russia, recommended that NES rector Shlomo Weber invite Page to give the commencement address based on his connection to the Trump Campaign.[553] Denis Klimentov, an employee of NES, said that when Russians learned of Page's involvement in the Trump Campaign in March 2016, the excitement was palpable.[554] Weber recalled that in summer 2016 there was substantial interest in the Trump Campaign in Moscow, and he felt that bringing a member of the Campaign to the school would be beneficial.[555]

Page was eager to accept the invitation to speak at NES, and he sought approval from Trump Campaign officials to make the trip to Russia.[556] On May 16, 2016, while that request was still under consideration, Page emailed Clovis, J.D. Gordon, and Walid Phares and suggested that candidate Trump take his place speaking at the commencement ceremony in Moscow.[557] On June 19, 2016, Page followed up again to request approval to speak at the NES event and to reiterate that NES "would love to have Mr. Trump speak at this annual celebration" in Page's place.[558] Campaign manager Corey Lewandowski responded the same day, saying, "If you want to do this, it would be out side [sic] of your role with the DJT for President campaign. I am certain Mr. Trump will not be able to attend."[559]

In early July 2016, Page traveled to Russia for the NES events. On July 5, 2016, Denis Klimentov, copying his brother, Dmitri Klimentov,[560] emailed Maria Zakharova, the Director of the Russian Ministry of Foreign Affairs' Information and Press Department, about Page's visit and his connection to the Trump Campaign.[561] Denis Klimentov said in the email that he wanted to draw the Russian government's attention to Page's visit in Moscow.[562] His message to Zakharova

---

[550] Page 3/16/17 302, at 2-3; Page 3/10/17 302, at 3.

[551] S. Weber 7/28/17 302, at 3.

[552] Y. Weber 6/1/17 302, at 4-5; S. Weber 7/28/17 302, at 3.

[553] *See* Y. Weber 6/1/17 302, at 4; S. Weber 7/28/17 302, at 3.

[554] De. Klimentov 6/9/17 302, at 2.

[555] S. Weber 7/28/17 302, at 3.

[556] *See* 5/16/16 Email, Page to Phares et al. (referring to submission of a "campaign advisor request form").

[557] Grand Jury ; 5/16/16 Email, Page to Phares et al.

[558] 6/19/16 Email, Page to Gordon et al.

[559] 6/19/16 Email, Lewandowski to Page et al.

[560] Dmitri Klimentov is a New York-based public relations consultant.

[561] 7/5/16 Email, Klimentov to Zakharova (translated).

[562] 7/5/16 Email, Klimentov to Zakharova (translated).

U.S. Department of Justice

~~Attorney Work Product // May Contain Material Protected Under Fed. R. Crim. P. 6(e)~~

continued: "Page is Trump's adviser on foreign policy. He is a known businessman; he used to work in Russia. . . . If you have any questions, I will be happy to help contact him."[563] Dmitri Klimentov then contacted Russian Press Secretary Dmitry Peskov about Page's visit to see if Peskov wanted to introduce Page to any Russian government officials.[564] The following day, Peskov responded to what appears to have been the same Denis Klimentov-Zakharova email thread. Peskov wrote, "I have read about [Page]. Specialists say that he is far from being the main one. So I better not initiate a meeting in the Kremlin."[565]

On July 7, 2016, Page delivered the first of his two speeches in Moscow at NES.[566] In the speech, Page criticized the U.S. government's foreign policy toward Russia, stating that "Washington and other Western capitals have impeded potential progress through their often hypocritical focus on ideas such as democratization, inequality, corruption and regime change."[567] On July 8, 2016, Page delivered a speech during the NES commencement.[568] After Page delivered his commencement address, Russian Deputy Prime Minister and NES board member Arkady Dvorkovich spoke at the ceremony and stated that the sanctions the United States had imposed on Russia had hurt the NES.[569] Page and Dvorkovich shook hands at the commencement ceremony, and Weber recalled that Dvorkovich made statements to Page about working together in the future.[570] ██████ Grand Jury ██████[571] .

Page said that, during his time in Moscow, he met with friends and associates he knew from when he lived in Russia, including Andrey Baranov, a former Gazprom employee who had become the head of investor relations at Rosneft, a Russian energy company.[572] Page stated that he and Baranov talked about "immaterial non-public" information.[573] Page believed he and Baranov discussed Rosneft president Igor Sechin, and he thought Baranov might have mentioned

---

[563] 7/5/16 Email, Klimentov to Zakharova (translated).

[564] Dm. Klimentov 11/27/18 302, at 1-2.

[565] 7/6/16 Email, Peskov to Klimentov (translated).

[566] Page 3/10/17 302, at 3.

[567] *See* Carter W. Page, *The Lecture of Trump's Advisor Carter Page in Moscow,* YouTube Channel Katehon Think Tank, Posted July 7, 2016, *available at* https://www.youtube.com/watch?time_continue=28&v=1CYF29saA9w. Page also provided the FBI with a copy of his speech and slides from the speech. *See* Carter Page, "The Evolution of the World Economy: Trends and Potential," Speech at National Economic Speech (July 7, 2016).

[568] Page 3/10/17 302, at 3.

[569] Page 3/16/17 302, at 3.

[570] S. Weber 7/28/17 302, at 4.

[571] ██████ Grand Jury ██████ .

[572] Page 3/10/17 302, at 3; Page 3/30/17 302, at 3; Page 3/31/17 302, at 2.

[573] Page 3/30/17 302, at 3.

U.S. Department of Justice

~~Attorney Work Product // May Contain Material Protected Under Fed. R. Crim. P. 6(e)~~

the possibility of a sale of a stake in Rosneft in passing.[574]   Page recalled mentioning his involvement in the Trump Campaign with Baranov, although he did not remember details of the conversation.[575]   Page also met with individuals from Tatneft, a Russian energy company, to discuss possible business deals, including having Page work as a consultant.[576]

On July 8, 2016, while he was in Moscow, Page emailed several Campaign officials and stated he would send "a readout soon regarding some incredible insights and outreach I've received from a few Russian legislators and senior members of the Presidential Administration here."[577] On July 9, 2016, Page emailed Clovis, writing in pertinent part:

> Russian Deputy Prime minister and NES board member Arkady Dvorkovich also spoke before the event. In a private conversation, Dvorkovich expressed strong support for Mr. Trump and a desire to work together toward devising better solutions in response to the vast range of current international problems. Based on feedback from a diverse array of other sources close to the Presidential Administration, it was readily apparent that this sentiment is widely held at all levels of government.[578]

Despite these representations to the Campaign, Grand Jury

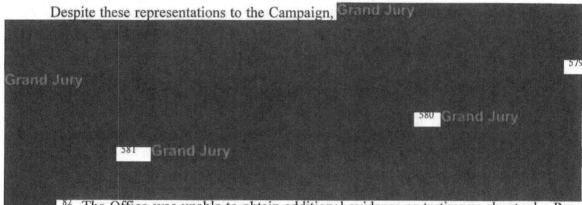

[82]   The Office was unable to obtain additional evidence or testimony about who Page may have met or communicated with in Moscow; thus, Page's activities in Russia—as described in his emails with the Campaign—were not fully explained.

---

[574] Page 3/30/17 302, at 9. Grand Jury

[575] Grand Jury   Page 3/30/17 302, at 3.

[576] Page 3/10/17 302, at 3; Page 3/30/17 302, at 7; Page 3/31/17 302, at 2.

[577] Grand Jury   7/8/16 Email, Page to Dahl & Gordon.

[578] Grand Jury   7/9/16 Email, Page to Clovis.

[579] Grand Jury

[580] Grand Jury

[581] Grand Jury

[582] Grand Jury

U.S. Department of Justice

~~Attorney Work Product~~ // ~~May Contain Material Protected Under Fed. R. Crim. P. 6(e)~~

d. Later Campaign Work and Removal from the Campaign

In July 2016, after returning from Russia, Page traveled to the Republican National Convention in Cleveland.[583] While there, Page met Russian Ambassador to the United States Sergey Kislyak; that interaction is described in Volume I, Section IV.A.6.a, *infra*.[584] Page later emailed Campaign officials with feedback he said he received from ambassadors he had met at the Convention, and he wrote that Ambassador Kislyak was very worried about candidate Clinton's world views.[585] ████Grand Jury████

████.[586]

Following the Convention, Page's trip to Moscow and his advocacy for pro-Russia foreign policy drew the media's attention and began to generate substantial press coverage. The Campaign responded by distancing itself from Page, describing him as an "informal foreign policy advisor" who did "not speak for Mr. Trump or the campaign."[587] On September 23, 2016, Yahoo! News reported that U.S. intelligence officials were investigating whether Page had opened private communications with senior Russian officials to discuss U.S. sanctions policy under a possible Trump Administration.[588] A Campaign spokesman told Yahoo! News that Page had "no role" in the Campaign and that the Campaign was "not aware of any of his activities, past or present."[589] On September 24, 2016, Page was formally removed from the Campaign.[590]

Although Page had been removed from the Campaign, after the election he sought a position in the Trump Administration.[591] On November 14, 2016, he submitted an application to the Transition Team that inflated his credentials and experiences, stating that in his capacity as a Trump Campaign foreign policy advisor he had met with "top world leaders" and "effectively

---

[583] Page 3/10/17 302, at 4; Page 3/16/17 302, at 3.

[584] Page 3/10/17 302, at 4; Page 3/16/17 302, at 3.

[585] ████Grand Jury████; 7/23/16 Email, Page to Clovis; 7/25/16 Email, Page to Gordon & Schmitz.

[586] ████Grand Jury████

[587] *See, e.g.,* Steven Mufson & Tom Hamburger, *Trump Advisor's Public Comments, Ties to Moscow Stir Unease in Both Parties,* Washington Post (Aug. 5, 2016).

[588] Michael Isikoff, *U.S. Intel Officials Probe Ties Between Trump Adviser and Kremlin,* Yahoo! News (Sept. 23, 2016).

[589] Michael Isikoff, *U.S. Intel Officials Probe Ties Between Trump Adviser and Kremlin,* Yahoo! News (Sept. 23, 2016); *see also* 9/25/16 Email, Hicks to Conway & Bannon (instructing that inquiries about Page should be answered with "[h]e was announced as an informal adviser in March. Since then he has had no role or official contact with the campaign. We have no knowledge of activities past or present and he now officially has been removed from all lists etc.").

[590] Page 3/16/17 302, at 2; *see, e.g.,* 9/23/16 Email, J. Miller to Bannon & S. Miller (discussing plans to remove Page from the campaign).

[591] ████Grand Jury████, "Transition Online Form," 11/14/16 (████
████Grand Jury████

U.S. Department of Justice

~~Attorney Work Product // May Contain Material Protected Under Fed. R. Crim. P. 6(e)~~

responded to diplomatic outreach efforts from senior government officials in Asia, Europe, the Middle East, Africa, [and] the Americas."[592] Page received no response from the Transition Team. When Page took a personal trip to Moscow in December 2016, he met again with at least one Russian government official. That interaction and a discussion of the December trip are set forth in Volume I, Section IV.B.6, *infra*.

4. Dimitri Simes and the Center for the National Interest

Members of the Trump Campaign interacted on several occasions with the Center for the National Interest (CNI), principally through its President and Chief Executive Officer, Dimitri Simes. CNI is a think tank with expertise in and connections to the Russian government. Simes was born in the former Soviet Union and immigrated to the United States in the 1970s. In April 2016, candidate Trump delivered his first speech on foreign policy and national security at an event hosted by the *National Interest*, a publication affiliated with CNI. Then-Senator Jeff Sessions and Russian Ambassador Kislyak both attended the event and, as a result, it gained some attention in relation to Sessions's confirmation hearings to become Attorney General. Sessions had various other contacts with CNI during the campaign period on foreign-policy matters, including Russia. Jared Kushner also interacted with Simes about Russian issues during the campaign. The investigation did not identify evidence that the Campaign passed or received any messages to or from the Russian government through CNI or Simes.

a. CNI and Dimitri Simes Connect with the Trump Campaign

CNI is a Washington-based non-profit organization that grew out of a center founded by former President Richard Nixon.[593] CNI describes itself "as a voice for strategic realism in U.S. foreign policy," and publishes a bi-monthly foreign policy magazine, the *National Interest*.[594] CNI is overseen by a board of directors and an advisory council that is largely honorary and whose members at the relevant time included Sessions, who served as an advisor to candidate Trump on national security and foreign policy issues.[595]

Dimitri Simes is president and CEO of CNI and the publisher and CEO of the *National Interest*.[596] Simes was born in the former Soviet Union, emigrated to the United States in the early 1970s, and joined CNI's predecessor after working at the Carnegie Endowment for International

---

[592] Grand Jury   Grand Jury   , "Transition Online Form," 11/14/16

[593] Simes 3/8/18 302, at 1-2.

[594] *About the Center*, CNI, *available at* https://cftni.org/about/.

[595] *Advisory Counsel*, CNI, *available at* https://web.archive.org/web/20161030025331/http://cftni.org/about/advisory-council/; Simes 3/8/18 302, at 3-4; Saunders 2/15/18 302, at 4; Sessions 1/17/18 302, at 16.

[596] Simes 3/8/18 302, at 2.

U.S. Department of Justice

~~Attorney Work Product // May Contain Material Protected Under Fed. R. Crim. P. 6(e)~~

Peace.[597] Simes personally has many contacts with current and former Russian government officials,[598] as does CNI collectively. As CNI stated when seeking a grant from the Carnegie Corporation in 2015, CNI has "unparalleled access to Russian officials and politicians among Washington think tanks,"[599] in part because CNI has arranged for U.S. delegations to visit Russia and for Russian delegations to visit the United States as part of so-called "Track II" diplomatic efforts.[600]

On March 14, 2016, CNI board member Richard Plepler organized a luncheon for CNI and its honorary chairman, Henry Kissinger, at the Time Warner Building in New York.[601] The idea behind the event was to generate interest in CNI's work and recruit new board members for CNI.[602] Along with Simes, attendees at the event included Jared Kushner, son-in-law of candidate Trump.[603] Kushner told the Office that the event came at a time when the Trump Campaign was having trouble securing support from experienced foreign policy professionals and that, as a result, he decided to seek Simes's assistance during the March 14 event.[604]

Simes and Kushner spoke again on a March 24, 2016 telephone call,[605] three days after Trump had publicly named the team of foreign policy advisors that had been put together on short notice.[606] On March 31, 2016, Simes and Kushner had an in-person, one-on-one meeting in Kushner's New York office.[607] During that meeting, Simes told Kushner that the best way to handle foreign-policy issues for the Trump Campaign would be to organize an advisory group of experts to meet with candidate Trump and develop a foreign policy approach that was consistent with Trump's voice.[608] Simes believed that Kushner was receptive to that suggestion.[609]

Simes also had contact with other individuals associated with the Trump Campaign regarding the Campaign's foreign policy positions. For example, on June 17, 2016, Simes sent J.D. Gordon an email with a "memo to Senator Sessions that we discussed at our recent meeting"

---

[597] Simes 3/8/18 302, at 1-2; Simes 3/27/18 302, at 19.

[598] Simes 3/27/18 302, at 10-15.

[599] C00011656 (*Rethinking U.S.-Russia Relations*, CNI (Apr. 18, 2015)).

[600] Simes 3/8/18 302, at 5; Saunders 2/15/18 302, at 29-30; Zakheim 1/25/18 302, at 3.

[601] Simes 3/8/18 302, at 6; C00006784 (3/11/16 Email, Gilbride to Saunders (3:43:12 p.m.); *cf.* Zakheim 1/25/18 302, at 1 (Kissinger was CNI's "Honorary Chairman of the Board"); Boyd 1/24/18 302, at 2; P. Sanders 2/15/18 302, at 5.

[602] Simes 3/8/18 302, at 5-6; Simes 3/27/18 302, at 2.

[603] Simes 3/8/18 302, at 6; Kushner 4/11/18 302 at 2.

[604] Kushner 4/11/18 302, at 2.

[605] Simes 3/8/18 302, at 6-7.

[606] Grand Jury ████████████ *see* Volume I, Section IV.A.2, *supra*.

[607] Simes 3/8/18 302, at 7-9.

[608] Simes 3/8/18 302, at 7-8.

[609] Simes 3/8/18 302, at 8; *see also* Boyd 1/24/18 302, at 2.

U.S. Department of Justice

~~Attorney Work Product // May Contain Material Protected Under Fed. R. Crim. P. 6(e)~~

and asked Gordon to both read it and share it with Sessions. The memorandum proposed building a "small and carefully selected group of experts" to assist Sessions with the Campaign, operating under the assumption "that Hillary Clinton is very vulnerable on national security and foreign policy issues." The memorandum outlined key issues for the Campaign, including a "new beginning with Russia."[610]

b. National Interest Hosts a Foreign Policy Speech at the Mayflower Hotel

During both their March 24 phone call and their March 31 in-person meeting, Simes and Kushner discussed the possibility of CNI hosting a foreign policy speech by candidate Trump.[611] Following those conversations, Simes agreed that he and others associated with CNI would provide behind-the-scenes input on the substance of the foreign-policy speech and that CNI officials would coordinate the logistics of the speech with Sessions and his staff, including Sessions's chief of staff, Rick Dearborn.[612]

In mid-April 2016, Kushner put Simes in contact with senior policy advisor Stephen Miller and forwarded to Simes an outline of the foreign-policy speech that Miller had prepared.[613] Simes sent back to the Campaign bullet points with ideas for the speech that he had drafted with CNI Executive Director Paul Saunders and board member Richard Burt.[614] Simes received subsequent draft outlines from Miller, and he and Saunders spoke to Miller by phone about substantive changes to the speech.[615] It is not clear, however, whether CNI officials received an actual draft of the speech for comment; while Saunders recalled having received an actual draft, Simes did not, and the emails that CNI produced to this Office do not contain such a draft.[616]

After board members expressed concern to Simes that CNI's hosting the speech could be perceived as an endorsement of a particular candidate, CNI decided to have its publication, the *National Interest*, serve as the host and to have the event at the National Press Club.[617] Kushner later requested that the event be moved to the Mayflower Hotel, which was another venue that Simes had mentioned during initial discussions with the Campaign, in order to address concerns about security and capacity.[618]

---

[610] C00008187 (6/17/16 Email, Simes to Gordon (3:35:45 p.m.)).

[611] Simes 3/8/18 302, at 7.

[612] Simes 3/8/18 302, at 8-11; C00008923 (4/6/16 Email, Simes to Burt (2:22:28 p.m.)); Burt 2/9/18 302, at 7.

[613] C00008551 (4/17/16 Email, Kushner to Simes (2:44:25 p.m.)); C00006759 (4/14/16 Email Kushner to Simes & S. Miller (12:30 p.m.)).

[614] Burt 2/9/18 302, at 7; Saunders 2/15/18 302, at 7-8.

[615] Simes 3/8/18 302, at 13; Saunders 2/15/18 302, at 7-8.

[616] Simes 3/8/18 302, at 13; Saunders 2/15/18 302, at 7-8.

[617] Saunders 2/15/18 302, at 8; Simes 3/8/18 302, at 12; C00003834-43 (4/22/16 Email, Simes to Boyd et al. (8:47 a.m.)).

[618] Simes 3/8/18 302, at 12, 18; Saunders 2/15/18 302, at 11.

U.S. Department of Justice

Attorney Work Product // May Contain Material Protected Under Fed. R. Crim. P. 6(e)

On April 25, 2016, Saunders booked event rooms at the Mayflower to host both the speech and a VIP reception that was to be held beforehand.[619] Saunders understood that the reception—at which invitees would have the chance to meet candidate Trump—would be a small event.[620] Saunders decided who would attend by looking at the list of CNI's invitees to the speech itself and then choosing a subset for the reception.[621] CNI's invitees to the reception included Sessions and Kislyak.[622] The week before the speech Simes had informed Kislyak that he would be invited to the speech, and that he would have the opportunity to meet Trump.[623]

When the pre-speech reception began on April 27, a receiving line was quickly organized so that attendees could meet Trump.[624] Sessions first stood next to Trump to introduce him to the members of Congress who were in attendance.[625] After those members had been introduced, Simes stood next to Trump and introduced him to the CNI invitees in attendance, including Kislyak.[626] Simes perceived the introduction to be positive and friendly, but thought it clear that Kislyak and Trump had just met for the first time.[627] Kislyak also met Kushner during the pre-speech reception. The two shook hands and chatted for a minute or two, during which Kushner recalled Kislyak saying, "we like what your candidate is saying . . . it's refreshing."[628]

Several public reports state that, in addition to speaking to Kushner at the pre-speech reception, Kislyak also met or conversed with Sessions at that time.[629] Sessions stated to investigators, however, that he did not remember any such conversation.[630] Nor did anyone else affiliated with CNI or the *National Interest* specifically recall a conversation or meeting between Sessions and Kislyak at the pre-speech reception.[631] It appears that, if a conversation occurred at the pre-speech reception, it was a brief one conducted in public view, similar to the exchange between Kushner and Kislyak.

---

[619] Saunders 2/15/18 302, at 11-12; C00006651-57 (Mayflower Group Sales Agreement).

[620] Saunders 2/15/18 302, at 12-13.

[621] Saunders 2/15/18 302, at 12.

[622] C00002575 (Attendee List); C00008536 (4/25/16 Email, Simes to Kushner (4:53:45 p.m.)).

[623] Simes 3/8/18 302, at 19-20.

[624] Simes 3/8/18 302, at 21.

[625] Simes 3/8/18 302, at 21.

[626] Simes 3/8/18 302, at 21.

[627] Simes 3/8/18 302, at 21.

[628] Kushner 4/11/18 302, at 4.

[629] *See, e.g.*, Ken Dilanian, *Did Trump, Kushner, Sessions Have an Undisclosed Meeting With Russian?*, NBC News (June 1, 2016); Julia Ioffe, *Why Did Jeff Sessions Really Meet With Sergey Kislyak*, The Atlantic (June 13, 2017).

[630] Sessions 1/17/18 302, at 22.

[631] Simes 3/8/18 302, at 21; Saunders 2/15/18 302, at 14, 21; Boyd 1/24/18 302, at 3-4; Heilbrunn 2/1/18 302, at 6; *Statement Regarding President Trump's April 27, 2016 Foreign Policy Speech at the Center for the National Interest*, CNI (Mar. 8, 2017).

U.S. Department of Justice

~~Attorney Work Product // May Contain Material Protected Under Fed. R. Crim. P. 6(e)~~

The Office found no evidence that Kislyak conversed with either Trump or Sessions after the speech, or would have had the opportunity to do so. Simes, for example, did not recall seeing Kislyak at the post-speech luncheon,[632] and the only witness who accounted for Sessions's whereabouts stated that Sessions may have spoken to the press after the event but then departed for Capitol Hill.[633] Saunders recalled, based in part on a food-related request he received from a Campaign staff member, that Trump left the hotel a few minutes after the speech to go to the airport.[634]

c. Jeff Sessions's Post-Speech Interactions with CNI

In the wake of Sessions's confirmation hearings as Attorney General, questions arose about whether Sessions's campaign-period interactions with CNI apart from the Mayflower speech included any additional meetings with Ambassador Kislyak or involved Russian-related matters. With respect to Kislyak contacts, on May 23, 2016, Sessions attended CNI's Distinguished Service Award dinner at the Four Seasons Hotel in Washington, D.C.[635] Sessions attended a pre-dinner reception and was seated at one of two head tables for the event.[636] A seating chart prepared by Saunders indicates that Sessions was scheduled to be seated next to Kislyak, who appears to have responded to the invitation by indicating he would attend the event.[637] Sessions, however, did not remember seeing, speaking with, or sitting next to Kislyak at the dinner.[638] Although CNI board member Charles Boyd said he may have seen Kislyak at the dinner,[639] Simes, Saunders, and Jacob Heilbrunn—editor of the *National Interest*—all had no recollection of seeing Kislyak at the May 23 event.[640] Kislyak also does not appear in any of the photos from the event that the Office obtained.

In the summer of 2016, CNI organized at least two dinners in Washington, D.C. for Sessions to meet with experienced foreign policy professionals.[641] The dinners included CNI-affiliated individuals, such as Richard Burt and Zalmay Khalilzad, a former U.S. ambassador to Afghanistan and Iraq and the person who had introduced Trump before the April 27, 2016 foreign-

---

[632] Simes 3/8/18 302, at 22; Heilbrunn 2/1/18 302, at 7.

[633] Luff 1/30/18 302, at 4.

[634] Saunders 2/15/18 302, at 15.

[635] Sessions 1/17/18 302, at 22; Saunders 2/15/18 302, at 17.

[636] Saunders 2/15/18 302, at 17; C00004779-80 (5/23/16 Email, Cantelmo to Saunders & Hagberg (9:30:12 a.m.); C00004362 (5/23/16 Email, Bauman to Cantelmo et al. (2:02:32 a.m.).

[637] C00004362 (5/23/16 Email Bauman to Cantelmo et al. (2:02:32 a.m.).

[638] Sessions 1/17/18 302, at 22.

[639] Boyd 1/24/18 302, at 4.

[640] Simes 3/8/18 302, at 23; Saunders 2/15/18 302, at 18; Heilbrunn 2/1/18 302, at 7.

[641] Simes 3/8/18 302, at 31; Saunders 2/15/18 302, at 19; Burt 2/9/18 302, at 9-10; Khalilzad 1/9/18 302, at 5.

U.S. Department of Justice

~~Attorney Work Product // May Contain Material Protected Under Fed. R. Crim. P. 6(e)~~

policy speech.[642] Khalilzad also met with Sessions one-on-one separately from the dinners.[643] At the dinners and in the meetings, the participants addressed U.S. relations with Russia, including how U.S. relations with NATO and European countries affected U.S. policy toward Russia.[644] But the discussions were not exclusively focused on Russia.[645] Khalilzad, for example, recalled discussing "nation-building" and violent extremism with Sessions.[646] In addition, Sessions asked Saunders (of CNI) to draft two memoranda not specific to Russia: one on Hillary Clinton's foreign policy shortcomings and another on Egypt.[647]

d. Jared Kushner's Continuing Contacts with Simes

Between the April 2016 speech at the Mayflower Hotel and the presidential election, Jared Kushner had periodic contacts with Simes.[648] Those contacts consisted of both in-person meetings and phone conversations, which concerned how to address issues relating to Russia in the Campaign and how to move forward with the advisory group of foreign policy experts that Simes had proposed.[649] Simes recalled that he, not Kushner, initiated all conversations about Russia, and that Kushner never asked him to set up back-channel conversations with Russians.[650] According to Simes, after the Mayflower speech in late April, Simes raised the issue of Russian contacts with Kushner, advised that it was bad optics for the Campaign to develop hidden Russian contacts, and told Kushner both that the Campaign should not highlight Russia as an issue and should handle any contacts with Russians with care.[651] Kushner generally provided a similar account of his interactions with Simes.[652]

Among the Kushner-Simes meetings was one held on August 17, 2016, at Simes's request, in Kushner's New York office. The meeting was to address foreign policy advice that CNI was providing and how to respond to the Clinton Campaign's Russia-related attacks on candidate

---

[642] Burt 2/9/18 302, at 9-10; Khalilzad 1/9/18 302, at 1-2, 5.

[643] Khalilzad 1/9/18 302, at 5-6.

[644] Simes 3/8/18 302, at 31; Burt 2/9/18 302, at 9-10; Khalilzad 1/9/18 302, at 5.

[645] Saunders 2/15/18 302, at 20.

[646] Khalilzad 1/9/18 302, at 6.

[647] Saunders 2/15/18 302, at 19-20.

[648] Simes 3/8/18 302, at 27.

[649] Simes 3/8/18 302, at 27.

[650] Simes 3/8/18 302, at 27.

[651] Simes 3/8/18 302, at 27. During this period of time, the Campaign received a request for a high-level Campaign official to meet with an officer at a Russian state-owned bank "to discuss an offer [that officer] claims to be carrying from President Putin to meet with" candidate Trump. NOSC00005653 (5/17/16 Email, Dearborn to Kushner (8:12 a.m.)). Copying Manafort and Gates, Kushner responded, "Pass on this. A lot of people come claiming to carry messages. Very few are able to verify. For now I think we decline such meetings. Most likely these people go back home and claim they have special access to gain importance for themselves. Be careful." NOSC00005653 (5/17/16 Email, Kushner to Dearborn).

[652] Kushner 4/11/18 302, at 11-13.

U.S. Department of Justice

~~Attorney Work Product // May Contain Material Protected Under Fed. R. Crim. P. 6(e)~~

Trump.[653] In advance of the meeting, Simes sent Kushner a "Russia Policy Memo" laying out "what Mr. Trump may want to say about Russia."[654] In a cover email transmitting that memo and a phone call to set up the meeting, Simes mentioned "a well-documented story of highly questionable connections between Bill Clinton" and the Russian government, "parts of [which]" (according to Simes) had even been "discussed with the CIA and the FBI in the late 1990s and shared with the [Independent Counsel] at the end of the Clinton presidency."[655] Kushner forwarded the email to senior Trump Campaign officials Stephen Miller, Paul Manafort, and Rick Gates, with the note "suggestion only."[656] Manafort subsequently forwarded the email to his assistant and scheduled a meeting with Simes.[657] (Manafort was on the verge of leaving the Campaign by the time of the scheduled meeting with Simes, and Simes ended up meeting only with Kushner).

During the August 17 meeting, Simes provided Kushner the Clinton-related information that he had promised.[658] Simes told Kushner that, Personal Privacy

[659] Simes claimed that he had received this information from former CIA and Reagan White House official Fritz Ermarth, who claimed to have learned it from U.S. intelligence sources, not from Russians.[660]

Simes perceived that Kushner did not find the information to be of interest or use to the Campaign because it was, in Simes's words, "old news."[661] When interviewed by the Office, Kushner stated that he believed that there was little chance of something new being revealed about the Clintons given their long career as public figures, and that he never received from Simes information that could be "operationalized" for the Trump Campaign.[662] Despite Kushner's

---

[653] Simes 3/8/18 302, at 29-30; Simes 3/27/18 302, at 6; Kushner 4/11/18 302, at 12; C00007269 (8/10/16 Meeting Invitation, Vargas to Simes et al.); DJTFP00023484 (8/11/16 Email, Hagan to Manafort (5:57:15 p.m.)).

[654] C00007981-84 (8/9/16 Email, Simes to Kushner (6:09:21 p.m.)). The memorandum recommended "downplaying Russia as a U.S. foreign policy priority at this time" and suggested that "some tend to exaggerate Putin's flaws." The memorandum also recommended approaching general Russian-related questions in the framework of "how to work with Russia to advance important U.S. national interests" and that a Trump Administration "not go abroad in search of monsters to destroy." The memorandum did not discuss sanctions but did address how to handle Ukraine-related questions, including questions about Russia's invasion and annexation of Crimea.

[655] C00007981 (8/9/16 Email, Simes to Kushner (6:09:21 p.m.)).

[656] DJTFP00023459 (8/10/16 Email, Kushner to S. Miller et al. (11:30:13 a.m.)).

[657] DJTFP00023484 (8/11/16 Email, Hagan to Manafort (5:57:15 p.m.)).

[658] Simes 3/8/18 302, at 29-30; Simes 3/27/18 302, at 6; Kushner 4/11/18 302, at 12.

[659] Simes 3/8/18 302, at 30; Simes 3/27/18 302, at 6.

[660] Simes 3/8/18 302, at 30.

[661] Simes 3/8/18 302, at 30; Simes 3/27/18 302, at 6.

[662] Kushner 4/11/18 302, at 12.

U.S. Department of Justice

~~Attorney Work Product~~ // ~~May Contain Material Protected Under Fed. R. Crim. P. 6(e)~~

reaction, Simes believed that he provided the same information at a small group meeting of foreign policy experts that CNI organized for Sessions.[663]

5. June 9, 2016 Meeting at Trump Tower

On June 9, 2016, senior representatives of the Trump Campaign met in Trump Tower with a Russian attorney expecting to receive derogatory information about Hillary Clinton from the Russian government. The meeting was proposed to Donald Trump Jr. in an email from Robert Goldstone, at the request of his then-client Emin Agalarov, the son of Russian real-estate developer Aras Agalarov. Goldstone relayed to Trump Jr. that the "Crown prosecutor of Russia . . . offered to provide the Trump Campaign with some official documents and information that would incriminate Hillary and her dealings with Russia" as "part of Russia and its government's support for Mr. Trump." Trump Jr. immediately responded that "if it's what you say I love it," and arranged the meeting through a series of emails and telephone calls.

Trump Jr. invited campaign chairman Paul Manafort and senior advisor Jared Kushner to attend the meeting, and both attended. Members of the Campaign discussed the meeting before it occurred, and Michael Cohen recalled that Trump Jr. may have told candidate Trump about an upcoming meeting to receive adverse information about Clinton, without linking the meeting to Russia. According to written answers submitted by President Trump, he has no recollection of learning of the meeting at the time, and the Office found no documentary evidence showing that he was made aware of the meeting—or its Russian connection—before it occurred.

The Russian attorney who spoke at the meeting, Natalia Veselnitskaya, had previously worked for the Russian government and maintained a relationship with that government throughout this period of time. She claimed that funds derived from illegal activities in Russia were provided to Hillary Clinton and other Democrats. Trump Jr. requested evidence to support those claims, but Veselnitskaya did not provide such information. She and her associates then turned to a critique of the origins of the Magnitsky Act, a 2012 statute that imposed financial and travel sanctions on Russian officials and that resulted in a retaliatory ban on adoptions of Russian children. Trump Jr. suggested that the issue could be revisited when and if candidate Trump was elected. After the election, Veselnitskaya made additional efforts to follow up on the meeting, but the Trump Transition Team did not engage.

a. Setting Up the June 9 Meeting

i. Outreach to Donald Trump Jr.

Aras Agalarov is a Russian real-estate developer with ties to Putin and other members of the Russian government, including Russia's Prosecutor General, Yuri Chaika.[664] Aras Agalarov is the president of the Crocus Group, a Russian enterprise that holds substantial Russian government construction contracts and that—as discussed above, Volume I, Section IV.A.1, *supra*

---

[663] Simes 3/8/18 302, at 30.

[664] Grand Jury ▮▮▮▮▮▮▮▮▮▮▮▮▮▮▮▮▮▮▮▮▮▮ Goldstone 2/8/18 302, at 4.

U.S. Department of Justice

~~Attorney Work Product // May Contain Material Protected Under Fed. R. Crim. P. 6(e)~~

—worked with Trump in connection with the 2013 Miss Universe pageant in Moscow and a potential Trump Moscow real-estate project.[665] The relationship continued over time, as the parties pursued the Trump Moscow project in 2013-2014 and exchanged gifts and letters in 2016.[666] For example, in April 2016, Trump responded to a letter from Aras Agalarov with a handwritten note.[667] Aras Agalarov expressed interest in Trump's campaign, passed on "congratulations" for winning in the primary and—according to one email drafted by Goldstone—an "offer" of his "support and that of many of his important Russian friends and colleagues[,] especially with reference to U.S./Russian relations."[668]

On June 3, 2016, Emin Agalarov called Goldstone, Emin's then-publicist.[669] Goldstone is a music and events promoter who represented Emin Agalarov from approximately late 2012 until late 2016.[670] While representing Emin Agalarov, Goldstone facilitated the ongoing contact between the Trumps and the Agalarovs—including an invitation that Trump sent to Putin to attend the 2013 Miss Universe Pageant in Moscow.[671] Grand Jury

.[672] Goldstone understood Grand Jury a Russian political connection, and Emin Agalarov indicated that the attorney was a prosecutor.[673] Goldstone recalled that the information that might interest the Trumps involved Hillary Clinton Grand Jury [674] Grand Jury

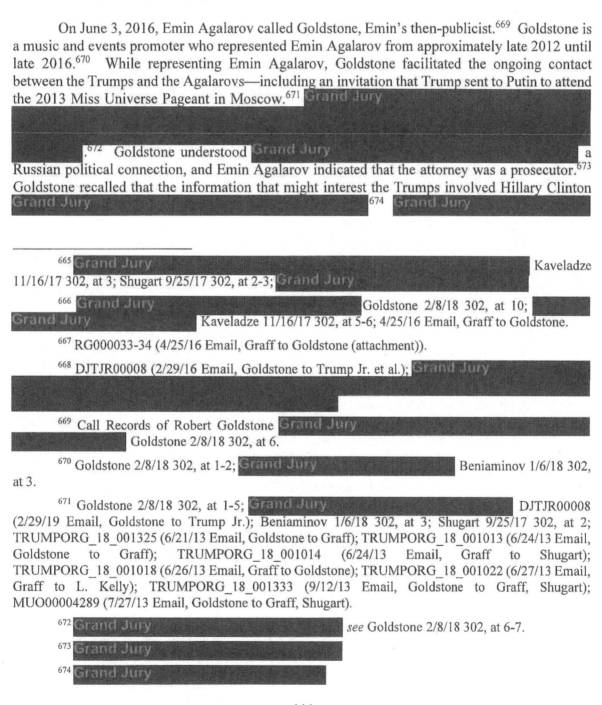

---

[665] Grand Jury Kaveladze 11/16/17 302, at 3; Shugart 9/25/17 302, at 2-3; Grand Jury

[666] Grand Jury Goldstone 2/8/18 302, at 10; Grand Jury Kaveladze 11/16/17 302, at 5-6; 4/25/16 Email, Graff to Goldstone.

[667] RG000033-34 (4/25/16 Email, Graff to Goldstone (attachment)).

[668] DJTJR00008 (2/29/16 Email, Goldstone to Trump Jr. et al.); Grand Jury

[669] Call Records of Robert Goldstone Grand Jury Goldstone 2/8/18 302, at 6.

[670] Goldstone 2/8/18 302, at 1-2; Grand Jury Beniaminov 1/6/18 302, at 3.

[671] Goldstone 2/8/18 302, at 1-5; Grand Jury DJTJR00008 (2/29/19 Email, Goldstone to Trump Jr.); Beniaminov 1/6/18 302, at 3; Shugart 9/25/17 302, at 2; TRUMPORG_18_001325 (6/21/13 Email, Goldstone to Graff); TRUMPORG_18_001013 (6/24/13 Email, Goldstone to Graff); TRUMPORG_18_001014 (6/24/13 Email, Graff to Shugart); TRUMPORG_18_001018 (6/26/13 Email, Graff to Goldstone); TRUMPORG_18_001022 (6/27/13 Email, Graff to L. Kelly); TRUMPORG_18_001333 (9/12/13 Email, Goldstone to Graff, Shugart); MUO00004289 (7/27/13 Email, Goldstone to Graff, Shugart).

[672] Grand Jury see Goldstone 2/8/18 302, at 6-7.

[673] Grand Jury

[674] Grand Jury

U.S. Department of Justice

~~Attorney Work Product // May Contain Material Protected Under Fed. R. Crim. P. 6(e)~~

███Grand Jury███ [675]

The ███Grand Jury███ mentioned by Emin Agalarov was Natalia Veselnitskaya.[676] From approximately 1998 until 2001, Veselnitskaya worked as a prosecutor for the Central Administrative District of the Russian Prosecutor's Office,[677] and she continued to perform government-related work and maintain ties to the Russian government following her departure.[678] She lobbied and testified about the Magnitsky Act, which imposed financial sanctions and travel restrictions on Russian officials and which was named for a Russian tax specialist who exposed a fraud and later died in a Russian prison.[679] Putin called the statute "a purely political, unfriendly act," and Russia responded by barring a list of current and former U.S. officials from entering Russia and by halting the adoption of Russian children by U.S. citizens.[680] Veselnitskaya performed legal work for Denis Katsyv,[681] the son of Russian businessman Peter Katsyv, and for his company Prevezon Holdings Ltd., which was a defendant in a civil-forfeiture action alleging the laundering of proceeds from the fraud exposed by Magnitsky.[682] She also

---

[675] ███Grand Jury███

[676] In December 2018, a grand jury in the Southern District of New York returned an indictment charging Veselnitskaya with obstructing the *Prevezon* litigation discussed in the text above. *See* Indictment, *United States v. Natalia Vladimirovna Veselnitskaya*, No. 18-cr-904 (S.D.N.Y.). The indictment alleges, among other things, that Veselnitskaya lied to the district court about her relationship to the Russian Prosecutor General's Office and her involvement in responding to a U.S. document request sent to the Russian government.

[677] Veselnitskaya 11/20/17 Statement to the Senate Committee on the Judiciary, at 2; ███████
███Grand Jury███

[678] Testimony of Natalia Veselnitskaya Before the Senate Committee on Judiciary (Nov. 20, 2017) at 33; Keir Simmons & Rachel Elbaum, *Russian Lawyer Veselnitskaya Says She Didn't Give Trump Jr. Info on Clinton*, NBC News (July 11, 2017); Maria Tsvetkova & Jack Stubbs, *Moscow Lawyer Who Met Trump Jr. Had Russian Spy Agency As Client*, Reuters (July 21, 2017); Andrew E. Kramer & Sharon LaFraniere, *Lawyer Who Was Said to Have Dirt on Clinton Had Closer Ties to Kremlin than She Let On*, New York Times (Apr. 27, 2018).

[679] *See* Pub. L. No. 112-208 §§ 402, 404(a)(1), 126 Stat. 1502, 1502-1506. Sergei Magnitsky was a Russian tax specialist who worked for William Browder, a former investment fund manager in Russia. Browder hired Magnitsky to investigate tax fraud by Russian officials, and Magnitsky was charged with helping Browder embezzle money. After Magnitsky died in a Russian prison, Browder lobbied Congress to pass the Magnitsky Act. *See, e.g.*, Andrew E. Kramer, *Turning Tables in Magnitsky Case, Russia Accuses Nemesis of Murder*, New York Times (Oct. 22, 2017); Testimony of Natalia Veselnitskaya Before the Senate Committee on Judiciary (Nov. 20, 2017), Exhibits at 1-4; Rosie Gray, *Bill Browder's Testimony to the Senate Judiciary Committee*, The Atlantic (July 25, 2017).

[680] Ellen Barry, *Russia Bars 18 Americans After Sanctions by US*, New York Times (Apr. 13, 2013); Tom Porter, *Supporters of the Magnitsky Act Claim They've Been Targets of Russian Assassination and Kidnapping Bids*, Newsweek (July 16, 2017).

[681] Testimony of Natalia Veselnitskaya Before the Senate Committee on Judiciary (Nov. 20, 2017), at 21.

[682] *See* Veselnitskaya Decl., *United States v. Prevezon Holdings, Ltd.*, No. 13-cv-6326 (S.D.N.Y.); *see Prevezon Holdings*, Second Amended Complaint; *Prevezon Holdings*, Mem. and Order; *Prevezon Holdings*, Deposition of Oleg Lurie.

U.S. Department of Justice

Attorney Work Product // May Contain Material Protected Under Fed. R. Crim. P. 6(e)

appears to have been involved in an April 2016 approach to a U.S. congressional delegation in Moscow offering "confidential information" from "the Prosecutor General of Russia" about "interactions between certain political forces in our two countries."[683]

Shortly after his June 3 call with Emin Agalarov, Goldstone emailed Trump Jr.[684] The email stated:

Good morning
Emin just called and asked me to contact you with something very interesting.
The Crown prosecutor of Russia met with his father Aras this morning and in their meeting offered to provide the Trump campaign with some official documents and information that would incriminate Hillary and her dealings with Russia and would be very useful to your father. This is obviously very high level and sensitive information but is part of Russia and its government's support for Mr. Trump - helped along by Aras and Emin.
What do you think is the best way to handle this information and would you be able to speak to Emin about it directly?
I can also send this info to your father via Rhona, but it is ultra sensitive so wanted to send to you first.
Best
Rob Goldstone

Within minutes of this email, Trump Jr. responded, emailing back: "Thanks Rob I appreciate that. I am on the road at the moment but perhaps I just speak to Emin first. Seems we have some time and if it's what you say I love it especially later in the summer. Could we do a call first thing next week when I am back?"[685] Goldstone conveyed Trump Jr.'s interest to Emin Agalarov, emailing that Trump Jr. "wants to speak personally on the issue."[686]

On June 6, 2016, Emin Agalarov asked Goldstone if there was "[a]ny news," and Goldstone explained that Trump Jr. was likely still traveling for the "final elections . . . where [T]rump will be 'crowned' the official nominee."[687] On the same day, Goldstone again emailed Trump Jr. and asked when Trump Jr. was "free to talk with Emin about this Hillary info."[688] Trump Jr. asked if

[683] *See* Gribbin 8/31/17 302, at 1-2 & 1A (undated one-page document given to congressional delegation). The Russian Prosecutor General is an official with broad national responsibilities in the Russian legal system. *See Federal Law on the Prosecutor's Office of the Russian Federation* (1992, amended 2004).

[684] RG000061 (6/3/16 Email, Goldstone to Trump Jr.); DJTJR00446 (6/3/16 Email, Goldstone to Donald Trump Jr.); @DonaldJTrumpJr 07/11/17 (11:00) Tweet.

[685] DJTJR00446 (6/3/16 Email, Trump Jr. to Goldstone); @DonaldJTrumpJr 07/11/17 (11:00) Tweet; RG000061 (6/3/16 Email, Trump Jr. to Goldstone).

[686] Grand Jury RG000062 (6/3/16 Email, Goldstone & Trump Jr.).

[687] RG000063 (6/6/16 Email, A. Agalarov to Goldstone); RG000064 (6/6/16 Email, Goldstone to A. Agalarov).

[688] RG000065 (6/6/16 Email, Goldstone to Trump Jr.); DJTJR00446 (6/6/16 Email, Goldstone to Trump Jr.).

U.S. Department of Justice

~~Attorney Work Product // May Contain Material Protected Under Fed. R. Crim. P. 6(e)~~

they could "speak now," and Goldstone arranged a call between Trump Jr. and Emin Agalarov.[689] On June 6 and June 7, Trump Jr. and Emin Agalarov had multiple brief calls.[690]

Also on June 6, 2016, Aras Agalarov called Ike Kaveladze and asked him to attend a meeting in New York with the Trump Organization.[691] Kaveladze is a Georgia-born, naturalized U.S. citizen who worked in the United States for the Crocus Group and reported to Aras Agalarov.[692] Kaveladze told the Office that, in a second phone call on June 6, 2016, Aras Agalarov asked Kaveladze if he knew anything about the Magnitsky Act, and Aras sent him a short synopsis for the meeting and Veselnitskaya's business card. According to Kaveladze, Aras Agalarov said the purpose of the meeting was to discuss the Magnitsky Act, and he asked Kaveladze to translate.[693]

ii. Awareness of the Meeting Within the Campaign

On June 7, Goldstone emailed Trump Jr. and said that "Emin asked that I schedule a meeting with you and [t]he Russian government attorney who is flying over from Moscow."[694] Trump Jr. replied that Manafort (identified as the "campaign boss"), Jared Kushner, and Trump Jr. would likely attend.[695] Goldstone was surprised to learn that Trump Jr., Manafort, and Kushner would attend.[696] Kaveladze ▓Grand Jury▓ "puzzled" by the list of attendees and that he checked with one of Emin Agalarov's assistants, Roman Beniaminov, who said that the purpose of the meeting was for Veselnitskaya to convey "negative information on Hillary Clinton."[697] Beniaminov, however, stated that he did not recall having known or said that.[698]

Early on June 8, 2016 Kushner emailed his assistant, asking her to discuss a 3:00 p.m.

---

[689] DJTJR00445 (6/6/16 Email, Goldstone and Trump Jr.); RG000065-67 (6/6/16 Email, Goldstone and Trump Jr.); ▓Grand Jury▓

[690] DJTJR00499 (Call Records of Donald Trump Jr. ▓Grand Jury▓); Call Records of Donald Trump Jr. ▓Grand Jury▓ .

[691] Kaveladze 11/16/17 302, at 6; ▓Grand Jury▓

[692] Kaveladze 11/16/17 302, at 1-2; ▓Grand Jury▓ Beniaminov 1/6/18 302, at 2-3; ▓Grand Jury▓

[693] Kaveladze 11/16/17 302, at 6.

[694] DJTJR00467 (6/7/16 Email, Goldstone to Trump Jr.); @DonaldJTrumpJr 07/11/17 (11:00) Tweet; RG000068 (6/7/16 Email, Goldstone to Trump Jr.); ▓Grand Jury▓

[695] DJTJR00469 (6/7/16 Email, Trump Jr. to Goldstone); @DonaldJTrumpJr 07/11/17 (11:00) Tweet; RG000071 (6/7/16 Email, Trump Jr. to Goldstone); OSC-KAV_00048 (6/7/16 Email, Goldstone to Kaveladze); ▓Grand Jury▓

[696] Goldstone 2/8/18 302, at 7; ▓Grand Jury▓

[697] ▓Grand Jury▓ see Kaveladze 11/16/17 302 at 7; OSC-KAV_00048 (6/7/16 Email, Goldstone to Kaveladze).

[698] Beniaminov 1/6/18 302, at 3.

U.S. Department of Justice

~~Attorney Work Product // May Contain Material Protected Under Fed. R. Crim. P. 6(e)~~

meeting the following day with Trump Jr.[699] Later that day, Trump Jr. forwarded the entirety of his email correspondence regarding the meeting with Goldstone to Manafort and Kushner, under the subject line "FW: Russia - Clinton – private and confidential," adding a note that the "[m]eeting got moved to 4 tomorrow at my offices."[700] Kushner then sent his assistant a second email, informing her that the "[m]eeting with don jr is 4pm now."[701] Manafort responded, "See you then. P."[702]

Rick Gates, who was the deputy campaign chairman, stated during interviews with the Office that in the days before June 9, 2016 Trump Jr. announced at a regular morning meeting of senior campaign staff and Trump family members that he had a lead on negative information about the Clinton Foundation.[703] Gates believed that Trump Jr. said the information was coming from a group in Kyrgyzstan and that he was introduced to the group by a friend.[704] Gates recalled that the meeting was attended by Trump Jr., Eric Trump, Paul Manafort, Hope Hicks, and, joining late, Ivanka Trump and Jared Kushner. According to Gates, Manafort warned the group that the meeting likely would not yield vital information and they should be careful.[705] Hicks denied any knowledge of the June 9 meeting before 2017,[706] and Kushner did not recall if the planned June 9 meeting came up at all earlier that week.[707]

Michael Cohen recalled being in Donald J. Trump's office on June 6 or 7 when Trump Jr. told his father that a meeting to obtain adverse information about Clinton was going forward.[708] Cohen did not recall Trump Jr. stating that the meeting was connected to Russia.[709] From the tenor of the conversation, Cohen believed that Trump Jr. had previously discussed the meeting with his father, although Cohen was not involved in any such conversation.[710] In an interview with the Senate Judiciary Committee, however, Trump Jr. stated that he did not inform his father about the

---

[699] NOSC0000007-08 (6/8/18 Email, Kushner to Vargas).

[700] NOSC00000039-42 (6/8/16 Email, Trump Jr. to Kushner & Manafort); DJTJR00485 (6/8/16 Email, Trump Jr. to Kushner & Manafort).

[701] NOSC0000004 (6/8/16 Email, Kushner to Vargas).

[702] 6/8/16 Email, Manafort to Trump Jr.

[703] Gates 1/30/18 302, at 7; Gates 3/1/18 302, at 3-4. Although the March 1 302 refers to "June 19," that is likely a typographical error; external emails indicate that a meeting with those participants occurred on June 6. See NOSC00023603 (6/6/16 Email, Gates to Trump Jr. et al.).

[704] Gates 1/30/18 302, at 7. Aras Agalarov is originally from Azerbaijan, and public reporting indicates that his company, the Crocus Group, has done substantial work in Kyrgyzstan. See Neil MacFarquhar, *A Russian Developer Helps Out the Kremlin on Occasion. Was He a Conduit to Trump?*, New York Times (July 16, 2017).

[705] Gates 3/1/18 302, at 3-4.

[706] Hicks 12/7/17 302, at 6.

[707] Kushner 4/11/18 302, at 8.

[708] Cohen 8/7/18 302, at 4-6.

[709] Cohen 8/7/18 302, at 4-5.

[710] Cohen 9/12/18 302, at 15-16.

U.S. Department of Justice

~~Attorney Work Product // May Contain Material Protected Under Fed. R. Crim. P. 6(e)~~

emails or the upcoming meeting.[711] Similarly, neither Manafort nor Kushner recalled anyone informing candidate Trump of the meeting, including Trump Jr.[712] President Trump has stated to this Office, in written answers to questions, that he has "no recollection of learning at the time" that his son, Manafort, or "Kushner was considering participating in a meeting in June 2016 concerning potentially negative information about Hillary Clinton."[713]

b. The Events of June 9, 2016

i. Arrangements for the Meeting

Veselnitskaya was in New York on June 9, 2016, for appellate proceedings in the *Prevezon* civil forfeiture litigation.[714] That day, Veselnitskaya called Rinat Akhmetshin, a Soviet-born U.S. lobbyist, ███Grand Jury███ and when she learned that he was in New York, invited him to lunch.[715] Akhmetshin told the Office that he had worked on issues relating to the Magnitsky Act and had worked on the *Prevezon* litigation.[716] Kaveladze and Anatoli Samochornov, a

---

[711] *Interview of: Donald J. Trump, Jr., Senate Judiciary Committee,* 115th Cong. 28-29, 84, 94-95 (Sept. 7, 2017). The Senate Judiciary Committee interview was not under oath, but Trump Jr. was advised that it is a violation of 18 U.S.C. § 1001 to make materially false statements in a congressional investigation. *Id.* at 10-11.

[712] Manafort 9/11/18 302, at 3-4; Kushner 4/11/18 302, at 10.

[713] Written Responses of Donald J. Trump (Nov. 20, 2018), at 8 (Response to Question I, Parts (a)-(c)). We considered whether one sequence of events suggested that candidate Trump had contemporaneous knowledge of the June 9 meeting. On June 7, 2016 Trump announced his intention to give "a major speech" "probably Monday of next week"—which would have been June 13—about "all of the things that have taken place with the Clintons." *See, e.g.,* Phillip Bump, *What we know about the Trump Tower meeting,* Washington Post (Aug. 7, 2018). Following the June 9 meeting, Trump changed the subject of his planned speech to national security. But the Office did not find evidence that the original idea for the speech was connected to the anticipated June 9 meeting or that the change of topic was attributable to the failure of that meeting to produce concrete evidence about Clinton. Other events, such as the Pulse nightclub shooting on June 12, could well have caused the change. The President's written answers to our questions state that the speech's focus was altered "[i]n light of" the Pulse nightclub shooting. *See* Written Responses, *supra.* As for the original topic of the June 13 speech, Trump has said that "he expected to give a speech referencing the publicly available, negative information about the Clintons," and that the draft of the speech prepared by Campaign staff "was based on publicly available material, including, in particular, information from the book *Clinton Cash* by Peter Schweizer." Written Responses, *supra.* In a later June 22 speech, Trump did speak extensively about allegations that Clinton was corrupt, drawing from the *Clinton Cash* book. *See Full Transcript: Donald Trump NYC Speech on Stakes of the Election,* politico.com (June 22, 2016).

[714] Testimony of Natalia Veselnitskaya Before the Senate Committee on Judiciary (Nov. 20, 2017) at 41, 42; Alison Frankel, *How Did Russian Lawyer Veselnitskaya Get into U.S. for Trump Tower Meeting?* Reuters, (Nov. 6, 2017); Michael Kranish et al., *Russian Lawyer who Met with Trump Jr. Has Long History Fighting Sanctions,* Washington Post (July 11, 2017); *see* OSC-KAV00113 (6/8/16 Email, Goldstone to Kaveladze); RG000073 (6/8/16 Email, Goldstone to Trump Jr.); Lieberman 12/13/17 302, at 5; *see also Prevezon Holdings* Order (Oct. 17, 2016).

[715] ███Grand Jury███

[716] Akhmetshin 11/14/17 302, at 4-6; ███Grand Jury███

Russian-born translator who had assisted Veselnitskaya with Magnitsky-related lobbying and the *Prevezon* case, also attended the lunch.[717] Grand Jury Veselnitskaya said she was meeting Grand Jury and asked Akhmetshin what she should tell him.[718] According to several participants in the lunch, Veselnitskaya showed Akhmetshin a document alleging financial misconduct by Bill Browder and the Ziff brothers (Americans with business in Russia), and those individuals subsequently making political donations to the DNC.[719] Grand Jury

[20]

The group then went to Trump Tower for the meeting.[721]

ii. Conduct of the Meeting

Trump Jr., Manafort, and Kushner participated on the Trump side, while Kaveladze, Samochornov, Akhmetshin, and Goldstone attended with Veselnitskaya.[722] The Office spoke to every participant except Veselnitskaya and Trump Jr., the latter of whom declined to be voluntarily interviewed by the Office Grand Jury

The meeting lasted approximately 20 minutes.[723] Grand Jury

[24] Goldstone recalled that Trump Jr. invited Veselnitskaya to begin but did not say anything about the subject of the meeting.[725] Participants agreed that Veselnitskaya stated that the Ziff brothers had broken Russian laws and had donated their profits to the DNC or the Clinton Campaign.[726] She asserted that the Ziff brothers had engaged in tax evasion and money laundering

---

[717] Kaveladze 11/16/17 302, at 7; Grand Jury Samochornov 7/13/17 302, at 2, 4; Grand Jury

[718] Grand Jury .

[719] Grand Jury Kaveladze 11/16/17 302, at 7; Grand Jury Samochornov did not recall the planned subject matter of the Trump Tower meeting coming up at lunch. Grand Jury Samochornov 7/12/17 302, at 4. In her later Senate statement and interactions with the press, Veselnitskaya produced what she claimed were the talking points that she brought to the June 9 meeting.

[720] Grand Jury

[721] *E.g.*, Samochornov 7/12/17 302, at 4.

[722] *E.g.*, Samochornov 7/12/17 302, at 4.

[723] *E.g.*, Samochornov 7/12/17 302, at 4; Goldstone 2/8/18 302, at 9.

[724] Grand Jury

[725] Grand Jury

[726] Grand Jury

U.S. Department of Justice

~~Attorney Work Product // May Contain Material Protected Under Fed. R. Crim. P. 6(e)~~

in both the United States and Russia,[727] ▓▓▓Grand Jury▓▓▓
▓▓▓[728] According to Akhmetshin, Trump Jr. asked follow-up questions about how the alleged payments could be tied specifically to the Clinton Campaign, but Veselnitskaya indicated that she could not trace the money once it entered the United States.[729] Kaveladze similarly recalled that Trump Jr. asked what they have on Clinton, and Kushner became aggravated and asked "[w]hat are we doing here?"[730]

Akhmetshin then spoke about U.S. sanctions imposed under the Magnitsky Act and Russia's response prohibiting U.S. adoption of Russian children.[731] Several participants recalled that Trump Jr. commented that Trump is a private citizen, and there was nothing they could do at that time.[732] Trump Jr. also said that they could revisit the issue if and when they were in government.[733] Notes that Manafort took on his phone reflect the general flow of the conversation, although not all of its details.[734]

At some point in the meeting, Kushner sent an iMessage to Manafort stating "waste of time," followed immediately by two separate emails to assistants at Kushner Companies with requests that

---

[727] ▓▓▓Grand Jury▓▓▓

[728] ▓▓▓Grand Jury▓▓▓

[729] ▓▓▓Grand Jury▓▓▓ Akhmetshin 11/14/17 302, at 12.

[730] Kaveladze 11/16/17 302, at 8; ▓▓▓Grand Jury▓▓▓
▓▓▓

[731] Samochornov 7/13/17 302, at 3; ▓▓▓Grand Jury▓▓▓
▓▓▓

[732] *E.g.*, Akhmetshin 11/14/17 302, at 12-13; ▓▓▓Grand Jury▓▓▓

[733] Akhmetshin 11/14/17 302, at 12-13; ▓▓▓Grand Jury▓▓▓ Samochornov 7/13/17 302, at 3. Trump Jr. confirmed this in a statement he made in July 2017 after news of the June 2016 meeting broke. *Interview of: Donald J. Trump, Jr., Senate Judiciary Committee U.S. Senate Washington DC*, 115th Cong. 57 (Sept. 7, 2017).

[734] Manafort's notes state:

Bill browder
Offshore - Cyprus
133m shares
Companies
Not invest - loan
Value in Cyprus as inter
Illici
Active sponsors of RNC
Browder hired Joanna Glover
Tied into Cheney
Russian adoption by American families

PJM-SJC-00000001-02 (Notes Produced to Senate Judiciary Committee).

U.S. Department of Justice

~~Attorney Work Product // May Contain Material Protected Under Fed. R. Crim. P. 6(e)~~

they call him to give him an excuse to leave.[735] Samochornov recalled that Kushner departed the meeting before it concluded; Veselnitskaya recalled the same when interviewed by the press in July 2017.[736]

Veselnitskaya's press interviews and written statements to Congress differ materially from other accounts. In a July 2017 press interview, Veselnitskaya claimed that she has no connection to the Russian government and had not referred to any derogatory information concerning the Clinton Campaign when she met with Trump Campaign officials.[737] Veselnitskaya's November 2017 written submission to the Senate Judiciary Committee stated that the purpose of the June 9 meeting was not to connect with "the Trump Campaign" but rather to have "a private meeting with Donald Trump Jr.—a friend of my good acquaintance's son on the matter of assisting me or my colleagues in informing the Congress members as to the criminal nature of manipulation and interference with the legislative activities of the US Congress."[738] In other words, Veselnitskaya claimed her focus was on Congress and not the Campaign. No witness, however, recalled any reference to Congress during the meeting. Veselnitskaya also maintained that she "attended the meeting as a lawyer of Denis Katsyv," the previously mentioned owner of Prevezon Holdings, but she did not "introduce [her]self in this capacity."[739]

In a July 2017 television interview, Trump Jr. stated that while he had no way to gauge the reliability, credibility, or accuracy of what Goldstone had stated was the purpose of the meeting, if "someone has information on our opponent . . . maybe this is something. I should hear them out."[740] Trump Jr. further stated in September 2017 congressional testimony that he thought he should "listen to what Rob and his colleagues had to say."[741] Depending on what, if any, information was provided, Trump Jr. stated he could then "consult with counsel to make an informed decision as to whether to give it any further consideration."[742]

---

[735] NOSC00003992 (6/9/16 Text Message, Kushner to Manafort); Kushner 4/11/18 302, at 9; Vargas 4/4/18 302, at 7; NOSC00000044 (6/9/16 Email, Kushner to Vargas); NOSC00000045 (6/9/16 Email, Kushner to Cain).

[736] Samochornov 7/12/17 302, at 4; Grand Jury   Kushner 4/11/18 302, at 9-10; *see also Interview of: Donald J. Trump, Jr., Senate Judiciary Committee,* 115th Cong. 48-49 (Sept. 7, 2017).

[737] *Russian Lawyer Veselnitskaya Says She Didn't Give Trump Jr. Info on Clinton,* NBC News (July 11, 2017).

[738] *Testimony of Natalia Veselnitskaya before the United States Senate Committee on the Judiciary,* 115th Cong. 10 (Nov 20, 2017).

[739] *Testimony of Natalia Veselnitskaya before the United States Senate Committee on the Judiciary,* 115th Cong. 21 (Nov. 20, 2017).

[740] Sean Hannity, *Transcript-Donald Trump Jr,* Fox News (July 11, 2017).

[741] *Interview of: Donald J. Trump, Jr, Senate Judiciary Committee,* 115th Cong. 16 (Sept. 7, 2017).

[742] *Interview of: Donald J. Trump, Jr, Senate Judiciary Committee,* 115th Cong. 16-17 (Sept. 7, 2017).

U.S. Department of Justice

~~Attorney Work Product // May Contain Material Protected Under Fed. R. Crim. P. 6(e)~~

After the June 9 meeting concluded, Goldstone apologized to Trump Jr.[743] According to Goldstone, he told Trump Jr. ████████ [744] and told Emin Agalarov in a phone call that the meeting was about adoption ████ [745] ██ [46] Aras Agalarov asked Kaveladze to report in after the meeting, but before Kaveladze could call, Aras Agalarov called him.[747] With Veselnitskaya next to him, Kaveladze reported that the meeting had gone well, but he later told Aras Agalarov that the meeting about the Magnitsky Act had been a waste of time because it was not with lawyers and they were "preaching to the wrong crowd."[748]

c. Post-June 9 Events

Veselnitskaya and Aras Agalarov made at least two unsuccessful attempts after the election to meet with Trump representatives to convey similar information about Browder and the Magnitsky Act.[749] On November 23, 2016, Kaveladze emailed Goldstone about setting up another meeting "with T people" and sent a document bearing allegations similar to those conveyed on June 9.[750] Kaveladze followed up with Goldstone, stating that "Mr. A," which Goldstone understood to mean Aras Agalarov, called to ask about the meeting.[751] Goldstone emailed the document to Rhona Graff, saying that "Aras Agalarov has asked me to pass on this document in the hope it can be passed on to the appropriate team. If needed, a lawyer representing the case is

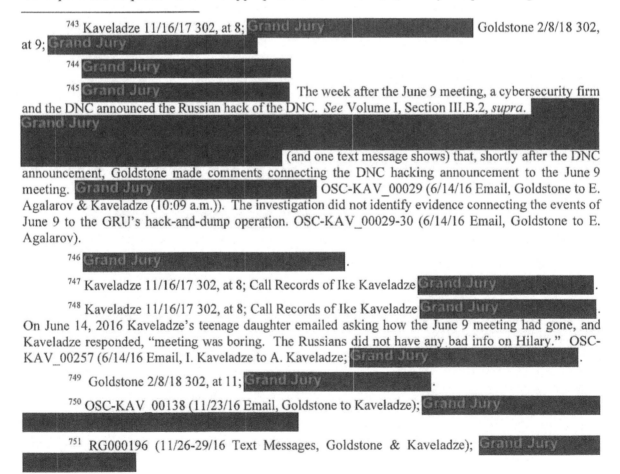

[743] Kaveladze 11/16/17 302, at 8; ████████████ Goldstone 2/8/18 302, at 9; ████████

[744] ████████████████

[745] ████████████ The week after the June 9 meeting, a cybersecurity firm and the DNC announced the Russian hack of the DNC. *See* Volume I, Section III.B.2, *supra.* ████████ ████████████████████████████ (and one text message shows) that, shortly after the DNC announcement, Goldstone made comments connecting the DNC hacking announcement to the June 9 meeting. ████████████ OSC-KAV_00029 (6/14/16 Email, Goldstone to E. Agalarov & Kaveladze (10:09 a.m.)). The investigation did not identify evidence connecting the events of June 9 to the GRU's hack-and-dump operation. OSC-KAV_00029-30 (6/14/16 Email, Goldstone to E. Agalarov).

[746] ████████████████

[747] Kaveladze 11/16/17 302, at 8; Call Records of Ike Kaveladze ████████ .

[748] Kaveladze 11/16/17 302, at 8; Call Records of Ike Kaveladze ████████ . On June 14, 2016 Kaveladze's teenage daughter emailed asking how the June 9 meeting had gone, and Kaveladze responded, "meeting was boring. The Russians did not have any bad info on Hilary." OSC-KAV_00257 (6/14/16 Email, I. Kaveladze to A. Kaveladze; ████████ .

[749] Goldstone 2/8/18 302, at 11; ████████ .

[750] OSC-KAV_00138 (11/23/16 Email, Goldstone to Kaveladze); ████████ ████████

[751] RG000196 (11/26-29/16 Text Messages, Goldstone & Kaveladze); ████████ ████████

U.S. Department of Justice

~~Attorney Work Product // May Contain Material Protected Under Fed. R. Crim. P. 6(e)~~

in New York currently and happy to meet with any member of his transition team."[752] According to Goldstone, around January 2017, Kaveladze contacted him again to set up another meeting, but Goldstone did not make the request.[753] The investigation did not identify evidence of the transition team following up.

Participants in the June 9, 2016 meeting began receiving inquiries from attorneys representing the Trump Organization starting in approximately June 2017.[754] On approximately June 2, 2017, Goldstone spoke with Alan Garten, general counsel of the Trump Organization, about his participation in the June 9 meeting.[755] The same day, Goldstone emailed Veselnitskaya's name to Garten, identifying her as the "woman who was the attorney who spoke at the meeting from Moscow."[756] Later in June 2017, Goldstone participated in a lengthier call with Garten and Alan Futerfas, outside counsel for the Trump Organization (and, subsequently, personal counsel for Trump Jr.).[757] On June 27, 2017, Goldstone emailed Emin Agalarov with the subject "Trump attorneys" and stated that he was "interviewed by attorneys" about the June 9 meeting who were "concerned because it links Don Jr. to officials from Russia—which he has always denied meeting."[758] Goldstone stressed that he "did say at the time this was an awful idea and a terrible meeting."[759] Emin Agalarov sent a screenshot of the message to Kaveladze.[760]

The June 9 meeting became public in July 2017. In a July 9, 2017 text message to Emin Agalarov, Goldstone wrote "I made sure I kept you and your father out of [t]his story,"[761] and "[i]f contacted I can do a dance and keep you out of it."[762] Goldstone added, "FBI now investigating," and "I hope this favor was worth for your dad—it could blow up."[763] On July 12, 2017 Emin Agalarov complained to Kaveladze that his father, Aras, "never listens" to him and that their

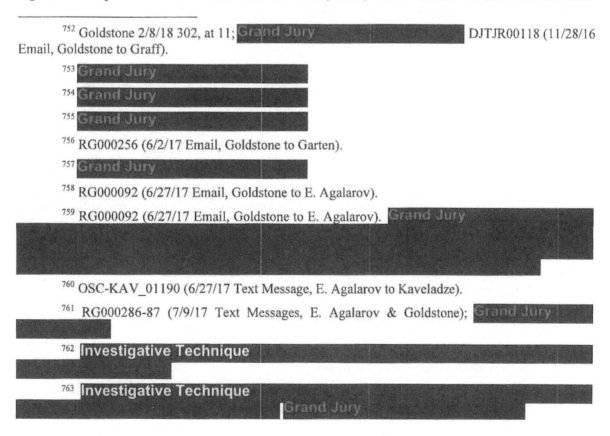

[752] Goldstone 2/8/18 302, at 11; ▓▓Grand Jury▓▓ DJTJR00118 (11/28/16 Email, Goldstone to Graff).

[753] ▓▓Grand Jury▓▓

[754] ▓▓Grand Jury▓▓

[755] ▓▓Grand Jury▓▓

[756] RG000256 (6/2/17 Email, Goldstone to Garten).

[757] ▓▓Grand Jury▓▓

[758] RG000092 (6/27/17 Email, Goldstone to E. Agalarov).

[759] RG000092 (6/27/17 Email, Goldstone to E. Agalarov). ▓▓Grand Jury▓▓

[760] OSC-KAV_01190 (6/27/17 Text Message, E. Agalarov to Kaveladze).

[761] RG000286-87 (7/9/17 Text Messages, E. Agalarov & Goldstone); ▓▓Grand Jury▓▓

[762] ▓▓Investigative Technique▓▓

[763] ▓▓Investigative Technique▓▓ ▓▓Grand Jury▓▓

relationship with "mr T has been thrown down the drain."[764] The next month, Goldstone commented to Emin Agalarov about the volume of publicity the June 9 meeting had generated, stating that his "reputation [was] basically destroyed by this dumb meeting which your father insisted on even though Ike and Me told him would be bad news and not to do."[765] Goldstone added, "I am not able to respond out of courtesy to you and your father. So am painted as some mysterious link to Putin."[766]

After public reporting on the June 9 meeting began, representatives from the Trump Organization again reached out to participants. On July 10, 2017, Futerfas sent Goldstone an email with a proposed statement for Goldstone to issue, which read:

> As the person who arranged the meeting, I can definitively state that the statements I have read by Donald Trump Jr. are 100% accurate. The meeting was a complete waste of time and Don was never told Ms. Veselnitskaya's name prior to the meeting. Ms. Veselnitskaya mostly talked about the Magnitsky Act and Russian adoption laws and the meeting lasted 20 to 30 minutes at most. There was never any follow up and nothing ever came of the meeting.[767]

[Grand Jury] the statement drafted by Trump Organization representatives was [Grand Jury] [768] He proposed a different statement, asserting that he had been asked "by [his] client in Moscow – Emin Agalarov – to facilitate a meeting between a Russian attorney (Natalia Veselnitzkaya [sic]) and Donald Trump Jr. The lawyer had apparently stated that she had some information regarding funding to the DNC from Russia, which she believed Mr. Trump Jr. might find interesting."[769] Goldstone never released either statement.[770]

On the Russian end, there were also communications about what participants should say about the June 9 meeting. Specifically, the organization that hired Samochornov—an anti-Magnitsky Act group controlled by Veselnitskaya and the owner of Prevezon—offered to pay $90,000 of Samochornov's legal fees.[771] At Veselnitskaya's request, the organization sent Samochornov a transcript of a Veselnitskaya press interview, and Samochornov understood that the organization would pay his legal fees only if he made statements consistent with Veselnitskaya's.[772] Samochornov declined, telling the Office that he did not want to perjure

---

[764] OSC-KAV_01197 (7/11-12/17 Text Messages, Kaveladze & E. Agalarov); [Grand Jury]

[765] [Investigative Technique]

[766] [Investigative Technique]

[767] 7/10/17 Email, Goldstone to Futerfas & Garten.

[768] [Grand Jury]

[769] 7/10/17 Email, Goldstone to Futerfas & Garten.

[770] [Grand Jury]

[771] Samochornov 7/13/17 302, at 1; [Grand Jury]

[772] [Grand Jury] Samochornov 7/13/17 302, at 1.

U.S. Department of Justice

~~Attorney Work Product // May Contain Material Protected Under Fed. R. Crim. P. 6(e)~~

himself.[773] The individual who conveyed Veselnitskaya's request to Samochornov stated that he did not expressly condition payment on following Veselnitskaya's answers but, in hindsight, recognized that by sending the transcript, Samochornov could have interpreted the offer of assistance to be conditioned on his not contradicting Veselnitskaya's account.[774]

Volume II, Section II.G, *infra*, discusses interactions between President Trump, Trump Jr., and others in June and July 2017 regarding the June 9 meeting.

6. Events at the Republican National Convention

Trump Campaign officials met with Russian Ambassador Sergey Kislyak during the week of the Republican National Convention. The evidence indicates that those interactions were brief and non-substantive. During platform committee meetings immediately before the Convention, J.D. Gordon, a senior Campaign advisor on policy and national security, diluted a proposed amendment to the Republican Party platform expressing support for providing "lethal" assistance to Ukraine in response to Russian aggression. Gordon requested that platform committee personnel revise the proposed amendment to state that only "appropriate" assistance be provided to Ukraine. The original sponsor of the "lethal" assistance amendment stated that Gordon told her (the sponsor) that he was on the phone with candidate Trump in connection with his request to dilute the language. Gordon denied making that statement to the sponsor, although he acknowledged it was possible he mentioned having previously spoken to the candidate about the subject matter. The investigation did not establish that Gordon spoke to or was directed by the candidate to make that proposal. Gordon said that he sought the change because he believed the proposed language was inconsistent with Trump's position on Ukraine.

a. Ambassador Kislyak's Encounters with Senator Sessions and J.D. Gordon the Week of the RNC

In July 2016, Senator Sessions and Gordon spoke at the Global Partners in Diplomacy event, a conference co-sponsored by the State Department and the Heritage Foundation held in Cleveland, Ohio the same week as the Republican National Convention (RNC or "Convention").[775] Approximately 80 foreign ambassadors to the United States, including Kislyak, were invited to the conference.[776]

On July 20, 2016, Gordon and Sessions delivered their speeches at the conference.[777] In his speech, Gordon stated in pertinent part that the United States should have better relations with

---

[773] Samochornov 7/13/17 302, at 1.

[774] ▮▮Grand Jury▮▮▮▮▮▮▮▮▮▮▮▮▮

[775] Gordon 8/29/17 302, at 9; Sessions 1/17/18 302, at 22; Allan Smith, *We Now Know More About why Jeff Sessions and a Russian Ambassador Crossed Paths at the Republican Convention*, Business Insider (Mar. 2, 2017).

[776] Gordon 8/29/17 302, at 9; Laura DeMarco, *Global Cleveland and Sen. Bob Corker Welcome International Republican National Convention Guests*, Cleveland Plain Dealer (July 20, 2016).

[777] Gordon 8/29/17 302, at 9; Sessions 1/17/18 302, at 22.

U.S. Department of Justice

~~Attorney Work Product~~ // ~~May Contain Material Protected Under Fed. R. Crim. P. 6(e)~~

Russia.[778] During Sessions's speech, he took questions from the audience, one of which may have been asked by Kislyak.[779] When the speeches concluded, several ambassadors lined up to greet the speakers.[780] Gordon shook hands with Kislyak and reiterated that he had meant what he said in the speech about improving U.S.-Russia relations.[781] Sessions separately spoke with between six and 12 ambassadors, including Kislyak.[782] Although Sessions stated during interviews with the Office that he had no specific recollection of what he discussed with Kislyak, he believed that the two spoke for only a few minutes and that they would have exchanged pleasantries and said some things about U.S.-Russia relations.[783]

Later that evening, Gordon attended a reception as part of the conference.[784] Gordon ran into Kislyak as the two prepared plates of food, and they decided to sit at the same table to eat.[785] They were joined at that table by the ambassadors from Azerbaijan and Kazakhstan, and by Trump Campaign advisor Carter Page.[786] As they ate, Gordon and Kislyak talked for what Gordon estimated to have been three to five minutes, during which Gordon again mentioned that he meant what he said in his speech about improving U.S.-Russia relations.[787]

b. Change to Republican Party Platform

In preparation for the 2016 Convention, foreign policy advisors to the Trump Campaign, working with the Republican National Committee, reviewed the 2012 Convention's foreign policy platform to identify divergence between the earlier platform and candidate Trump's positions.[788] The Campaign team discussed toning down language from the 2012 platform that identified Russia as the country's number one threat, given the candidate's belief that there needed to be better U.S. relations with Russia.[789] The RNC Platform Committee sent the 2016 draft platform to the National Security and Defense Platform Subcommittee on July 10, 2016, the evening before its

---

[778] Gordon 8/29/17 302, at 9.

[779] Sessions 1/17/18 302, at 22; Luff 1/30/18 302, at 3.

[780] Gordon 8/29/17 302, at 9; Luff 1/30/18 302, at 3.

[781] Gordon 8/29/17 302, at 9.

[782] Sessions 1/17/18 302, at 22; Luff 1/30/18 302, at 3; *see also* Volume I, Section IV.A.4.b, *supra* (explaining that Sessions and Kislyak may have met three months before this encounter during a reception held on April 26, 2016, at the Mayflower Hotel).

[783] Sessions 1/17/18 302, at 22.

[784] Gordon 8/29/17 302, at 9-10.

[785] Gordon 8/29/17 302, at 9-10.

[786] Gordon 8/29/17 302, at 10; *see also* Volume I, Section IV.A.3.d, *supra* (explaining that Page acknowledged meeting Kislyak at this event).

[787] Gordon 8/29/17 302, at 10.

[788] Gordon 8/29/17 302, at 10.

[789] Gordon 8/29/17 302, at 10.

U.S. Department of Justice

Attorney Work Product // May Contain Material Protected Under Fed. R. Crim. P. 6(e)

first meeting to propose amendments.[790]

Although only delegates could participate in formal discussions and vote on the platform, the Trump Campaign could request changes, and members of the Trump Campaign attended committee meetings.[791] John Mashburn, the Campaign's policy director, helped oversee the Campaign's involvement in the platform committee meetings.[792] He told the Office that he directed Campaign staff at the Convention, including J.D. Gordon, to take a hands-off approach and only to challenge platform planks if they directly contradicted Trump's wishes.[793]

On July 11, 2016, delegate Diana Denman submitted a proposed platform amendment that included provision of armed support for Ukraine.[794] The amendment described Russia's "ongoing military aggression" in Ukraine and announced "support" for "maintaining (and, if warranted, increasing) sanctions against Russia until Ukraine's sovereignty and territorial integrity are fully restored" and for "providing lethal defensive weapons to Ukraine's armed forces and greater coordination with NATO on defense planning."[795] Gordon reviewed the proposed platform changes, including Denman's.[796] Gordon stated that he flagged this amendment because of Trump's stated position on Ukraine, which Gordon personally heard the candidate say at the March 31 foreign policy meeting—namely, that the Europeans should take primary responsibility for any assistance to Ukraine, that there should be improved U.S.-Russia relations, and that he did not want to start World War III over that region.[797] Gordon told the Office that Trump's statements on the campaign trail following the March meeting underscored those positions to the point where Gordon felt obliged to object to the proposed platform change and seek its dilution.[798]

On July 11, 2016, at a meeting of the National Security and Defense Platform Subcommittee, Denman offered her amendment.[799] Gordon and another Campaign staffer, Matt Miller, approached a committee co-chair and asked him to table the amendment to permit further discussion.[800] Gordon's concern with the amendment was the language about providing "lethal

---

[790] Gordon 8/29/17 302, at 10; Hoff 5/26/17 302, at 1-2.

[791] Hoff 5/26/17 302, at 1; Gordon 9/7/17 302, at 10.

[792] Mashburn 6/25/18 302, at 4; Manafort 9/20/18 302, at 7-8.

[793] Mashburn 6/25/18 302, at 4; Gordon 8/29/17 302, at 10.

[794] DENMAN 000001-02, DENMAN 000012, DENMAN 000021-22; Denman 12/4/17 302, at 1; Denman 6/7/17 302, at 2.

[795] DENMAN 000001-02, DENMAN 000012, DENMAN 000021-22.

[796] Gordon 8/29/17 302, at 10-11.

[797] Gordon 8/29/17 302, at 11; Gordon 9/7/17 302, at 11; Gordon 2/14/19 302, at 1-2, 5-6.

[798] Gordon 2/14/19 302, at 5-6.

[799] Denman 6/7/17 302, at 2; see DENMAN 000014.

[800] Denman 6/7/17 302, at 2; Denman 12/4/17 302, at 2; Gordon 9/7/17 302, at 11-12; see Hoff 5/26/17 302, at 2.

U.S. Department of Justice

~~Attorney Work Product // May Contain Material Protected Under Fed. R. Crim. P. 6(e)~~

defensive weapons to Ukraine."[801] Miller did not have any independent basis to believe that this language contradicted Trump's views and relied on Gordon's recollection of the candidate's views.[802]

According to Denman, she spoke with Gordon and Matt Miller, and they told her that they had to clear the language and that Gordon was "talking to New York."[803] Denman told others that she was asked by the two Trump Campaign staffers to strike "lethal defense weapons" from the proposal but that she refused.[804] Denman recalled Gordon saying that he was on the phone with candidate Trump, but she was skeptical whether that was true.[805] Gordon denied having told Denman that he was on the phone with Trump, although he acknowledged it was possible that he mentioned having previously spoken to the candidate about the subject matter.[806] Gordon's phone records reveal a call to Sessions's office in Washington that afternoon, but do not include calls directly to a number associated with Trump.[807] And according to the President's written answers to the Office's questions, he does not recall being involved in the change in language of the platform amendment.[808]

Gordon stated that he tried to reach Rick Dearborn, a senior foreign policy advisor, and Mashburn, the Campaign policy director. Gordon stated that he connected with both of them (he could not recall if by phone or in person) and apprised them of the language he took issue with in the proposed amendment. Gordon recalled no objection by either Dearborn or Mashburn and that all three Campaign advisors supported the alternative formulation ("appropriate assistance").[809] Dearborn recalled Gordon warning them about the amendment, but not weighing in because Gordon was more familiar with the Campaign's foreign policy stance.[810] Mashburn stated that Gordon reached him, and he told Gordon that Trump had not taken a stance on the issue and that the Campaign should not intervene.[811]

When the amendment came up again in the committee's proceedings, the subcommittee changed the amendment by striking the "lethal defense weapons" language and replacing it with

---

[801] Denman 6/7/17 302, at 3.

[802] M. Miller 10/25/17 302 at 3.

[803] Denman 12/4/17 302, at 2; Denman 6/7/17 302, at 2.

[804] Hoff 5/26/17 302, at 2.

[805] Denman 6/7/17 302, at 2-3, 3-4; Denman 12/4/17 302, at 2.

[806] Gordon 2/14/19 302, at 7.

[807] Call Records of J.D. Gordon ▮Grand Jury▮▮▮▮▮▮▮▮. Gordon stated to the Office that his calls with Sessions were unrelated to the platform change. Gordon 2/14/19 302, at 7.

[808] Written Responses of Donald J. Trump (Nov. 20, 2018), at 17 (Response to Question IV, Part (f)).

[809] Gordon 2/14/19 302, at 6-7; Gordon 9/7/17 302, at 11-12; see Gordon 8/29/17 302, at 11.

[810] Dearborn 11/28/17 302, at 7-8.

[811] Mashburn 6/25/18 302, at 4.

"appropriate assistance."[812]   Gordon stated that he and the subcommittee co-chair ultimately agreed to replace the language about armed assistance with "appropriate assistance."[813]   The subcommittee accordingly approved Denman's amendment but with the term "appropriate assistance."[814]   Gordon stated that, to his recollection, this was the only change sought by the Campaign.[815]   Sam Clovis, the Campaign's national co-chair and chief policy advisor, stated he was surprised by the change and did not believe it was in line with Trump's stance.[816]   Mashburn stated that when he saw the word "appropriate assistance," he believed that Gordon had violated Mashburn's directive not to intervene.[817]

7.   Post-Convention Contacts with Kislyak

Ambassador Kislyak continued his efforts to interact with Campaign officials with responsibility for the foreign-policy portfolio—among them Sessions and Gordon—in the weeks after the Convention. The Office did not identify evidence in those interactions of coordination between the Campaign and the Russian government.

a.   *Ambassador Kislyak Invites J.D. Gordon to Breakfast at the Ambassador's Residence*

On August 3, 2016, an official from the Embassy of the Russian Federation in the United States wrote to Gordon "[o]n behalf of" Ambassador Kislyak inviting Gordon "to have breakfast/tea with the Ambassador at his residence" in Washington, D.C. the following week.[818]   Gordon responded five days later to decline the invitation. He wrote, "[t]hese days are not optimal for us, as we are busily knocking down a constant stream of false media stories while also preparing for the first debate with HRC. Hope to take a raincheck for another time when things quiet down a bit. Please pass along my regards to the Ambassador."[819]   The investigation did not identify evidence that Gordon made any other arrangements to meet (or met) with Kislyak after this email.

b.   *Senator Sessions's September 2016 Meeting with Ambassador Kislyak*

Also in August 2016, a representative of the Russian Embassy contacted Sessions's Senate office about setting up a meeting with Kislyak.[820]   At the time, Sessions was a member of the

---

[812] Hoff 5/26/17 302, at 2-3; *see* Denman 12/4/17 302, at 2-3; Gordon 8/29/17 302, at 11.

[813] Gordon 8/29/17 302, at 11; Gordon 9/7/17 302, at 12.

[814] Hoff 5/26/17 302, at 2-3.

[815] Gordon 2/14/19 302, at 6.

[816] Clovis 10/3/17 302, at 10-11.

[817] Mashburn 6/25/18 302, at 4.

[818] DJTFP00004828 (8/3/16 Email, Pchelyakov [embassy@russianembassy.org] to Gordon).

[819] DJTFP00004953 (8/8/16 Email, Gordon to embassy@russianembassy.org).

[820] Luff 1/30/18 302, at 5.

U.S. Department of Justice

~~Attorney Work Product // May Contain Material Protected Under Fed. R. Crim. P. 6(e)~~

Senate Foreign Relations Committee and would meet with foreign officials in that capacity.[821] But Sessions's staff reported, and Sessions himself acknowledged, that meeting requests from ambassadors increased substantially in 2016, as Sessions assumed a prominent role in the Trump Campaign and his name was mentioned for potential cabinet-level positions in a future Trump Administration.[822]

On September 8, 2016, Sessions met with Kislyak in his Senate office.[823] Sessions said that he believed he was doing the Campaign a service by meeting with foreign ambassadors, including Kislyak.[824] He was accompanied in the meeting by at least two of his Senate staff: Sandra Luff, his legislative director; and Pete Landrum, who handled military affairs.[825] The meeting lasted less than 30 minutes.[826] Sessions voiced concerns about Russia's sale of a missile-defense system to Iran, Russian planes buzzing U.S. military assets in the Middle East, and Russian aggression in emerging democracies such as Ukraine and Moldova.[827] Kislyak offered explanations on these issues and complained about NATO land forces in former Soviet-bloc countries that border Russia.[828] Landrum recalled that Kislyak referred to the presidential campaign as "an interesting campaign,"[829] and Sessions also recalled Kislyak saying that the Russian government was receptive to the overtures Trump had laid out during his campaign.[830] None of the attendees, though, remembered any discussion of Russian election interference or any request that Sessions convey information from the Russian government to the Trump Campaign.[831]

During the meeting, Kislyak invited Sessions to further discuss U.S.-Russia relations with him over a meal at the ambassador's residence.[832] Sessions was non-committal when Kislyak extended the invitation. After the meeting ended, Luff advised Sessions against accepting the one-on-one meeting with Kislyak, whom she assessed to be an "old school KGB guy."[833] Neither Luff nor Landrum recalled that Sessions followed up on the invitation or made any further effort to dine

---

[821] Sessions 1/17/18 302, at 23-24; Luff 1/30/18 302, at 5.

[822] Sessions 1/17/18 302, at 23-24; Luff 1/30/18 302, at 5; Landrum 2/27/18 302, at 3-5.

[823] Sessions 1/17/18 302, at 23.

[824] Sessions 1/17/18 302, at 23.

[825] Sessions 1/17/18 302, at 23; Luff 1/30/18 302, at 5-6; Landrum 2/27/18 302, at 4-5 (stating he could not remember if election was discussed).

[826] Luff 1/30/18 302, at 6; Landrum 2/27/18 302, at 5.

[827] Luff 1/30/18 302, at 6; Landrum 2/27/18 302, at 4-5.

[828] Luff 1/30/18 302, at 6; Landrum 2/27/18 302 at 4-5.

[829] Landrum 2/27/18 302, at 5.

[830] Sessions 1/17/18 302, at 23. Sessions also noted that ambassadors came to him for information about Trump and hoped he would pass along information to Trump. Sessions 1/17/18 302, at 23-24.

[831] Sessions 1/17/18 302, at 23; Luff 1/30/18 302, at 6; Landrum 2/27/18 302, at 5.

[832] Luff 1/30/18 302, at 5; Landrum 2/27/18 302, at 4.

[833] Luff 1/30/18 302, at 5.

U.S. Department of Justice

~~Attorney Work Product // May Contain Material Protected Under Fed. R. Crim. P. 6(e)~~

or meet with Kislyak before the November 2016 election.[834] Sessions and Landrum recalled that, after the election, some efforts were made to arrange a meeting between Sessions and Kislyak.[835] According to Sessions, the request came through CNI and would have involved a meeting between Sessions and Kislyak, two other ambassadors, and the Governor of Alabama.[836] Sessions, however, was in New York on the day of the anticipated meeting and was unable to attend.[837] The investigation did not identify evidence that the two men met at any point after their September 8 meeting.

8. Paul Manafort

Paul Manafort served on the Trump Campaign, including a period as campaign chairman, from March to August 2016.[838] Manafort had connections to Russia through his prior work for Russian oligarch Oleg Deripaska and later through his work for a pro-Russian regime in Ukraine. Manafort stayed in touch with these contacts during the campaign period through Konstantin Kilimnik, a longtime Manafort employee who previously ran Manafort's office in Kiev and who the FBI assesses to have ties to Russian intelligence.

Manafort instructed Rick Gates, his deputy on the Campaign and a longtime employee,[839] to provide Kilimnik with updates on the Trump Campaign—including internal polling data, although Manafort claims not to recall that specific instruction. Manafort expected Kilimnik to share that information with others in Ukraine and with Deripaska. Gates periodically sent such polling data to Kilimnik during the campaign.

---

[834] Luff 1/30/18 302, at 6; Landrum 2/27/18 302, at 4-5.

[835] Sessions 1/17/18 302, at 23.

[836] Sessions 1/17/18 302, at 23.

[837] Sessions 1/17/18 302, at 23.

[838] On August 21, 2018, Manafort was convicted in the Eastern District of Virginia on eight tax, Foreign Bank Account Registration (FBAR), and bank fraud charges. On September 14, 2018, Manafort pleaded guilty in the District of Columbia to (1) conspiracy to defraud the United States and conspiracy to commit offenses against the United States (money laundering, tax fraud, FBAR, Foreign Agents Registration Act (FARA), and FARA false statements), and (2) conspiracy to obstruct justice (witness tampering). Manafort also admitted criminal conduct with which he had been charged in the Eastern District of Virginia, but as to which the jury hung. The conduct at issue in both cases involved Manafort's work in Ukraine and the money he earned for that work, as well as crimes after the Ukraine work ended. On March 7, 2019, Manafort was sentenced to 47 months of imprisonment in the Virginia prosecution. On March 13, the district court in D.C. sentenced Manafort to a total term of 73 months: 60 months on the Count 1 conspiracy (with 30 of those months to run concurrent to the Virginia sentence), and 13 months on the Count 1 conspiracy, to be served consecutive to the other two sentences. The two sentences resulted in a total term of 90 months.

[839] As noted in Volume I, Section III.D.1.b, *supra*, Gates pleaded guilty to two criminal charges in the District of Columbia, including making a false statement to the FBI, pursuant to a plea agreement. He has provided information and in-court testimony that the Office has deemed to be reliable. *See also* Transcript at 16, *United States v. Paul J. Manafort, Jr.*, 1:17-cr-201 (D.D.C. Feb. 13, 2019), Doc. 514 ("*Manafort 2/13/19 Transcript*") (court's explanation of reasons to credit Gates's statements in one instance).

U.S. Department of Justice

~~Attorney Work Product // May Contain Material Protected Under Fed. R. Crim. P. 6(e)~~

Manafort also twice met Kilimnik in the United States during the campaign period and conveyed campaign information. The second meeting took place on August 2, 2016, in New York City. Kilimnik requested the meeting to deliver in person a message from former Ukrainian President Viktor Yanukovych, who was then living in Russia. The message was about a peace plan for Ukraine that Manafort has since acknowledged was a "backdoor" means for Russia to control eastern Ukraine. Several months later, after the presidential election, Kilimnik wrote an email to Manafort expressing the view—which Manafort later said he shared—that the plan's success would require U.S. support to succeed: "all that is required to start the process is a very minor 'wink' (or slight push) from [Donald Trump]."[840] The email also stated that if Manafort were designated as the U.S. representative and started the process, Yanukovych would ensure his reception in Russia "at the very top level."

Manafort communicated with Kilimnik about peace plans for Ukraine on at least four occasions after their first discussion of the topic on August 2: December 2016 (the Kilimnik email described above); January 2017; February 2017; and again in the spring of 2018. The Office reviewed numerous Manafort email and text communications, and asked President Trump about the plan in written questions.[841] The investigation did not uncover evidence of Manafort's passing along information about Ukrainian peace plans to the candidate or anyone else in the Campaign or the Administration. The Office was not, however, able to gain access to all of Manafort's electronic communications (in some instances, messages were sent using encryption applications). And while Manafort denied that he spoke to members of the Trump Campaign or the new Administration about the peace plan, he lied to the Office and the grand jury about the peace plan and his meetings with Kilimnik, and his unreliability on this subject was among the reasons that the district judge found that he breached his cooperation agreement.[842]

The Office could not reliably determine Manafort's purpose in sharing internal polling data with Kilimnik during the campaign period. Manafort ▮▮▮Grand Jury▮▮▮ did not see a downside to sharing campaign information, and told Gates that his role in the Campaign would

---

[840] The email was drafted in Kilimnik's DMP email account (in English) ▮▮▮Investigative Technique▮▮▮

[841] According to the President's written answers, he does not remember Manafort communicating to him any particular positions that Ukraine or Russia would want the United States to support. Written Responses of Donald J. Trump (Nov. 20, 2018), at 16-17 (Response to Question IV, Part (d)).

[842] Manafort made several false statements during debriefings. Based on that conduct, the Office determined that Manafort had breached his plea agreement and could not be a cooperating witness. The judge presiding in Manafort's D.C. criminal case found by a preponderance of the evidence that Manafort intentionally made multiple false statements to the FBI, the Office, and the grand jury concerning his interactions and communications with Kilimnik (and concerning two other issues). Although the report refers at times to Manafort's statements, it does so only when those statements are sufficiently corroborated to be trustworthy, to identify issues on which Manafort's untruthful responses may themselves be of evidentiary value, or to provide Manafort's explanations for certain events, even when we were unable to determine whether that explanation was credible.

U.S. Department of Justice

~~Attorney Work Product~~ // ~~May Contain Material Protected Under Fed. R. Crim. P. 6(e)~~

be "good for business" and potentially a way to be made whole for work he previously completed in the Ukraine. As to Deripaska, Manafort claimed that by sharing campaign information with him, Deripaska might see value in their relationship and resolve a "disagreement"—a reference to one or more outstanding lawsuits. Because of questions about Manafort's credibility and our limited ability to gather evidence on what happened to the polling data after it was sent to Kilimnik, the Office could not assess what Kilimnik (or others he may have given it to) did with it. The Office did not identify evidence of a connection between Manafort's sharing polling data and Russia's interference in the election, which had already been reported by U.S. media outlets at the time of the August 2 meeting. The investigation did not establish that Manafort otherwise coordinated with the Russian government on its election-interference efforts.

a. Paul Manafort's Ties to Russia and Ukraine

Manafort's Russian contacts during the campaign and transition periods stem from his consulting work for Deripaska from approximately 2005 to 2009 and his separate political consulting work in Ukraine from 2005 to 2015, including through his company DMP International LLC (DMI). Kilimnik worked for Manafort in Kiev during this entire period and continued to communicate with Manafort through at least June 2018. Kilimnik, who speaks and writes Ukrainian and Russian, facilitated many of Manafort's communications with Deripaska and Ukrainian oligarchs.

i. Oleg Deripaska Consulting Work

In approximately 2005, Manafort began working for Deripaska, a Russian oligarch who has a global empire involving aluminum and power companies and who is closely aligned with Vladimir Putin.[843] A memorandum describing work that Manafort performed for Deripaska in 2005 regarding the post-Soviet republics referenced the need to brief the Kremlin and the benefits that the work could confer on "the Putin Government."[844] Gates described the work Manafort did for Deripaska as "political risk insurance," and explained that Deripaska used Manafort to install friendly political officials in countries where Deripaska had business interests.[845] Manafort's company earned tens of millions of dollars from its work for Deripaska and was loaned millions of dollars by Deripaska as well.[846]

In 2007, Deripaska invested through another entity in Pericles Emerging Market Partners L.P. ("Pericles"), an investment fund created by Manafort and former Manafort business partner Richard Davis. The Pericles fund was established to pursue investments in Eastern Europe.[847] Deripaska was the sole investor.[848] Gates stated in interviews with the Office that the venture led

---

[843] Pinchuk et al., *Russian Tycoon Deripaska in Putin Delegation to China*, Reuters (June 8, 2018).

[844] 6/23/05 Memo, Manafort & Davis to Deripaska & Rothchild.

[845] Gates 2/2/18 302, at 7.

[846] Manafort 9/20/18 302, at 2-5; Manafort Income by Year, 2005 – 2015; Manafort Loans from Wire Transfers, 2005 – 2015.

[847] Gates 3/12/18 302, at 5.

[848] Manafort 12/16/15 Dep., at 157:8-11.

U.S. Department of Justice

~~Attorney Work Product // May Contain Material Protected Under Fed. R. Crim. P. 6(e)~~

to a deterioration of the relationship between Manafort and Deripaska.[849] In particular, when the fund failed, litigation between Manafort and Deripaska ensued. Gates stated that, by 2009, Manafort's business relationship with Deripaska had "dried up."[850] According to Gates, various interactions with Deripaska and his intermediaries over the past few years have involved trying to resolve the legal dispute.[851] As described below, in 2016, Manafort, Gates, Kilimnik, and others engaged in efforts to revive the Deripaska relationship and resolve the litigation.

ii. Political Consulting Work

Through Deripaska, Manafort was introduced to Rinat Akhmetov, a Ukrainian oligarch who hired Manafort as a political consultant.[852] In 2005, Akhmetov hired Manafort to engage in political work supporting the Party of Regions,[853] a political party in Ukraine that was generally understood to align with Russia. Manafort assisted the Party of Regions in regaining power, and its candidate, Viktor Yanukovych, won the presidency in 2010. Manafort became a close and trusted political advisor to Yanukovych during his time as President of Ukraine. Yanukovych served in that role until 2014, when he fled to Russia amidst popular protests.[854]

iii. Konstantin Kilimnik

Kilimnik is a Russian national who has lived in both Russia and Ukraine and was a longtime Manafort employee.[855] Kilimnik had direct and close access to Yanukovych and his senior entourage, and he facilitated communications between Manafort and his clients, including Yanukovych and multiple Ukrainian oligarchs.[856] Kilimnik also maintained a relationship with Deripaska's deputy, Viktor Boyarkin,[857] a Russian national who previously served in the defense attaché office of the Russian Embassy to the United States.[858]

---

[849] Gates 2/2/18 302, at 9.

[850] Gates 2/2/18 302, at 6.

[851] Gates 2/2/18 302, at 9-10.

[852] Manafort 7/30/14 302, at 1; Manafort 9/20/18 302, at 2.

[853] Manafort 9/11/18 302, at 5-6.

[854] Gates 3/16/18 302, at 1; Davis 2/8/18 302, at 9; Devine 7/6/18 302, at 2-3.

[855] Patten 5/22/18 302, at 5; Gates 1/29/18 302, at 18-19; 10/28/97 Kilimnik Visa Record, U.S. Department of State.

[856] Gates 1/29/18 302, at 18-19; Patten 5/22/18 302, at 8; Gates 1/31/18 302, at 4-5; Gates 1/30/18 302, at 2; Gates 2/2/18 302, at 11.

[857] Gates 1/29/18 302, at 18; Patten 5/22/18 302, at 8.

[858] Boyarkin Visa Record, U.S. Department of State.

U.S. Department of Justice

~~Attorney Work Product // May Contain Material Protected Under Fed. R. Crim. P. 6(e)~~

Manafort told the Office that he did not believe Kilimnik was working as a Russian "spy."[859] The FBI, however, assesses that Kilimnik has ties to Russian intelligence.[860] Several pieces of the Office's evidence—including witness interviews and emails obtained through court-authorized search warrants—support that assessment:

- Kilimnik was born on April 27, 1970, in Dnipropetrovsk Oblast, then of the Soviet Union, and attended the Military Institute of the Ministry of Defense from 1987 until 1992.[861] Sam Patten, a business partner to Kilimnik,[862] stated that Kilimnik told him that he was a translator in the Russian army for seven years and that he later worked in the Russian armament industry selling arms and military equipment.[863]

- U.S. government visa records reveal that Kilimnik obtained a visa to travel to the United States with a Russian diplomatic passport in 1997.[864]

- Kilimnik worked for the International Republican Institute's (IRI) Moscow office, where he did translation work and general office management from 1998 to 2005.[865] While another official recalled the incident differently,[866] one former associate of Kilimnik's at IRI told the FBI that Kilimnik was fired from his post because his links to Russian intelligence were too strong. The same individual stated that it was well known at IRI that Kilimnik had links to the Russian government.[867]

- Jonathan Hawker, a British national who was a public relations consultant at FTI Consulting, worked with DMI on a public relations campaign for Yanukovych. After Hawker's work for DMI ended, Kilimnik contacted Hawker about working for a Russian

---

[859] Manafort 9/11/18 302, at 5.

[860] The Office has noted Kilimnik's assessed ties to Russian intelligence in public court filings. *E.g.*, Gov't Opp. to Mot. to Modify, *United States v. Paul J. Manafort, Jr.*, 1:17-cr-201 (D.D.C. Dec. 4, 2017), Doc. 73, at 2 ("*Manafort* (D.D.C.) Gov't Opp. to Mot. to Modify").

[861] 12/17/16 Kilimnik Visa Record, U.S. Department of State.

[862] In August 2018, Patten pleaded guilty pursuant to a plea agreement to violating the Foreign Agents Registration Act, and admitted in his Statement of Offense that he also misled and withheld documents from the Senate Select Committee on Intelligence in the course of its investigation of Russian election interference. Plea Agreement, *United States v. W. Samuel Patten*, 1:18-cr-260 (D.D.C. Aug. 31, 2018), Doc. 6; Statement of Offense, *United States v. W. Samuel Patten*, 1:18-cr-260 (D.D.C. Aug. 31, 2018), Doc. 7.

[863] Patten 5/22/18 302, at 5-6.

[864] 10/28/97 Kilimnik Visa Record, U.S. Department of State.

[865] Nix 3/30/18 302, at 1-2.

[866] Nix 3/30/18 302, at 2.

[867] Lenzi 1/30/18 302, at 2.

U.S. Department of Justice

~~Attorney Work Product // May Contain Material Protected Under Fed. R. Crim. P. 6(e)~~

government entity on a public-relations project that would promote, in Western and Ukrainian media, Russia's position on its 2014 invasion of Crimea.[868]

- Gates suspected that Kilimnik was a "spy," a view that he shared with Manafort, Hawker, and Alexander van der Zwaan,[869] an attorney who had worked with DMI on a report for the Ukrainian Ministry of Foreign Affairs.[870]

Investigative Technique

b. Contacts during Paul Manafort's Time with the Trump Campaign

i. Paul Manafort Joins the Campaign

Manafort served on the Trump Campaign from late March to August 19, 2016. On March 29, 2016, the Campaign announced that Manafort would serve as the Campaign's "Convention Manager."[871] On May 19, 2016, Manafort was promoted to campaign chairman and chief strategist, and Gates, who had been assisting Manafort on the Campaign, was appointed deputy campaign chairman.[872]

Thomas Barrack and Roger Stone both recommended Manafort to candidate Trump.[873] In early 2016, at Manafort's request, Barrack suggested to Trump that Manafort join the Campaign to manage the Republican Convention.[874] Stone had worked with Manafort from approximately 1980 until the mid-1990s through various consulting and lobbying firms. Manafort met Trump in 1982 when Trump hired the Black, Manafort, Stone and Kelly lobbying firm.[875] Over the years, Manafort saw Trump at political and social events in New York City and at Stone's wedding, and Trump requested VIP status at the 1988 and 1996 Republican conventions worked by Manafort.[876]

---

[868] Hawker 1/9/18 302, at 13; 3/18/14 Email, Hawker & Tulukbaev.

[869] van der Zwaan pleaded guilty in the U.S. District Court for the District of Columbia to making false statements to the Special Counsel's Office. Plea Agreement, *United States v. Alex van der Zwaan*, 1:18-cr-31 (D.D.C. Feb. 20, 2018), Doc. 8.

[870] Hawker 6/9/18 302, at 4; van der Zwaan 11/3/17 302, at 22. Manafort said in an interview that Gates had joked with Kilimnik about Kilimnik's going to meet with his KGB handler. Manafort 10/16/18 302, at 7.

[871] *Press Release – Donald J. Trump Announces Campaign Convention Manager Paul J. Manafort*, The American Presidency Project – U.C. Santa Barbara (Mar. 29, 2016).

[872] Gates 1/29/18 302, at 8; Meghan Keneally, *Timeline of Manafort's role in the Trump Campaign*, ABC News (Oct. 20, 2017).

[873] Gates 1/29/18 302, at 7-8; Manafort 9/11/18 302, at 1-2; Barrack 12/12/17 302, at 3.

[874] Barrack 12/12/17 302, at 3; Gates 1/29/18 302, at 7-8.

[875] Manafort 10/16/18 302, at 6.

[876] Manafort 10/16/18 302, at 6.

U.S. Department of Justice

~~Attorney Work Product~~ // ~~May Contain Material Protected Under Fed. R. Crim. P. 6(e)~~

According to Gates, in March 2016, Manafort traveled to Trump's Mar-a-Lago estate in Florida to meet with Trump. Trump hired him at that time.[877] Manafort agreed to work on the Campaign without pay. Manafort had no meaningful income at this point in time, but resuscitating his domestic political campaign career could be financially beneficial in the future. Gates reported that Manafort intended, if Trump won the Presidency, to remain outside the Administration and monetize his relationship with the Administration.[878]

ii. Paul Manafort's Campaign-Period Contacts

Immediately upon joining the Campaign, Manafort directed Gates to prepare for his review separate memoranda addressed to Deripaska, Akhmetov, Serhiy Lyovochkin, and Boris Kolesnikov,[879] the last three being Ukrainian oligarchs who were senior Opposition Bloc officials.[880] The memoranda described Manafort's appointment to the Trump Campaign and indicated his willingness to consult on Ukrainian politics in the future. On March 30, 2016, Gates emailed the memoranda and a press release announcing Manafort's appointment to Kilimnik for translation and dissemination.[881] Manafort later followed up with Kilimnik to ensure his messages had been delivered, emailing on April 11, 2016 to ask whether Kilimnik had shown "our friends" the media coverage of his new role.[882] Kilimnik replied, "Absolutely. Every article." Manafort further asked: "How do we use to get whole. Has Ovd [Oleg Vladimirovich Deripaska] operation seen?" Kilimnik wrote back the same day, "Yes, I have been sending everything to Victor [Boyarkin, Deripaska's deputy], who has been forwarding the coverage directly to OVD."[883]

Gates reported that Manafort said that being hired on the Campaign would be "good for business" and increase the likelihood that Manafort would be paid the approximately $2 million he was owed for previous political consulting work in Ukraine.[884] Gates also explained to the Office that Manafort thought his role on the Campaign could help "confirm" that Deripaska had dropped the Pericles lawsuit, and that Gates believed Manafort sent polling data to Deripaska (as

---

[877] Gates 2/2/18 302, at 10.

[878] Gates 1/30/18 302, at 4.

[879] Gates 2/2/18 302, at 11.

[880] *See* Sharon LaFraniere, *Manafort's Trial Isn't About Russia, but It Will Be in the Air*, New York Times (July 30, 2018); Tierney Sneed, *Prosecutors Believe Manafort Made $60 Million Consulting in Ukraine*, Talking Points Memo (July 30, 2018); Mykola Vorobiov, *How Pro-Russian Forces Will Take Revenge on Ukraine*, Atlantic Council (Sept. 23, 2018); Sergii Leshchenko, *Ukraine's Oligarchs Are Still Calling the Shots*, Foreign Policy (Aug. 14, 2014); Interfax-Ukraine, *Kolesnikov: Inevitability of Punishment Needed for Real Fight Against Smuggling in Ukraine*, Kyiv Post (June 23, 2018); Igor Kossov, *Kyiv Hotel Industry Makes Room for New Entrants*, Kyiv Post (Mar. 7, 2019); Markian Kuzmowycz, *How the Kremlin Can Win Ukraine's Elections*, Atlantic Council (Nov. 19, 2018). The Opposition Bloc is a Ukraine political party that largely reconstituted the Party of Regions.

[881] 3/30/16 Email, Gates to Kilimnik.

[882] 4/11/16 Email, Manafort & Kilimnik.

[883] 4/11/16 Email, Manafort & Kilimnik.

[884] Gates 2/2/18 302, at 10.

U.S. Department of Justice

~~Attorney Work Product // May Contain Material Protected Under Fed. R. Crim. P. 6(e)~~

discussed further below) so that Deripaska would not move forward with his lawsuit against Manafort.[885] Gates further stated that Deripaska wanted a visa to the United States, that Deripaska could believe that having Manafort in a position inside the Campaign or Administration might be helpful to Deripaska, and that Manafort's relationship with Trump could help Deripaska in other ways as well.[886] Gates stated, however, that Manafort never told him anything specific about what, if anything, Manafort might be offering Deripaska.[887]

Gates also reported that Manafort instructed him in April 2016 or early May 2016 to send Kilimnik Campaign internal polling data and other updates so that Kilimnik, in turn, could share it with Ukrainian oligarchs.[888] Gates understood that the information would also be shared with Deripaska. Grand Jury .[889] Gates reported to the Office that he did not know why Manafort wanted him to send polling information, but Gates thought it was a way to showcase Manafort's work, and Manafort wanted to open doors to jobs after the Trump Campaign ended.[890] Gates said that Manafort's instruction included sending internal polling data prepared for the Trump Campaign by pollster Tony Fabrizio.[891] Fabrizio had worked with Manafort for years and was brought into the Campaign by Manafort. Gates stated that, in accordance with Manafort's instruction, he periodically sent Kilimnik polling data via WhatsApp; Gates then deleted the communications on a daily basis.[892] Gates further told the Office that, after Manafort left the Campaign in mid-August, Gates sent Kilimnik polling data less frequently and that the data he sent was more publicly available information and less internal data.[893]

Gates's account about polling data is consistent Grand Jury [94] with multiple emails that Kilimnik sent to U.S. associates and press contacts between late July and mid-August of 2016. Those emails referenced "internal polling," described the status of the Trump Campaign and

---

[885] Gates 2/2/18 302, at 11; Gates 9/27/18 302 (serial 740), at 2.

[886] Gates 2/2/18 302, at 12.

[887] Gates 2/2/18 302, at 12.

[888] Gates 1/31/18 302, at 17; Gates 9/27/18 302 (serial 740), at 2. In a later interview with the Office, Gates stated that Manafort directed him to send polling data to Kilimnik after a May 7, 2016 meeting between Manafort and Kilimnik in New York, discussed in Volume I, Section IV.A.8.b.iii, *infra*. Gates 11/7/18 302, at 3.

[889] Gates 9/27/18 302, Part II, at 2; Grand Jury .

[890] Gates 2/12/18 302, at 10; Gates 1/31/18 302, at 17.

[891] Gates 9/27/18 302 (serial 740), at 2; Gates 2/7/18 302, at 15.

[892] Gates 1/31/18 302, at 17.

[893] Gates 2/12/18 302, at 11-12. According to Gates, his access to internal polling data was more limited because Fabrizio was himself distanced from the Campaign at that point.

[894] Grand Jury

Manafort's role in it, and assessed Trump's prospects for victory.[895]   Manafort did not acknowledge instructing Gates to send Kilimnik internal data, Grand Jury

[896]

The Office also obtained contemporaneous emails that shed light on the purpose of the communications with Deripaska and that are consistent with Gates's account. For example, in response to a July 7, 2016, email from a Ukrainian reporter about Manafort's failed Deripaska-backed investment, Manafort asked Kilimnik whether there had been any movement on "this issue with our friend."[897]   Gates stated that "our friend" likely referred to Deripaska,[898] and Manafort told the Office that the "issue" (and "our biggest interest," as stated below) was a solution to the Deripaska-Pericles issue.[899]   Kilimnik replied:

> I am carefully optimistic on the question of our biggest interest.
>
> Our friend [Boyarkin] said there is lately significantly more attention to the campaign in his boss' [Deripaska's] mind, and he will be most likely looking for ways to reach out to you pretty soon, understanding all the time sensitivity. I am more than sure that it will be resolved and we will get back to the original relationship with V.'s boss [Deripaska].[900]

Eight minutes later, Manafort replied that Kilimnik should tell Boyarkin's "boss," a reference to Deripaska, "that if he needs private briefings we can accommodate."[901]   Manafort has alleged to the Office that he was willing to brief Deripaska only on public campaign matters and gave an example: why Trump selected Mike Pence as the Vice-Presidential running mate.[902]   Manafort said he never gave Deripaska a briefing.[903]   Manafort noted that if Trump won, Deripaska would want to use Manafort to advance whatever interests Deripaska had in the United States and elsewhere.[904]

---

[895] 8/18/16 Email, Kilimnik to Dirkse; 8/18/16 Email, Kilimnik to Schultz; 8/18/16 Email, Kilimnik to Marson; 7/27/16 Email, Kilimnik to Ash; 8/18/16 Email, Kilimnik to Ash; 8/18/16 Email, Kilimnik to Jackson; 8/18/16 Email, Kilimnik to Mendoza-Wilson; 8/19/16 Email, Kilimnik to Patten.

[896] Grand Jury

[897] 7/7/16 Email, Manafort to Kilimnik.

[898] Gates 2/2/18 302, at 13.

[899] Manafort 9/11/18 302, at 6.

[900] 7/8/16 Email, Kilimnik to Manafort.

[901] 7/8/16 Email, Kilimnik to Manafort; Gates 2/2/18 302, at 13.

[902] Manafort 9/11/18 302, at 6.

[903] Manafort 9/11/18 302, at 6.

[904] Manafort 9/11/18 302, at 6.

U.S. Department of Justice

~~Attorney Work Product // May Contain Material Protected Under Fed. R. Crim. P. 6(e)~~

iii. Paul Manafort's Two Campaign-Period Meetings with Konstantin Kilimnik in the United States

Manafort twice met with Kilimnik in person during the campaign period—once in May and again in August 2016. The first meeting took place on May 7, 2016, in New York City.[905] In the days leading to the meeting, Kilimnik had been working to gather information about the political situation in Ukraine. That included information gleaned from a trip that former Party of Regions official Yuriy Boyko had recently taken to Moscow—a trip that likely included meetings between Boyko and high-ranking Russian officials.[906] Kilimnik then traveled to Washington, D.C. on or about May 5, 2016; while in Washington, Kilimnik had pre-arranged meetings with State Department employees.[907]

Late on the evening of May 6, Gates arranged for Kilimnik to take a 3:00 a.m. train to meet Manafort in New York for breakfast on May 7.[908] According to Manafort, during the meeting, he and Kilimnik talked about events in Ukraine, and Manafort briefed Kilimnik on the Trump Campaign, expecting Kilimnik to pass the information back to individuals in Ukraine and elsewhere.[909] Manafort stated that Opposition Bloc members recognized Manafort's position on the Campaign was an opportunity, but Kilimnik did not ask for anything.[910] Kilimnik spoke about a plan of Boyko to boost election participation in the eastern zone of Ukraine, which was the base for the Opposition Bloc.[911] Kilimnik returned to Washington, D.C. right after the meeting with Manafort.

Manafort met with Kilimnik a second time at the Grand Havana Club in New York City on the evening of August 2, 2016. The events leading to the meeting are as follows. On July 28, 2016, Kilimnik flew from Kiev to Moscow.[912] The next day, Kilimnik wrote to Manafort requesting that they meet, using coded language about a conversation he had that day.[913] In an email with a subject line "Black Caviar," Kilimnik wrote:

> I met today with the guy who gave you your biggest black caviar jar several years ago. We spent about 5 hours talking about his story, and I have several important messages from him to you. He asked me to go and brief you on our conversation. I said I have to run it by you first, but in principle I am prepared to do it. . . . It has to do about the future of his

---

[905] ▆▆Investigative Technique▆▆

[906] 4/26/16 Email, Kilimnik to Purcell, at 2; Gates 2/2/18 302, at 12; Patten 5/22/18 302, at 6-7; Gates 11/7/18 302, at 3.

[907] 5/7/16 Email, Kilimnik to Charap & Kimmage; 5/7/16 Email, Kasanof to Kilimnik.

[908] 5/6/16 Email, Manafort to Gates; 5/6/16 Email, Gates to Kilimnik.

[909] Manafort 10/11/18 302, at 1.

[910] Manafort 10/11/18 302, at 1.

[911] Manafort 10/11/18 302, at 1.

[912] 7/25/16 Email, Kilimnik to katrin@yana.kiev.ua (2:17:34 a.m.).

[913] 7/29/16 Email, Kilimnik to Manafort (10:51 a.m.).

U.S. Department of Justice

~~Attorney Work Product // May Contain Material Protected Under Fed. R. Crim. P. 6(e)~~

country, and is quite interesting.[914]

Manafort identified "the guy who gave you your biggest black caviar jar" as Yanukovych. He explained that, in 2010, he and Yanukovych had lunch to celebrate the recent presidential election. Yanukovych gave Manafort a large jar of black caviar that was worth approximately $30,000 to $40,000.[915] Manafort's identification of Yanukovych as "the guy who gave you your biggest black caviar jar" is consistent with Kilimnik being in Moscow—where Yanukovych resided—when Kilimnik wrote "I met today with the guy," and with a December 2016 email in which Kilimnik referred to Yanukovych as "BG," Grand Jury [916] Manafort replied to Kilimnik's July 29 email, "Tuesday [August 2] is best . . . Tues or weds in NYC."[917]

Three days later, on July 31, 2016, Kilimnik flew back to Kiev from Moscow, and on that same day, wrote to Manafort that he needed "about 2 hours" for their meeting "because it is a long caviar story to tell."[918] Kilimnik wrote that he would arrive at JFK on August 2 at 7:30 p.m., and he and Manafort agreed to a late dinner that night.[919] Documentary evidence—including flight, phone, and hotel records, and the timing of text messages exchanged[920]—confirms the dinner took place as planned on August 2.[921]

As to the contents of the meeting itself, the accounts of Manafort and Gates—who arrived late to the dinner—differ in certain respects. But their versions of events, when assessed alongside available documentary evidence and what Kilimnik told business associate Sam Patten, indicate that at least three principal topics were discussed.

First, Manafort and Kilimnik discussed a plan to resolve the ongoing political problems in Ukraine by creating an autonomous republic in its more industrialized eastern region of Donbas,[922]

---

[914] 7/29/16 Email, Kilimnik to Manafort (10:51 a.m.).

[915] Manafort 9/12/18 302, at 3.

[916] 7/29/16 Email, Manafort to Kilimnik; Investigative Technique ; Grand Jury

[917] 7/29/16 Email, Manafort to Kilimnik.

[918] 7/31/16 Email, Manafort to Kilimnik.

[919] 7/31/16 Email, Manafort to Kilimnik.

[920] Kilimnik 8/2/16 CBP Record; Call Records of Konstantin Kilimnik Grand Jury ; Call Records of Rick Gates Grand Jury ; 8/2-3/16, Kilimnik Park Lane Hotel Receipt.

[921] Deripaska's private plane also flew to Teterboro Airport in New Jersey on the evening of August 2, 2016. According to Customs and Border Protection records, the only passengers on the plane were Deripaska's wife, daughter, mother, and father-in-law, and separate records obtained by our Office confirm that Kilimnik flew on a commercial flight to New York.

[922] The Luhansk and Donetsk People's Republics, which are located in the Donbas region of Ukraine, declared themselves independent in response to the popular unrest in 2014 that removed President Yanukovych from power. Pro-Russian Ukrainian militia forces, with backing from the Russian military, have occupied the region since 2014. Under the Yanukovych-backed plan, Russia would assist in withdrawing the military, and Donbas would become an autonomous region within Ukraine with its own

U.S. Department of Justice

~~Attorney Work Product // May Contain Material Protected Under Fed. R. Crim. P. 6(e)~~

and having Yanukovych, the Ukrainian President ousted in 2014, elected to head that republic.[923] That plan, Manafort later acknowledged, constituted a "backdoor" means for Russia to control eastern Ukraine.[924] Manafort initially said that, if he had not cut off the discussion, Kilimnik would have asked Manafort in the August 2 meeting to convince Trump to come out in favor of the peace plan, and Yanukovych would have expected Manafort to use his connections in Europe and Ukraine to support the plan.[925] Manafort also initially told the Office that he had said to Kilimnik that the plan was crazy, that the discussion ended, and that he did not recall Kilimnik asking Manafort to reconsider the plan after their August 2 meeting.[926] Manafort said ▇▇▇▇▇▇ ▇▇▇▇▇▇▇▇ that he reacted negatively to Yanukovych sending—years later—an "urgent" request when Yanukovych needed him.[927] When confronted with an email written by Kilimnik on or about December 8, 2016, however, Manafort acknowledged Kilimnik raised the peace plan again in that email.[928] Manafort ultimately acknowledged Kilimnik also raised the peace plan in January and February 2017 meetings with Manafort.▇▇▇▇▇ ▇▇▇▇ ▇▇▇▇▇▇▇[929]

Second, Manafort briefed Kilimnik on the state of the Trump Campaign and Manafort's plan to win the election.[930] That briefing encompassed the Campaign's messaging and its internal polling data. According to Gates, it also included discussion of "battleground" states, which Manafort identified as Michigan, Wisconsin, Pennsylvania, and Minnesota.[931] Manafort did not refer explicitly to "battleground" states in his telling of the August 2 discussion, ▇▇▇▇▇▇▇ ▇▇▇▇▇▇▇▇▇▇▇▇▇▇▇[9]32

---

prime minister. The plan emphasized that Yanukovych would be an ideal candidate to bring peace to the region as prime minister of the republic, and facilitate the reintegration of the region into Ukraine with the support of the U.S. and Russian presidents. As noted above, according to ▇▇▇▇ the written documentation describing the plan, for the plan to work, both U.S. and Russian support were necessary. ▇▇▇▇▇▇▇▇▇▇▇▇▇▇▇▇ 2/21/18 Email, Manafort, Ward, & Fabrizio, at 3-5.

[923] Manafort 9/11/18 302, at 4; ▇▇▇▇▇▇▇▇▇▇ ▇▇▇▇▇▇▇▇

[924] ▇▇▇▇▇▇▇▇

[925] Manafort 9/11/18 302, at 4.

[926] Manafort 9/12/18 302, at 4.

[927] ▇▇▇▇▇▇▇▇ Manafort 9/11/18 302, at 5; Manafort 9/12/18 302, at 4.

[928] Manafort 9/12/18 302, at 4; ▇▇▇▇Investigative Technique▇▇▇▇

[929] ▇▇▇▇▇▇▇▇▇▇▇▇▇▇▇▇ Documentary evidence confirms the peace-plan discussions in 2018. 2/19/18 Email, Fabrizio to Ward (forwarding email from Manafort); 2/21/18 Email, Manafort to Ward & Fabrizio.

[930] Manafort 9/11/18 302, at 5.

[931] Gates 1/30/18 302, at 3, 5.

[932] ▇▇▇▇▇▇▇▇

U.S. Department of Justice

~~Attorney Work Product // May Contain Material Protected Under Fed. R. Crim. P. 6(e)~~

Third, according to Gates and what Kilimnik told Patten, Manafort and Kilimnik discussed two sets of financial disputes related to Manafort's previous work in the region. Those consisted of the unresolved Deripaska lawsuit and the funds that the Opposition Bloc owed to Manafort for his political consulting work and how Manafort might be able to obtain payment.[933]

After the meeting, Gates and Manafort both stated that they left separately from Kilimnik because they knew the media was tracking Manafort and wanted to avoid media reporting on his connections to Kilimnik.[934]

c. Post-Resignation Activities

Manafort resigned from the Trump Campaign in mid-August 2016, approximately two weeks after his second meeting with Kilimnik, amidst negative media reporting about his political consulting work for the pro-Russian Party of Regions in Ukraine. Despite his resignation, Manafort continued to offer advice to various Campaign officials through the November election. Manafort told Gates that he still spoke with Kushner, Bannon, and candidate Trump,[935] and some of those post-resignation contacts are documented in emails. For example, on October 21, 2016, Manafort sent Kushner an email and attached a strategy memorandum proposing that the Campaign make the case against Clinton "as the failed and corrupt champion of the establishment" and that "Wikileaks provides the Trump campaign the ability to make the case in a very credible way – by using the words of Clinton, its campaign officials and DNC members."[936] Later, in a November 5, 2016 email to Kushner entitled "Securing the Victory," Manafort stated that he was "really feeling good about our prospects on Tuesday and focusing on preserving the victory," and that he was concerned the Clinton Campaign would respond to a loss by "mov[ing] immediately to discredit the [Trump] victory and claim voter fraud and cyber-fraud, including the claim that the Russians have hacked into the voting machines and tampered with the results."[937]

Trump was elected President on November 8, 2016. Manafort told the Office that, in the wake of Trump's victory, he was not interested in an Administration job. Manafort instead preferred to stay on the "outside," and monetize his campaign position to generate business given his familiarity and relationship with Trump and the incoming Administration.[938] Manafort appeared to follow that plan, as he traveled to the Middle East, Cuba, South Korea, Japan, and China and was paid to explain what a Trump presidency would entail.[939]

Manafort's activities in early 2017 included meetings relating to Ukraine and Russia. The

---

[933] Gates 1/30/18 302, at 2-4; Patten 5/22/18 302, at 7.

[934] Gates 1/30/18 302, at 5; Manafort 9/11/18 302, at 5.

[935] Gates 2/12/18 302, at 12.

[936] NOSC00021517-20 (10/21/16 Email, Manafort to Kushner).

[937] NOSC00021573-75 (11/5/16 Email, Manafort to Kushner).

[938] Manafort 9/12/18 302, at 1, 4-5; Gates 1/30/18 302, at 4.

[939] Manafort 9/12/18 302, at 1.

first meeting, which took place in Madrid, Spain in January 2017, was with Georgiy Oganov. Oganov, who had previously worked at the Russian Embassy in the United States, was a senior executive at a Deripaska company and was believed to report directly to Deripaska.[940] Manafort initially denied attending the meeting. When he later acknowledged it, he claimed that the meeting had been arranged by his lawyers and concerned only the Pericles lawsuit.[941] Other evidence, however, provides reason to doubt Manafort's statement that the sole topic of the meeting was the Pericles lawsuit. In particular, text messages to Manafort from a number associated with Kilimnik suggest that Kilimnik and Boyarkin—not Manafort's counsel—had arranged the meeting between Manafort and Oganov.[942] Kilimnik's message states that the meeting was supposed to be "not about money or Pericles" but instead "about recreating [the] old friendship"—ostensibly between Manafort and Deripaska—"and talking about global politics."[943] Manafort also replied by text that he "need[s] this finished before Jan. 20,"[944] which appears to be a reference to resolving Pericles before the inauguration.

On January 15, 2017, three days after his return from Madrid, Manafort emailed K.T. McFarland, who was at that time designated to be Deputy National Security Advisor and was formally appointed to that position on January 20, 2017.[945] Manafort's January 15 email to McFarland stated: "I have some important information I want to share that I picked up on my travels over the last month."[946] Manafort told the Office that the email referred to an issue regarding Cuba, not Russia or Ukraine, and Manafort had traveled to Cuba in the past month.[947] Either way, McFarland—who was advised by Flynn not to respond to the Manafort inquiry— appears not to have responded to Manafort.[948]

Manafort told the Office that around the time of the Presidential Inauguration in January, he met with Kilimnik and Ukrainian oligarch Serhiy Lyovochkin at the Westin Hotel in Alexandria, Virginia.[949] During this meeting, Kilimnik again discussed the Yanukovych peace plan that he had broached at the August 2 meeting and in a detailed December 8, 2016 message found in Kilimnik's DMP email account.[950] In that December 8 email, which Manafort

---

[940] Kalashnikova 5/17/18 302, at 4; Gary Lee, *Soviet Embassy's Identity Crisis*, Washington Post (Dec. 20, 1991); *Georgy S. Oganov Executive Profile & Biography*, Bloomberg (Mar. 12, 2019).

[941] Manafort 9/11/18 302, at 7.

[942] Text Message, Manafort & Kilimnik.

[943] Text Message, Manafort & Kilimnik; Manafort 9/12/18 302, at 5.

[944] Text Message, Manafort & Kilimnik.

[945] 1/15/17 Email, Manafort, McFarland, & Flynn.

[946] 1/15/17 Email, Manafort, McFarland, & Flynn.

[947] Manafort 9/11/18 302, at 7.

[948] 1/15/17 Email, Manafort, McFarland, & Flynn; McFarland 12/22/17 302, at 18-19.

[949] Grand Jury Manafort 9/11/18 302, at 7; Manafort 9/21/18 302, at 3; 1/19/17 & 1/22/17 Kilimnik CBP Records, Jan. 19 and 22, 2017; 2016-17 Text Messages, Kilimnik & Patten, at 1-2.

[950] Investigative Technique

U.S. Department of Justice

~~Attorney Work Product // May Contain Material Protected Under Fed. R. Crim. P. 6(e)~~

acknowledged having read,[951] Kilimnik wrote, "[a]ll that is required to start the process is a very minor 'wink' (or slight push) from DT"—an apparent reference to President-elect Trump—"and a decision to authorize you to be a 'special representative' and manage this process." Kilimnik assured Manafort, with that authority, he "could start the process and within 10 days visit Russia [Yanukovych] guarantees your reception at the very top level," and that "DT could have peace in Ukraine basically within a few months after inauguration."[952]

As noted above, Grand Jury and statements to the Office, Manafort sought to qualify his engagement on and support for the plan. Grand Jury

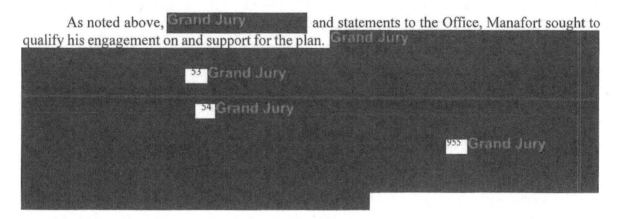

On February 26, 2017, Manafort met Kilimnik in Madrid, where Kilimnik had flown from Moscow.[956] In his first two interviews with the Office, Manafort denied meeting with Kilimnik on his Madrid trip and then—after being confronted with documentary evidence that Kilimnik was in Madrid at the same time as him—recognized that he met him in Madrid. Manafort said that Kilimnik had updated him on a criminal investigation into so-called "black ledger" payments to Manafort that was being conducted by Ukraine's National Anti-Corruption Bureau.[957] Grand Jury [958]

Manafort remained in contact with Kilimnik throughout 2017 and into the spring of 2018.

---

[951] Manafort 9/11/18 302, at 6; Grand Jury

[952] **Investigative Technique**

[953] Grand Jury

[954] Grand Jury .

[955] Grand Jury .

[956] 2/21/17 Email, Zatynaiko to Kilimnik.

[957] Manafort 9/13/18 302, at 1.

[958] Grand Jury In resolving whether Manafort breached his cooperation plea agreement by lying to the Office, the district court found that Manafort lied about, among other things, his contacts with Kilimnik regarding the peace plan, including the meeting in Madrid. *Manafort* 2/13/19 Transcript, at 29-31, 40.

U.S. Department of Justice

~~Attorney Work Product // May Contain Material Protected Under Fed. R. Crim. P. 6(e)~~

Those contacts included matters pertaining to the criminal charges brought by the Office,[959] and the Ukraine peace plan. In early 2018, Manafort retained his longtime polling firm to craft a draft poll in Ukraine, sent the pollsters a three-page primer on the plan sent by Kilimnik, and worked with Kilimnik to formulate the polling questions.[960] The primer sent to the pollsters specifically called for the United States and President Trump to support the Autonomous Republic of Donbas with Yanukovych as Prime Minister,[961] and a series of questions in the draft poll asked for opinions on Yanukovych's role in resolving the conflict in Donbas.[962] (The poll was not solely about Donbas; it also sought participants' views on leaders apart from Yanukovych as they pertained to the 2019 Ukraine presidential election.)

The Office has not uncovered evidence that Manafort brought the Ukraine peace plan to the attention of the Trump Campaign or the Trump Administration. Kilimnik continued his efforts to promote the peace plan to the Executive Branch (*e.g.*, U.S. Department of State) into the summer of 2018.[963]

B. Post-Election and Transition-Period Contacts

Trump was elected President on November 8, 2016. Beginning immediately after the election, individuals connected to the Russian government started contacting officials on the Trump Campaign and Transition Team through multiple channels—sometimes through Russian Ambassador Kislyak and at other times through individuals who sought reliable contacts through U.S. persons not formally tied to the Campaign or Transition Team. The most senior levels of the Russian government encouraged these efforts. The investigation did not establish that these efforts reflected or constituted coordination between the Trump Campaign and Russia in its election-interference activities.

1. Immediate Post-Election Activity

As soon as news broke that Trump had been elected President, Russian government officials and prominent Russian businessmen began trying to make inroads into the new Administration. They appeared not to have preexisting contacts and struggled to connect with senior officials around the President-Elect. As explained below, those efforts entailed both official contact through the Russian Embassy in the United States and outreaches—sanctioned at high levels of the Russian government—through business rather than political contacts.

---

[959] *Manafort* (D.D.C.) Gov't Opp. to Mot. to Modify, at 2; Superseding Indictment ¶¶ 48-51, *United States v. Paul J. Manafort, Jr.*, 1:17-cr-201 (D.D.C. June 8, 2018), Doc. 318.

[960] 2/12/18 Email, Fabrizio to Manafort & Ward; 2/16/18 Email, Fabrizio to Manafort; 2/19/18 Email, Fabrizio to Ward; 2/21/18 Email, Manafort to Ward & Fabrizio.

[961] 2/21/18 Email, Manafort to Ward & Fabrizio (7:16:49 a.m.) (attachment).

[962] 3/9/18 Email, Ward to Manafort & Fabrizio (attachment).

[963] Investigative Technique

144

a. Outreach from the Russian Government

At approximately 3 a.m. on election night, Trump Campaign press secretary Hope Hicks received a telephone call on her personal cell phone from a person who sounded foreign but was calling from a number with a DC area code.[964] Although Hicks had a hard time understanding the person, she could make out the words "Putin call."[965] Hicks told the caller to send her an email.[966]

The following morning, on November 9, 2016, Sergey Kuznetsov, an official at the Russian Embassy to the United States, emailed Hicks from his Gmail address with the subject line, "Message from Putin."[967] Attached to the email was a message from Putin, in both English and Russian, which Kuznetsov asked Hicks to convey to the President-Elect.[968] In the message, Putin offered his congratulations to Trump for his electoral victory, stating he "look[ed] forward to working with [Trump] on leading Russian-American relations out of crisis."[969]

Hicks forwarded the email to Kushner, asking, "Can you look into this? Don't want to get duped but don't want to blow off Putin!"[970] Kushner stated in Congressional testimony that he believed that it would be possible to verify the authenticity of the forwarded email through the Russian Ambassador, whom Kushner had previously met in April 2016.[971] Unable to recall the Russian Ambassador's name, Kushner emailed Dimitri Simes of CNI, whom he had consulted previously about Russia, *see* Volume I, Section IV.A.4, *supra*, and asked, "What is the name of Russian ambassador?"[972] Kushner forwarded Simes's response—which identified Kislyak by name—to Hicks.[973] After checking with Kushner to see what he had learned, Hicks conveyed Putin's letter to transition officials.[974] Five days later, on November 14, 2016, Trump and Putin spoke by phone in the presence of Transition Team members, including incoming National Security Advisor Michael Flynn.[975]

---

[964] Hicks 12/8/17 302, at 3.

[965] Hicks 12/8/17 302, at 3.

[966] Hicks 12/8/17 302, at 3.

[967] NOSC00044381 (11/9/16 Email, Kuznetsov to Hicks (5:27 a.m.)).

[968] NOSC00044381-82 (11/9/16 Email, Kuznetsov to Hicks (5:27 a.m.)).

[969] NOSC00044382 (11/9/16 Letter from Putin to President-Elect Trump (Nov. 9, 2016) (translation)).

[970] NOSC00044381 (11/9/16 Email, Hicks to Kushner (10:26 a.m.)).

[971] Statement of Jared C. Kushner to Congressional Committees, at 4 (Jul. 24, 2017).

[972] NOSC00000058 (11/9/16 Email, Kushner to Simes (10:28 a.m.)); Statement of Jared Kushner to Congressional Committees, at 4 (Jul. 24, 2017).

[973] NOSC00000058 (11/9/16 Email, Kushner to Hicks (11:05:44 a.m.)).

[974] Hicks 12/8/17 302, at 3-4.

[975] Flynn 11/16/17 302, at 8-10; *see* Doug G. Ware, *Trump, Russia's Putin Talk about Syria, Icy Relations in Phone Call*, UPI (Nov. 14, 2016).

U.S. Department of Justice

~~Attorney Work Product // May Contain Material Protected Under Fed. R. Crim. P. 6(e)~~

b. *High-Level Encouragement of Contacts through Alternative Channels*

As Russian officials in the United States reached out to the President-Elect and his team, a number of Russian individuals working in the private sector began their own efforts to make contact. Petr Aven, a Russian national who heads Alfa-Bank, Russia's largest commercial bank, described to the Office interactions with Putin during this time period that might account for the flurry of Russian activity.[976]

Aven told the Office that he is one of approximately 50 wealthy Russian businessmen who regularly meet with Putin in the Kremlin; these 50 men are often referred to as "oligarchs."[977] Aven told the Office that he met on a quarterly basis with Putin, including in the fourth quarter (Q4) of 2016, shortly after the U.S. presidential election.[978] Aven said that he took these meetings seriously and understood that any suggestions or critiques that Putin made during these meetings were implicit directives, and that there would be consequences for Aven if he did not follow through.[979] As was typical, the 2016 Q4 meeting with Putin was preceded by a preparatory meeting with Putin's chief of staff, Anton Vaino.[980]

According to Aven, at his Q4 2016 one-on-one meeting with Putin,[981] Putin raised the prospect that the United States would impose additional sanctions on Russian interests, including sanctions against Aven and/or Alfa-Bank.[982] Putin suggested that Aven needed to take steps to protect himself and Alfa-Bank.[983] Aven also testified that Putin spoke of the difficulty faced by the Russian government in getting in touch with the incoming Trump Administration.[984] According to Aven, Putin indicated that he did not know with whom formally to speak and generally did not know the people around the President-Elect.[985]

---

[976] Aven provided information to the Office in an interview and through an attorney proffer, ▮▮▮ Grand Jury ▮▮▮

[977] Aven 8/2/18 302, at 7.

[978] Grand Jury

[979] Aven 8/2/18 302, at 2-3.

[980] Grand Jury ▮▮▮ and interview with the Office, Aven referred to the high-ranking Russian government officials using numbers (*e.g.*, Official 1, Official 2). Aven separately confirmed through an attorney proffer that Official 1 was Putin and Official 2 was Putin's chief of staff, Vaino. *See* Affidavit of Ryan Junck (Aug. 2, 2018) (hard copy on file).

[981] At the time of his Q4 2016 meeting with Putin, Aven was generally aware of the press coverage about Russian interference in the U.S. election. According to Aven, he did not discuss that topic with Putin at any point, and Putin did not mention the rationale behind the threat of new sanctions. Aven 8/2/18 302, at 5-7.

[982] Grand Jury

[983] Grand Jury

[984] Grand Jury

[985] Grand Jury

U.S. Department of Justice

~~Attorney Work Product // May Contain Material Protected Under Fed. R. Crim. P. 6(e)~~

Aven ▓▓▓▓▓▓▓ told Putin he would take steps to protect himself and the Alfa-Bank shareholders from potential sanctions, and one of those steps would be to try to reach out to the incoming Administration to establish a line of communication.[986] Aven described Putin responding with skepticism about Aven's prospect for success.[987] According to Aven, although Putin did not expressly direct him to reach out to the Trump Transition Team, Aven understood that Putin expected him to try to respond to the concerns he had raised.[988] Aven's efforts are described in Volume I, Section IV.B.5, *infra*.

2. Kirill Dmitriev's Transition-Era Outreach to the Incoming Administration

Aven's description of his interactions with Putin is consistent with the behavior of Kirill Dmitriev, a Russian national who heads Russia's sovereign wealth fund and is closely connected to Putin. Dmitriev undertook efforts to meet members of the incoming Trump Administration in the months after the election. Dmitriev asked a close business associate who worked for the United Arab Emirates (UAE) royal court, George Nader, to introduce him to Trump transition officials, and Nader eventually arranged a meeting in the Seychelles between Dmitriev and Erik Prince, a Trump Campaign supporter and an associate of Steve Bannon.[989] In addition, the UAE national security advisor introduced Dmitriev to a hedge fund manager and friend of Jared Kushner, Rick Gerson, in late November 2016. In December 2016 and January 2017, Dmitriev and Gerson worked on a proposal for reconciliation between the United States and Russia, which Dmitriev implied he cleared through Putin. Gerson provided that proposal to Kushner before the inauguration, and Kushner later gave copies to Bannon and Secretary of State Rex Tillerson.

a. Background

Dmitriev is a Russian national who was appointed CEO of Russia's sovereign wealth fund, the Russian Direct Investment Fund (RDIF), when it was founded in 2011.[990] Dmitriev reported directly to Putin and frequently referred to Putin as his "boss."[991]

RDIF has co-invested in various projects with UAE sovereign wealth funds.[992] Dmitriev regularly interacted with Nader, a senior advisor to UAE Crown Prince Mohammed bin Zayed

---

[986] ▓▓▓▓▓▓▓

[987] ▓▓▓▓▓▓▓ Aven 8/2/18 302, at 6.

[988] Aven 8/2/18 302, at 4-8; ▓▓▓▓▓▓▓

[989] Nader provided information to the Office in multiple interviews, all but one of which were conducted under a proffer agreement ▓▓▓▓▓▓▓ . The investigators also interviewed Prince under a proffer agreement. Bannon was interviewed by the Office, ▓▓▓▓▓▓▓ under a proffer agreement.

[990] Kirill Dmitriev Biography, Russian Direct Investment Fund, *available at* https://rdif.ru/Eng_person_dmitriev_kirill/. *See also* Overview, Russian Direct Investment Fund, *available at* https://rdif.ru/Eng_About/.

[991] Gerson 6/15/18 302, at 1. *See also, e.g.*, 12/14/16 Text Message, Dmitriev to Gerson; 1/9/17 Text Message, Dmitriev to Gerson.

[992] ▓▓▓▓▓▓▓

U.S. Department of Justice

~~Attorney Work Product // May Contain Material Protected Under Fed. R. Crim. P. 6(e)~~

(Crown Prince Mohammed), in connection with RDIF's dealings with the UAE.[993] Putin wanted Dmitriev to be in charge of both the financial and the political relationship between Russia and the Gulf states, in part because Dmitriev had been educated in the West and spoke English fluently.[994] Nader considered Dmitriev to be Putin's interlocutor in the Gulf region, and would relay Dmitriev's views directly to Crown Prince Mohammed.[995]

Nader developed contacts with both U.S. presidential campaigns during the 2016 election, and kept Dmitriev abreast of his efforts to do so.[996] According to Nader, Dmitriev said that his and the government of Russia's preference was for candidate Trump to win, and asked Nader to assist him in meeting members of the Trump Campaign.[997] Grand Jury [998] Nader did not introduce Dmitriev to anyone associated with the Trump Campaign before the election.[999]

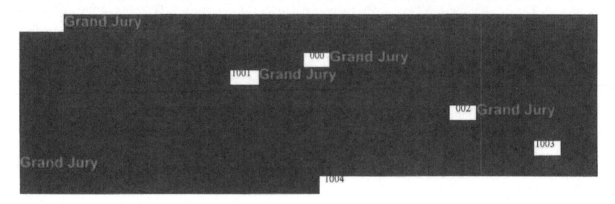

Erik Prince is a businessman who had relationships with various individuals associated with the Trump Campaign, including Steve Bannon, Donald Trump Jr., and Roger Stone.[1005] Prince did not have a formal role in the Campaign, although he offered to host a fundraiser for

---

[993] Nader 1/22/18 302, at 1-2; Nader 1/23/18 302, at 2-3; 5/3/16 Email, Nader to Phares; ▇▇▇ Grand Jury

[994] Nader 1/22/18 302, at 1-2.

[995] Nader 1/22/18 302, at 3.

[996] Nader 1/22/18 302, at 3; Grand Jury

[997] Nader 1/22/18 302, at 3; Grand Jury

[998] Grand Jury

[999] Nader 1/22/18 302, at 3.

[1000] Grand Jury

[1001] Grand Jury

[1002] Grand Jury

[1003] Grand Jury

[1004] Grand Jury

[1005] Prince 4/4/18 302, at 1-5; Bannon 2/14/18 302, at 21.

U.S. Department of Justice

~~Attorney Work Product // May Contain Material Protected Under Fed. R. Crim. P. 6(e)~~

Trump and sent unsolicited policy papers on issues such as foreign policy, trade, and Russian election interference to Bannon.[1006]

After the election, Prince frequently visited transition offices at Trump Tower, primarily to meet with Bannon but on occasion to meet Michael Flynn and others.[1007] Prince and Bannon would discuss, *inter alia*, foreign policy issues and Prince's recommendations regarding who should be appointed to fill key national security positions.[1008] Although Prince was not formally affiliated with the transition, Nader [Grand Jury] received assurances [Grand Jury] that the incoming Administration considered Prince a trusted associate.[1009]

b. Kirill Dmitriev's Post-Election Contacts With the Incoming Administration

Soon after midnight on election night, Dmitriev messaged [Investigative Technique] who was traveling to New York to attend the 2016 World Chess Championship. [Investigative Technique] Dmitry Peskov, the Russian Federation's press secretary, who was also attending the World Chess Championship.[1010] [Investigative Technique] [1011] [Investigative Technique] [1012] [Investigative Technique] [1013]

At approximately 2:40 a.m. on November 9, 2016, news reports stated that candidate Clinton had called President-Elect Trump to concede. At [Investigative Technique] [1014] [Investigative Technique] wrote to Dmitriev, "Putin has won."[1015]

[1006] Prince 4/4/18 302, at 1, 3-4; Prince 5/3/18 302, at 2; Bannon 2/14/18 302, at 19-20; 10/18/16 Email, Prince to Bannon.

[1007] Flynn 11/20/17 302, at 6; Flynn 1/11/18 302, at 5; Flynn 1/24/18 302, at 5-6; Flynn 5/1/18 302, at 11; Prince 4/4/18 302, at 5, 8; Bannon 2/14/18 302, at 20-21; 11/12/16 Email, Prince to Corallo.

[1008] Prince 4/4/18 302, at 5; Bannon 2/14/18 302, at 21.

[1009] [Grand Jury]

[1010] [Investigative Technique] Nader 1/22/18 302, at 5-6; [Grand Jury]

[1011] [Investigative Technique]

[1012] [Investigative Technique]

[1013] [Investigative Technique]

[1014] [Investigative Technique]

[1015] [Investigative Technique]

U.S. Department of Justice

~~Attorney Work Product // May Contain Material Protected Under Fed. R. Crim. P. 6(e)~~

Later that morning, Dmitriev contacted Nader, who was in New York, to request a meeting with the "key people" in the incoming Administration as soon as possible in light of the "[g]reat results."[1016] He asked Nader to convey to the incoming Administration that "we want to start rebuilding the relationship in whatever is a comfortable pace for them. We understand all of the sensitivities and are not in a rush."[1017] Dmitriev and Nader had previously discussed Nader introducing him to the contacts Nader had made within the Trump Campaign.[1018] Dmitriev also told Nader that he would ask Putin for permission to travel to the United States, where he would be able to speak to media outlets about the positive impact of Trump's election and the need for reconciliation between the United States and Russia.[1019]

Later that day, Dmitriev flew to New York, where Peskov was separately traveling to attend the chess tournament.[1020] Dmitriev invited Nader to the opening of the tournament and noted that, if there was "a chance to see anyone key from Trump camp," he "would love to start building for the future."[1021] Dmitriev also asked Nader to invite Kushner to the event so that he (Dmitriev) could meet him.[1022] Nader did not pass along Dmitriev's invitation to anyone connected with the incoming Administration.[1023] Although one World Chess Federation official recalled hearing from an attendee that President-Elect Trump had stopped by the tournament, the investigation did not establish that Trump or any Campaign or Transition Team official attended the event.[1024] And the President's written answers denied that he had.[1025]

Nader stated that Dmitriev continued to press him to set up a meeting with transition officials, and was particularly focused on Kushner and Trump Jr.[1026] Dmitriev told Nader that Putin would be very grateful to Nader and that a meeting would make history.[1027] [Grand Jury]

[1016] 11/9/16 Text Message, Dmitriev to Nader (9:34 a.m.); Nader 1/22/18 302, at 4.

[1017] 11/9/16 Text Message, Dmitriev to Nader (11:58 p.m.).

[1018] Nader 1/22/18 302, at 3.

[1019] 11/9/16 Text Message, Dmitriev to Nader (10:06 a.m.); 11/9/16 Text Message, Dmitriev to Nader (10:10 a.m.); [Grand Jury]

[1020] 11/9/16 Text Message, Dmitriev to Nader (10:08 a.m.); 11/9/16 Text Message, Dmitriev to Nader (3:40 p.m.); Nader 1/22/18 302, at 5.

[1021] 11/9/16 Text Message, Dmitriev to Nader (7:10 p.m.).

[1022] 11/10/16 Text Message, Dmitriev to Nader (5:20 a.m.).

[1023] Nader 1/22/18 302, at 5-6.

[1024] Marinello 5/31/18 302, at 2-3; Nader 1/22/18 302, at 5-6.

[1025] Written Responses of Donald J. Trump (Nov. 20, 2018), at 17-18 (Response to Question V, Part (a).

[1026] Nader 1/22/18 302, at 6; [Grand Jury]

[1027] Nader 1/22/18 302, at 6; [Grand Jury]

U.S. Department of Justice

~~Attorney Work Product // May Contain Material Protected Under Fed. R. Crim. P. 6(e)~~

GJ   [1028] Grand Jury

[029] According to Nader, Dmitriev was very anxious to connect with the incoming Administration and told Nader that he would try other routes to do so besides Nader himself.[1030] Nader did not ultimately introduce Dmitriev to anyone associated with the incoming Administration during Dmitriev's post-election trip to New York.[1031]

In early December 2016, Dmitriev again broached the topic of meeting incoming Administration officials with Nader in January or February.[1032] Dmitriev sent Nader a list of publicly available quotes of Dmitriev speaking positively about Donald Trump "in case they [were] helpful."[1033]

c. *Erik Prince and Kirill Dmitriev Meet in the Seychelles*

i. *George Nader and Erik Prince Arrange Seychelles Meeting with Dmitriev*

Nader traveled to New York in early January 2017 and had lunchtime and dinner meetings with Erik Prince on January 3, 2017.[1034] Nader and Prince discussed Dmitriev.[1035] Nader informed Prince that the Russians were looking to build a link with the incoming Trump Administration.[1036] [Grand Jury] he told Prince that Dmitriev had been pushing Nader to introduce him to someone from the incoming Administration [Grand Jury] .[1037] Nader suggested, in light of Prince's relationship with Transition Team officials, that Prince and Dmitriev meet to discuss issues of mutual concern.[1038] [Grand Jury] Prince told Nader that he needed to think further about it and to check with Transition Team officials.[1039]

After his dinner with Prince, Nader sent Prince a link to a Wikipedia entry about Dmitriev, and sent Dmitriev a message stating that he had just met "with some key people within the family and inner circle"—a reference to Prince—and that he had spoken at length and positively about

---

[1028] [Grand Jury]

[1029] [Grand Jury]

[1030] Nader 1/22/18 302, at 6.

[1031] Nader 1/22/18 302, at 5-7.

[1032] 12/8/16 Text Messages, Dmitriev to Nader (12:10:31 a.m.); Nader 1/22/18 302, at 11.

[1033] 12/8/16 Text Message, Dmitriev to Nader (12:10:31 a.m.); 12/8/16 Text Message, Dmitriev to Nader (12:10:57 a.m.).

[1034] Prince 4/4/18 302, at 8.

[1035] Prince 5/3/18 302, at 3; [Grand Jury]

[1036] [Grand Jury]

[1037] [Grand Jury]

[1038] [Grand Jury]

[1039] [Grand Jury]

U.S. Department of Justice

~~Attorney Work Product // May Contain Material Protected Under Fed. R. Crim. P. 6(e)~~

Dmitriev.[1040] Nader told Dmitriev that the people he met had asked for Dmitriev's bio, and Dmitriev replied that he would update and send it.[1041] Nader later received from Dmitriev two files concerning Dmitriev: one was a two-page biography, and the other was a list of Dmitriev's positive quotes about Donald Trump.[1042]

The next morning, Nader forwarded the message and attachments Dmitriev had sent him to Prince.[1043] Nader wrote to Prince that these documents were the versions "to be used with some additional details for them" (with "them" referring to members of the incoming Administration).[1044] Prince opened the attachments at Trump Tower within an hour of receiving them.[1045] Prince stated that, while he was at Trump Tower that day, he spoke with Kellyanne Conway, Wilbur Ross, Steve Mnuchin, and others while waiting to see Bannon.[1046] Cell-site location data for Prince's mobile phone indicates that Prince remained at Trump Tower for approximately three hours.[1047] Prince said that he could not recall whether, during those three hours, he met with Bannon and discussed Dmitriev with him.[1048] [Grand Jury]
[049]

Prince booked a ticket to the Seychelles on January 7, 2017.[1050] The following day, Nader wrote to Dmitriev that he had a "pleasant surprise" for him, namely that he had arranged for Dmitriev to meet "a Special Guest" from "the New Team," referring to Prince.[1051] Nader asked Dmitriev if he could come to the Seychelles for the meeting on January 12, 2017, and Dmitriev agreed.[1052]

The following day, Dmitriev sought assurance from Nader that the Seychelles meeting would be worthwhile.[1053] [Grand Jury] Dmitriev was not enthusiastic about the idea of meeting with Prince, and that Nader assured him that Prince wielded influence with the incoming

---

[1040] 1/4/17 Text Message, Nader to Prince; 1/4/17 Text Messages, Nader to Dmitriev (5:24 a.m. – 5:26 a.m.); Nader 1/22/18 302, at 8-9; [Grand Jury]

[1041] 1/4/17 Text Messages, Nader & Dmitriev (7:24:27 a.m.).

[1042] 1/4/17 Text Messages, Dmitriev to Nader (7:25-7:29 a.m.)

[1043] 1/4/17 Text Messages, Nader to Prince.

[1044] 1/4/17 Text Messages, Nader to Prince; [Grand Jury]

[1045] Prince 5/3/18 302, at 1-3.

[1046] Prince 5/3/18 302, at 2-3.

[1047] Cell-site location data for Prince's mobile phone [Investigative Technique]

[1048] Prince 5/3/18 302, at 3.

[1049] [Grand Jury]

[1050] 1/5/17 Email, Kasbo to Prince.

[1051] 1/8/17 Text Messages, Nader to Dmitriev (6:05 – 6:10 p.m.).

[1052] 1/8/17 Text Messages, Nader & Dmitriev (6:10 – 7:27 p.m.).

[1053] 1/9/17 Text Message, Dmitriev to Nader.

U.S. Department of Justice

~~Attorney Work Product // May Contain Material Protected Under Fed. R. Crim. P. 6(e)~~

Administration.[1054] Nader wrote to Dmitriev, "This guy [Prince] is designated by Steve [Bannon] to meet you! I know him and he is very very well connected and trusted by the New Team. His sister is now a Minister of Education."[1055] According to Nader, Prince had led him to believe that Bannon was aware of Prince's upcoming meeting with Dmitriev, and Prince acknowledged that it was fair for Nader to think that Prince would pass information on to the Transition Team.[1056] Bannon, however, told the Office that Prince did not tell him in advance about his meeting with Dmitriev.[1057]

ii. The Seychelles Meetings

Dmitriev arrived with his wife in the Seychelles on January 11, 2017, and checked into the Four Seasons Resort where Crown Prince Mohammed and Nader were staying.[1058] Prince arrived that same day.[1059] Prince and Dmitriev met for the first time that afternoon in Nader's villa, with Nader present.[1060] The initial meeting lasted approximately 30-45 minutes.[1061]

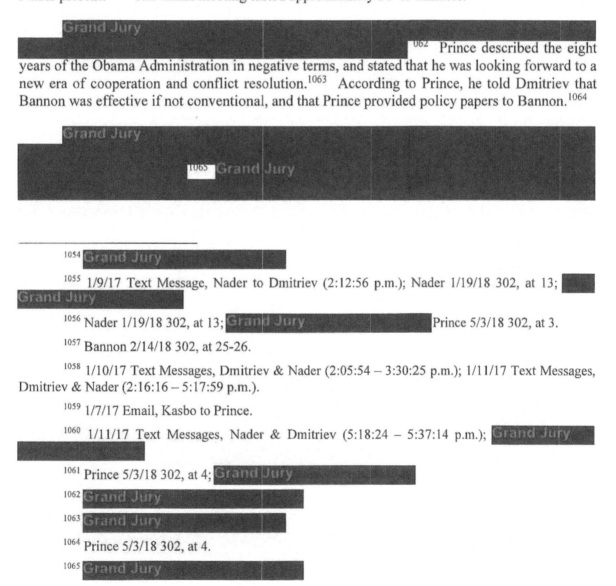

[1062] Prince described the eight years of the Obama Administration in negative terms, and stated that he was looking forward to a new era of cooperation and conflict resolution.[1063] According to Prince, he told Dmitriev that Bannon was effective if not conventional, and that Prince provided policy papers to Bannon.[1064]

[1054] [Grand Jury]

[1055] 1/9/17 Text Message, Nader to Dmitriev (2:12:56 p.m.); Nader 1/19/18 302, at 13; [Grand Jury]

[1056] Nader 1/19/18 302, at 13; [Grand Jury] Prince 5/3/18 302, at 3.

[1057] Bannon 2/14/18 302, at 25-26.

[1058] 1/10/17 Text Messages, Dmitriev & Nader (2:05:54 – 3:30:25 p.m.); 1/11/17 Text Messages, Dmitriev & Nader (2:16:16 – 5:17:59 p.m.).

[1059] 1/7/17 Email, Kasbo to Prince.

[1060] 1/11/17 Text Messages, Nader & Dmitriev (5:18:24 – 5:37:14 p.m.); [Grand Jury]

[1061] Prince 5/3/18 302, at 4; [Grand Jury]

[1062] [Grand Jury]

[1063] [Grand Jury]

[1064] Prince 5/3/18 302, at 4.

[1065] [Grand Jury]

U.S. Department of Justice

~~Attorney Work Product // May Contain Material Protected Under Fed. R. Crim. P. 6(e)~~

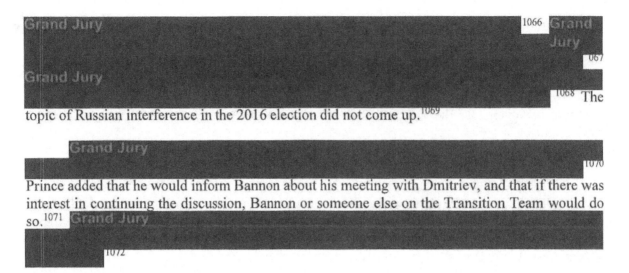

topic of Russian interference in the 2016 election did not come up.[1069]

Prince added that he would inform Bannon about his meeting with Dmitriev, and that if there was interest in continuing the discussion, Bannon or someone else on the Transition Team would do so.[1071] Grand Jury [1072]

Afterwards, Prince returned to his room, where he learned that a Russian aircraft carrier had sailed to Libya, which led him to call Nader and ask him to set up another meeting with Dmitriev.[1073] According to Nader, Prince called and said he had checked with his associates back home and needed to convey to Dmitriev that Libya was "off the table."[1074] Nader wrote to Dmitriev that Prince had "received an urgent message that he needs to convey to you immediately," and arranged for himself, Dmitriev, and Prince to meet at a restaurant on the Four Seasons property.[1075]

At the second meeting, Prince told Dmitriev that the United States could not accept any Russian involvement in Libya because it would make the situation there much worse.[1076] Grand Jury

---

[1066] Grand Jury

[1067] Grand Jury

[1068] Grand Jury

[1069] Prince 5/3/18 302, at 4-5.

[1070] Grand Jury

[1071] Prince 5/3/18 302, at 4; Grand Jury

[1072] Grand Jury

[1073] Prince 4/4/18 302, at 10; Prince 5/3/18 302, at 4; Grand Jury

[1074] Nader 1/22/18 302, at 14; Grand Jury

[1075] Grand Jury 1/11/17 Text Messages, Dmitriev & Nader (9:13:54 – 10:24:25 p.m.).

[1076] Grand Jury Prince, however, denied that and recalled that he was making these remarks to Dmitriev not in an official capacity for the transition but based on his experience as a former naval officer. Prince 5/3/18 302, at 4.

U.S. Department of Justice

~~Attorney Work Product // May Contain Material Protected Under Fed. R. Crim. P. 6(e)~~

[1077]

After the brief second meeting concluded, Nader and Dmitriev discussed what had transpired.[1078] Dmitriev told Nader that he was disappointed in his meetings with Prince for two reasons: first, he believed the Russians needed to be communicating with someone who had more authority within the incoming Administration than Prince had.[1079] Second, he had hoped to have a discussion of greater substance, such as outlining a strategic roadmap for both countries to follow.[1080] Dmitriev told Nader that Grand Jury Prince's comments Grand Jury were insulting Grand Jury [1081]

Hours after the second meeting, Prince sent two text messages to Bannon from the Seychelles.[1082] As described further below, investigators were unable to obtain the content of these or other messages between Prince and Bannon, and the investigation also did not identify evidence of any further communication between Prince and Dmitriev after their meetings in the Seychelles.

iii. Erik Prince's Meeting with Steve Bannon after the Seychelles Trip

After the Seychelles meetings, Prince told Nader that he would inform Bannon about his discussion with Dmitriev and would convey that someone within the Russian power structure was interested in seeking better relations with the incoming Administration.[1083] On January 12, 2017, Prince contacted Bannon's personal assistant to set up a meeting for the following week.[1084] Several days later, Prince messaged her again asking about Bannon's schedule.[1085]

Prince said that he met Bannon at Bannon's home after returning to the United States in mid-January and briefed him about several topics, including his meeting with Dmitriev.[1086] Prince told the Office that he explained to Bannon that Dmitriev was the head of a Russian sovereign wealth fund and was interested in improving relations between the United States and Russia.[1087] Prince had on his cellphone a screenshot of Dmitriev's Wikipedia page dated January 16, 2017,

---

[1077] Grand Jury

[1078] Nader 1/22/18 302, at 15; Grand Jury

[1079] Nader 1/22/18 302, at 9, 15; Grand Jury

[1080] Nader 1/22/18 302, at 15.

[1081] Grand Jury Nader 1/22/18 302, at 15.

[1082] Call Records of Erik Prince Grand Jury .

[1083] Prince 4/4/18 302, at 10; Prince 5/3/18 302, at 4; Grand Jury

[1084] 1/12/17 Text Messages, Prince to Preate.

[1085] 1/15/17 Text Message, Prince to Preate.

[1086] Prince 4/4/18 302, at 11; Prince 5/3/18 302, at 5.

[1087] Prince 4/4/18 302, at 11; Prince 5/3/18 302, at 5.

U.S. Department of Justice

~~Attorney Work Product // May Contain Material Protected Under Fed. R. Crim. P. 6(e)~~

and Prince told the Office that he likely showed that image to Bannon.[1088] Prince also believed he provided Bannon with Dmitriev's contact information.[1089] According to Prince, Bannon instructed Prince not to follow up with Dmitriev, and Prince had the impression that the issue was not a priority for Bannon.[1090] Prince related that Bannon did not appear angry, just relatively uninterested.[1091]

Bannon, by contrast, told the Office that he never discussed with Prince anything regarding Dmitriev, RDIF, or any meetings with Russian individuals or people associated with Putin.[1092] Bannon also stated that had Prince mentioned such a meeting, Bannon would have remembered it, and Bannon would have objected to such a meeting having taken place.[1093]

The conflicting accounts provided by Bannon and Prince could not be independently clarified by reviewing their communications, because neither one was able to produce any of the messages they exchanged in the time period surrounding the Seychelles meeting. Prince's phone contained no text messages prior to March 2017, though provider records indicate that he and Bannon exchanged dozens of messages.[1094] Prince denied deleting any messages but claimed he did not know why there were no messages on his device before March 2017.[1095] Bannon's devices similarly contained no messages in the relevant time period, and Bannon also stated he did not know why messages did not appear on his device.[1096] Bannon told the Office that, during both the months before and after the Seychelles meeting, he regularly used his personal Blackberry and personal email for work-related communications (including those with Prince), and he took no steps to preserve these work communications.[1097]

d. Kirill Dmitriev's Post-Election Contact with Rick Gerson Regarding U.S.-Russia Relations

Dmitriev's contacts during the transition period were not limited to those facilitated by Nader. In approximately late November 2016, the UAE national security advisor introduced Dmitriev to Rick Gerson, a friend of Jared Kushner who runs a hedge fund in New York.[1098] Gerson stated he had no formal role in the transition and had no involvement in the Trump

---

[1088] Prince 5/3/18 302, at 5; 1/16/17 Image on Prince Phone (on file with the Office).

[1089] Prince 5/3/18 302, at 5.

[1090] Prince 5/3/18 302, at 5.

[1091] Prince 5/3/18 302, at 5.

[1092] Bannon 10/26/18 302, at 10-11.

[1093] Bannon 10/26/18 302, at 10-11.

[1094] Call Records of Erik Prince ▓Grand Jury▓.

[1095] Prince 4/4/18 302, at 6.

[1096] Bannon 10/26/18 302, at 11; Bannon 2/14/18 302, at 36.

[1097] Bannon 10/26/18 302, at 11.

[1098] Gerson 6/5/18 302, at 1, 3; 11/26/16 Text Message, Dmitriev to Gerson; 1/25/17 Text Message, Dmitriev to Nader.

U.S. Department of Justice

~~Attorney Work Product // May Contain Material Protected Under Fed. R. Crim. P. 6(e)~~

Campaign other than occasional casual discussions about the Campaign with Kushner.[1099] After the election, Gerson assisted the transition by arranging meetings for transition officials with former UK prime minister Tony Blair and a UAE delegation led by Crown Prince Mohammed.[1100]

When Dmitriev and Gerson met, they principally discussed potential joint ventures between Gerson's hedge fund and RDIF.[1101] Dmitriev was interested in improved economic cooperation between the United States and Russia and asked Gerson who he should meet with in the incoming Administration who would be helpful towards this goal.[1102] Gerson replied that he would try to figure out the best way to arrange appropriate introductions, but noted that confidentiality would be required because of the sensitivity of holding such meetings before the new Administration took power, and before Cabinet nominees had been confirmed by the Senate.[1103] Gerson said he would ask Kushner and Michael Flynn who the "key person or people" were on the topics of reconciliation with Russia, joint security concerns, and economic matters.[1104]

Dmitriev told Gerson that he had been tasked by Putin to develop and execute a reconciliation plan between the United States and Russia. He noted in a text message to Gerson that if Russia was "approached with respect and willingness to understand our position, we can have Major Breakthroughs quickly."[1105] Gerson and Dmitriev exchanged ideas in December 2016 about what such a reconciliation plan would include.[1106] Gerson told the Office that the Transition Team had not asked him to engage in these discussions with Dmitriev, and that he did so on his own initiative and as a private citizen.[1107]

On January 9, 2017, the same day he asked Nader whether meeting Prince would be worthwhile, Dmitriev sent his biography to Gerson and asked him if he could "share it with Jared (or somebody else very senior in the team) – so that they know that we are focused from our side on improving the relationship and my boss asked me to play a key role in that."[1108] Dmitriev also asked Gerson if he knew Prince, and if Prince was somebody important or worth spending time

---

[1099] Gerson 6/5/18 302, at 1.

[1100] Gerson 6/5/18 302, at 1-2; Kushner 4/11/18 302, at 21.

[1101] Gerson 6/5/18 302, at 3-4; *see, e.g.*, 12/2/16 Text Messages, Dmitriev & Gerson; 12/14/16 Text Messages, Dmitriev & Gerson; 1/3/17 Text Message, Gerson to Dmitriev; 12/2/16 Email, Tolokonnikov to Gerson.

[1102] Gerson 6/5/18 302, at 3; 12/14/16 Text Message, Dmitriev to Gerson.

[1103] 12/14/16 Text Message, Gerson to Dmitriev.

[1104] 12/14/16 Text Message, Gerson to Dmitriev.

[1105] 12/14/16 Text Messages, Dmitriev & Gerson; Gerson 6/15/18 302, at 1.

[1106] 12/14/16 Text Messages, Dmitriev & Gerson.

[1107] Gerson 6/15/18 302, at 1.

[1108] 1/9/17 Text Messages, Dmitriev to Gerson; 1/9/17 Text Message, Dmitriev to Nader.

U.S. Department of Justice

~~Attorney Work Product // May Contain Material Protected Under Fed. R. Crim. P. 6(e)~~

with.[1109] After his trip to the Seychelles, Dmitriev told Gerson that Bannon had asked Prince to meet with Dmitriev and that the two had had a positive meeting.[1110]

On January 16, 2017, Dmitriev consolidated the ideas for U.S.-Russia reconciliation that he and Gerson had been discussing into a two-page document that listed five main points: (1) jointly fighting terrorism; (2) jointly engaging in anti-weapons of mass destruction efforts; (3) developing "win-win" economic and investment initiatives; (4) maintaining an honest, open, and continual dialogue regarding issues of disagreement; and (5) ensuring proper communication and trust by "key people" from each country.[1111] On January 18, 2017, Gerson gave a copy of the document to Kushner.[1112] Kushner had not heard of Dmitriev at that time.[1113] Gerson explained that Dmitriev was the head of RDIF, and Gerson may have alluded to Dmitriev's being well connected.[1114] Kushner placed the document in a file and said he would get it to the right people.[1115] Kushner ultimately gave one copy of the document to Bannon and another to Rex Tillerson; according to Kushner, neither of them followed up with Kushner about it.[1116] On January 19, 2017, Dmitriev sent Nader a copy of the two-page document, telling him that this was "a view from our side that I discussed in my meeting on the islands and with you and with our friends. Please share with them – we believe this is a good foundation to start from."[1117]

Gerson informed Dmitriev that he had given the document to Kushner soon after delivering it.[1118] On January 26, 2017, Dmitriev wrote to Gerson that his "boss"—an apparent reference to Putin—was asking if there had been any feedback on the proposal.[1119] Dmitriev said, "[w]e do not want to rush things and move at a comfortable speed. At the same time, my boss asked me to try to have the key US meetings in the next two weeks if possible."[1120] He informed Gerson that Putin and President Trump would speak by phone that Saturday, and noted that that information was "very confidential."[1121]

The same day, Dmitriev wrote to Nader that he had seen his "boss" again yesterday who had "emphasized that this is a great priority for us and that we need to build this communication

---

[1109] Gerson 6/5/18 302, at 4.

[1110] 1/18/17 Text Messages, Dmitriev & Gerson.

[1111] 1/16/17 Text Messages, Dmitriev & Gerson.

[1112] Gerson 6/5/18 302, at 3; Gerson 6/15/18 302, at 2.

[1113] Gerson 6/5/18 302, at 3.

[1114] Gerson 6/5/18 302, at 3; Gerson 6/15/18 302, at 1-2; Kushner 4/11/18 302, at 22.

[1115] Gerson 6/5/18 302, at 3.

[1116] Kushner 4/11/18 302, at 32.

[1117] 1/19/17 Text Message, Dmitriev to Nader (11:11:56 a.m.).

[1118] 1/18/17 Text Message, Gerson to Dmitriev; Gerson 6/15/18 302, at 2.

[1119] 1/26/17 Text Message, Dmitriev to Gerson.

[1120] 1/26/17 Text Message, Dmitriev to Gerson.

[1121] 1/26/17 Text Message, Dmitriev to Gerson.

U.S. Department of Justice

~~Attorney Work Product // May Contain Material Protected Under Fed. R. Crim. P. 6(e)~~

channel to avoid bureaucracy."[1122] On January 28, 2017, Dmitriev texted Nader that he wanted "to see if I can confirm to my boss that your friends may use some of the ideas from the 2 pager I sent you in the telephone call that will happen at 12 EST,"[1123] an apparent reference to the call scheduled between President Trump and Putin. Nader replied, "Definitely paper was so submitted to Team by Rick and me. They took it seriously!"[1124] After the call between President Trump and Putin occurred, Dmitriev wrote to Nader that "the call went very well. My boss wants me to continue making some public statements that us [sic] Russia cooperation is good and important."[1125] Gerson also wrote to Dmitriev to say that the call had gone well, and Dmitriev replied that the document they had drafted together "played an important role."[1126]

Gerson and Dmitriev appeared to stop communicating with one another in approximately March 2017, when the investment deal they had been working on together showed no signs of progressing.[1127]

3. Ambassador Kislyak's Meeting with Jared Kushner and Michael Flynn in Trump Tower Following the Election

On November 16, 2016, Catherine Vargas, an executive assistant to Kushner, received a request for a meeting with Russian Ambassador Sergey Kislyak.[1128] That same day, Vargas sent Kushner an email with the subject, "MISSED CALL: Russian Ambassador to the US, Sergey Ivanovich Kislyak . . . ."[1129] The text of the email read, "RE: setting up a time to meet w/you on 12/1. LMK how to proceed." Kushner responded in relevant part, "I think I do this one -- confirm with Dimitri [Simes of CNI] that this is the right guy."[1130] After reaching out to a colleague of Simes at CNI, Vargas reported back to Kushner that Kislyak was "the best go-to guy for routine matters in the US," while Yuri Ushakov, a Russian foreign policy advisor, was the contact for "more direct/substantial matters."[1131]

Bob Foresman, the UBS investment bank executive who had previously tried to transmit to candidate Trump an invitation to speak at an economic forum in Russia, *see* Volume I, Section IV.A.1.d.ii, *supra*, may have provided similar information to the Transition Team. According to

---

[1122] 1/26/17 Text Message, Dmitriev to Nader (10:04:41 p.m.).

[1123] 1/28/17 Text Message, Dmitriev to Nader (11:05:39 a.m.).

[1124] 1/28/17 Text Message, Nader to Dmitriev (11:11:33 a.m.).

[1125] 1/29/17 Text Message, Dmitriev to Nader (11:06:35 a.m.).

[1126] 1/28/17 Text Message, Gerson to Dmitriev; 1/29/17 Text Message, Dmitriev to Gerson.

[1127] Gerson 6/15/18 302, at 4; 3/21/17 Text Message, Gerson to Dmitriev.

[1128] *Statement of Jared C. Kushner to Congressional Committees* ("Kushner Stmt."), at 6 (7/24/17) (written statement by Kushner to the Senate Judiciary Committee).

[1129] NOSC00004356 (11/16/16 Email, Vargas to Kushner (6:44 p.m.)).

[1130] NOSC00004356 (11/16/16 Email, Kushner to Vargas (9:54 p.m.)).

[1131] 11/17/16 Email, Brown to Simes (10:41 a.m.); Brown 10/13/17 302, at 4; 11/17/16 Email, Vargas to Kushner (12:31:18).

U.S. Department of Justice

~~Attorney Work Product // May Contain Material Protected Under Fed. R. Crim. P. 6(e)~~

Foresman, at the end of an early December 2016 meeting with incoming National Security Advisor Michael Flynn and his designated deputy (K.T. McFarland) in New York, Flynn asked Foresman for his thoughts on Kislyak. Foresman had not met Kislyak but told Flynn that, while Kislyak was an important person, Kislyak did not have a direct line to Putin.[1132] Foresman subsequently traveled to Moscow, inquired of a source he believed to be close to Putin, and heard back from that source that Ushakov would be the official channel for the incoming U.S. national security advisor.[1133] Foresman acknowledged that Flynn had not asked him to undertake that inquiry in Russia but told the Office that he nonetheless felt obligated to report the information back to Flynn, and that he worked to get a face-to-face meeting with Flynn in January 2017 so that he could do so.[1134] Email correspondence suggests that the meeting ultimately went forward,[1135] but Flynn has no recollection of it or of the earlier December meeting.[1136] (The investigation did not identify evidence of Flynn or Kushner meeting with Ushakov after being given his name.[1137])

In the meantime, although he had already formed the impression that Kislyak was not necessarily the right point of contact,[1138] Kushner went forward with the meeting that Kislyak had requested on November 16. It took place at Trump Tower on November 30, 2016.[1139] At Kushner's invitation, Flynn also attended; Bannon was invited but did not attend.[1140] During the meeting, which lasted approximately 30 minutes, Kushner expressed a desire on the part of the incoming Administration to start afresh with U.S.-Russian relations.[1141] Kushner also asked Kislyak to identify the best person (whether Kislyak or someone else) with whom to direct future discussions—someone who had contact with Putin and the ability to speak for him.[1142]

The three men also discussed U.S. policy toward Syria, and Kislyak floated the idea of having Russian generals brief the Transition Team on the topic using a secure communications line.[1143] After Flynn explained that there was no secure line in the Transition Team offices,

---

[1132] Foresman 10/17/18 302, at 17.

[1133] Foresman 10/17/18 302, at 17-18.

[1134] Foresman 10/17/18 302, at 18.

[1135] RMF-SCO-00000015 (1/5/17 Email, Foresman to Atencio & Flaherty); RMF-SCO-00000015 (1/5/17 Email, Flaherty to Foresman & Atencio).

[1136] 9/26/18 Attorney Proffer from Covington & Burling LLP (reflected in email on file with the Office).

[1137] Vargas 4/4/18 302, at 5.

[1138] Kushner 11/1/17 302, at 4.

[1139] AKIN_GUMP_BERKOWITZ_0000016-019 (11/29/16 Email, Vargas to Kuznetsov).

[1140] Flynn 1/11/18 302, at 2; NOS00004240 (Calendar Invite, Vargas to Kushner & Flynn).

[1141] Kushner Stmt. at 6.

[1142] Kushner Stmt. at 6; Kushner 4/11/18 302, at 18.

[1143] Kushner Stmt. at 7; Kushner 4/11/18 302, at 18; Flynn 1/11/18 302, at 2.

U.S. Department of Justice

~~Attorney Work Product // May Contain Material Protected Under Fed. R. Crim. P. 6(e)~~

Kushner asked Kislyak if they could communicate using secure facilities at the Russian Embassy.[1144] Kislyak quickly rejected that idea.[1145]

4. Jared Kushner's Meeting with Sergey Gorkov

On December 6, 2016, the Russian Embassy reached out to Kushner's assistant to set up a second meeting between Kislyak and Kushner.[1146] Kushner declined several proposed meeting dates, but Kushner's assistant indicated that Kislyak was very insistent about securing a second meeting.[1147] Kushner told the Office that he did not want to take another meeting because he had already decided Kislyak was not the right channel for him to communicate with Russia, so he arranged to have one of his assistants, Avi Berkowitz, meet with Kislyak in his stead.[1148] Although embassy official Sergey Kuznetsov wrote to Berkowitz that Kislyak thought it "important" to "continue the conversation with Mr. Kushner in person,"[1149] Kislyak nonetheless agreed to meet instead with Berkowitz once it became apparent that Kushner was unlikely to take a meeting.

Berkowitz met with Kislyak on December 12, 2016, at Trump Tower.[1150] The meeting lasted only a few minutes, during which Kislyak indicated that he wanted Kushner to meet someone who had a direct line to Putin: Sergey Gorkov, the head of the Russian-government-owned bank Vnesheconombank (VEB).

Kushner agreed to meet with Gorkov.[1151] The one-on-one meeting took place the next day, December 13, 2016, at the Colony Capital building in Manhattan, where Kushner had previously scheduled meetings.[1152] VEB was (and is) the subject of Department of Treasury economic sanctions imposed in response to Russia's annexation of Crimea.[1153] Kushner did not, however, recall any discussion during his meeting with Gorkov about the sanctions against VEB or sanctions more generally.[1154] Kushner stated in an interview that he did not engage in any preparation for

---

[1144] Kushner 4/11/18 302, at 18.

[1145] Kushner 4/11/18 302, at 18.

[1146] Kushner Stmt. at 7; NOSC00000123 (12/6/16 Email, Vargas to Kushner (12:11:40 p.m.)).

[1147] Kushner 4/11/18 302, at 19; NOSC00000130 (12/12/16 Email, Kushner to Vargas (10:41 p.m.)).

[1148] Kushner 4/11/18 302, at 19; Kushner Stmt. at 7; DJTFP_SCO_01442290 (12/6/16 Email, Berkowitz to ▓▓▓▓▓▓▓▓

[1149] DJTFP_SCO_01442290 (12/7/16 Email ▓▓▓▓▓▓▓ to Berkowitz (12:31:39 p.m.)).

[1150] Berkowitz 1/12/18 302, at 7; AKIN_GUMP_BERKOWITZ_000001-04 (12/12/16 Text Messages, Berkowitz & 202-701-8532).

[1151] Kushner 4/11/18 302, at 19; NOSC00000130-135 (12/12/16 Email, Kushner to Berkowitz).

[1152] Kushner 4/11/18 302, at 19; NOSC00000130-135 (12/12/16 Email, Kushner to Berkowitz).

[1153] *Announcement of Treasury Sanctions on Entities Within the Financial Services and Energy Sectors of Russia, Against Arms or Related Materiel Entities, and those Undermining Ukraine's Sovereignty*, United States Department of the Treasury (Jul. 16, 2014).

[1154] Kushner 4/11/18 302, at 20.

U.S. Department of Justice

~~Attorney Work Product~~ // ~~May Contain Material Protected Under Fed. R. Crim. P. 6(e)~~

the meeting and that no one on the Transition Team even did a Google search for Gorkov's name.[1155]

At the start of the meeting, Gorkov presented Kushner with two gifts: a painting and a bag of soil from the town in Belarus where Kushner's family originated.[1156]

The accounts from Kushner and Gorkov differ as to whether the meeting was diplomatic or business in nature. Kushner told the Office that the meeting was diplomatic, with Gorkov expressing disappointment with U.S.-Russia relations under President Obama and hopes for improved relations with the incoming Administration.[1157] According to Kushner, although Gorkov told Kushner a little bit about his bank and made some statements about the Russian economy, the two did not discuss Kushner's companies or private business dealings of any kind.[1158] (At the time of the meeting, Kushner Companies had a debt obligation coming due on the building it owned at 666 Fifth Avenue, and there had been public reporting both about efforts to secure lending on the property and possible conflicts of interest for Kushner arising out of his company's borrowing from foreign lenders.[1159])

In contrast, in a 2017 public statement, VEB suggested Gorkov met with Kushner in Kushner's capacity as CEO of Kushner Companies for the purpose of discussing business, rather than as part of a diplomatic effort. In particular, VEB characterized Gorkov's meeting with Kushner as part of a series of "roadshow meetings" with "representatives of major US banks and business circles," which included "negotiations" and discussion of the "most promising business lines and sectors."[1160]

Foresman, the investment bank executive mentioned in Volume I, Sections IV.A.1 and IV.B.3, *supra*, told the Office that he met with Gorkov and VEB deputy chairman Nikolay Tsekhomsky in Moscow just before Gorkov left for New York to meet Kushner.[1161] According to Foresman, Gorkov and Tsekhomsky told him that they were traveling to New York to discuss post-election issues with U.S. financial institutions, that their trip was sanctioned by Putin, and that they would be reporting back to Putin upon their return.[1162]

[1155] Kushner 4/11/18 302, at 19. Berkowitz, by contrast, stated to the Office that he had googled Gorkov's name and told Kushner that Gorkov appeared to be a banker. Berkowitz 1/12/18 302, at 8.

[1156] Kushner 4/11/18 302, at 19-20.

[1157] Kushner Stmt. at 8.

[1158] Kushner Stmt. at 8.

[1159] *See, e.g.*, Peter Grant, *Donald Trump Son-in-Law Jared Kushner Could Face His Own Conflict-of-Interest Questions*, Wall Street Journal (Nov. 29, 2016).

[1160] Patrick Reevell & Matthew Mosk, *Russian Banker Sergey Gorkov Brushes off Questions About Meeting with Jared Kushner*, ABC News (June 1, 2017).

[1161] Foresman 10/17/18 302, at 14-15.

[1162] Foresman 10/17/18 302, at 15-16.

U.S. Department of Justice

~~Attorney Work Product // May Contain Material Protected Under Fed. R. Crim. P. 6(e)~~

The investigation did not resolve the apparent conflict in the accounts of Kushner and Gorkov or determine whether the meeting was diplomatic in nature (as Kushner stated), focused on business (as VEB's public statement indicated), or whether it involved some combination of those matters or other matters. Regardless, the investigation did not identify evidence that Kushner and Gorkov engaged in any substantive follow-up after the meeting.

Rather, a few days after the meeting, Gorkov's assistant texted Kushner's assistant, "Hi, please inform your side that the information about the meeting had a very positive response!"[1163] Over the following weeks, the two assistants exchanged a handful of additional cordial texts.[1164] On February 8, 2017, Gorkov's assistant texted Kushner's assistant (Berkowitz) to try to set up another meeting, and followed up by text at least twice in the days that followed.[1165] According to Berkowitz, he did not respond to the meeting request in light of the press coverage regarding the Russia investigation, and did not tell Kushner about the meeting request.[1166]

5. Petr Aven's Outreach Efforts to the Transition Team

In December 2016, weeks after the one-on-one meeting with Putin described in Volume I, Section IV.B.1.b, *supra*, Petr Aven attended what he described as a separate "all-hands" oligarch meeting between Putin and Russia's most prominent businessmen.[1167] As in Aven's one-on-one meeting, a main topic of discussion at the oligarch meeting in December 2016 was the prospect of forthcoming U.S. economic sanctions.[1168]

After the December 2016 all-hands meeting, Aven tried to establish a connection to the Trump team. Aven instructed Richard Burt to make contact with the incoming Trump Administration. Burt was on the board of directors for LetterOne (L1), another company headed by Aven, and had done work for Alfa-Bank.[1169] Burt had previously served as U.S. ambassador to Germany and Assistant Secretary of State for European and Canadian Affairs, and one of his primary roles with Alfa-Bank and L1 was to facilitate introductions to business contacts in the United States and other Western countries.[1170]

While at a L1 board meeting held in Luxembourg in late December 2016, Aven pulled Burt aside and told him that he had spoken to someone high in the Russian government who expressed

---

[1163] AKIN_GUMP_BERKOWITZ_0000011 (12/19/16 Text Message, Ivanchenko to Berkowitz (9:56 a.m.)).

[1164] AKIN_GUMP_BERKOWITZ_0000011-15 (12/19/16 – 2/16/17 Text Messages, Ivanchenko & Berkowitz).

[1165] AKIN_GUMP_BERKOWITZ_0000015 (2/8/17 Text Message, Ivanchenko to Berkowitz (10:41 a.m.)).

[1166] Berkowitz 3/22/18 302, at 4-5.

[1167] Aven 8/2/18 302, at 7; [Grand Jury]

[1168] [Grand Jury]

[1169] [Grand Jury] Aven 8/2/18 302, at 6.

[1170] [Grand Jury] Aven 8/2/18 302, at 6; Burt 2/9/18 302, at 2.

U.S. Department of Justice

~~Attorney Work Product // May Contain Material Protected Under Fed. R. Crim. P. 6(e)~~

interest in establishing a communications channel between the Kremlin and the Trump Transition Team.[1171] Aven asked for Burt's help in contacting members of the Transition Team.[1172] Although Burt had been responsible for helping Aven build connections in the past, Burt viewed Aven's request as unusual and outside the normal realm of his dealings with Aven.[1173]

Burt, who is a member of the board of CNI (discussed at Volume I, Section IV.A.4, *supra*),[1174] decided to approach CNI president Dimitri Simes for help facilitating Aven's request, recalling that Simes had some relationship with Kushner.[1175] At the time, Simes was lobbying the Trump Transition Team, on Burt's behalf, to appoint Burt U.S. ambassador to Russia.[1176]

Burt contacted Simes by telephone and asked if he could arrange a meeting with Kushner to discuss setting up a high-level communications channel between Putin and the incoming Administration.[1177] Simes told the Office that he declined and stated to Burt that setting up such a channel was not a good idea in light of the media attention surrounding Russian influence in the U.S. presidential election.[1178] According to Simes, he understood that Burt was seeking a secret channel, and Simes did not want CNI to be seen as an intermediary between the Russian government and the incoming Administration.[1179] Based on what Simes had read in the media, he stated that he already had concerns that Trump's business connections could be exploited by Russia, and Simes said that he did not want CNI to have any involvement or apparent involvement in facilitating any connection.[1180]

In an email dated December 22, 2016, Burt recounted for Aven his conversation with Simes:

> Through a trusted third party, I have reached out to the very influential person I mentioned in Luxembourg concerning Project A. There is an interest and an understanding for the need to establish such a channel. But the individual emphasized that at this moment, with so much intense interest in the Congress and the media over the question of cyber-hacking (and who ordered what), Project A was too explosive to discuss. The individual agreed to discuss it again after the New Year. I trust the individual's instincts on this.

[1171] Burt 2/9/18 302, at 2; Grand Jury

[1172] Grand Jury

[1173] Burt 2/9/18 302, at 4.

[1174] Burt 2/9/18 302, at 5.

[1175] Burt 2/9/18 302, at 3.

[1176] Burt 2/9/18 302, at 3.

[1177] Burt 2/9/18 302, at 3; Simes 3/27/18 302, at 4.

[1178] Burt 2/9/18 302, at 3; Simes 3/27/18 302, at 4.

[1179] Simes 3/27/18 302, at 5.

[1180] Simes 3/27/18 302, at 5.

U.S. Department of Justice

~~Attorney Work Product // May Contain Material Protected Under Fed. R. Crim. P. 6(e)~~

If this is unclear or you would like to discuss, don't hesitate to call.[1181]

According to Burt, the "very influential person" referenced in his email was Simes, and the reference to a "trusted third party" was a fabrication, as no such third party existed. "Project A" was a term that Burt created for Aven's effort to help establish a communications channel between Russia and the Trump team, which he used in light of the sensitivities surrounding what Aven was requesting, especially in light of the recent attention to Russia's influence in the U.S. presidential election.[1182] According to Burt, his report that there was "interest" in a communications channel reflected Simes's views, not necessarily those of the Transition Team, and in any event, Burt acknowledged that he added some "hype" to that sentence to make it sound like there was more interest from the Transition Team than may have actually existed.[1183]

Aven replied to Burt's email on the same day, saying "Thank you. All clear."[1184] According to Aven, this statement indicated that he did not want the outreach to continue.[1185] Burt spoke to Aven some time thereafter about his attempt to make contact with the Trump team, explaining to Aven that the current environment made it impossible, ▓▓▓Grand Jury▓▓▓ ▓▓▓▓▓▓▓▓▓▓.[1186] Burt did not recall discussing Aven's request with Simes again, nor did he recall speaking to anyone else about the request.[1187]

In the first quarter of 2017, Aven met again with Putin and other Russian officials.[1188] At that meeting, Putin asked about Aven's attempt to build relations with the Trump Administration, and Aven recounted his lack of success.[1189] ▓▓▓Grand Jury▓▓▓ ▓▓▓▓▓▓.[1190] Putin continued to inquire about Aven's efforts to connect to the Trump Administration in several subsequent quarterly meetings.[1191]

Aven also told Putin's chief of staff that he had been subpoenaed by the FBI.[1192] As part of that conversation, he reported that he had been asked by the FBI about whether he had worked to create a back channel between the Russian government and the Trump Administration.[1193]

[1181] 12/22/16 Email, Burt to Aven (7:23 p.m.).

[1182] Burt 2/9/18 302, at 3.

[1183] Burt 2/9/18 302, at 3-4.

[1184] 12/22/16 Email, Aven to Burt (4:58:22 p.m.).

[1185] Aven 8/2/18 302, at 7.

[1186] ▓▓▓Grand Jury▓▓▓

[1187] Burt 2/9/18 302, at 3-4.

[1188] ▓▓▓Grand Jury▓▓▓

[1189] ▓▓▓Grand Jury▓▓▓ Aven 8/2/18 302, at 7.

[1190] ▓▓▓Grand Jury▓▓▓

[1191] ▓▓▓Grand Jury▓▓▓

[1192] Aven 8/2/18 302, at 8.

[1193] Aven 8/2/18 302, at 8; ▓▓▓Grand Jury▓▓▓

U.S. Department of Justice

~~Attorney Work Product // May Contain Material Protected Under Fed. R. Crim. P. 6(e)~~

According to Aven, the official showed no emotion in response to this report and did not appear to care.[1194]

6. Carter Page Contact with Deputy Prime Minister Arkady Dvorkovich

In December 2016, more than two months after he was removed from the Trump Campaign, former Campaign foreign policy advisor Carter Page again visited Moscow in an attempt to pursue business opportunities.[1195] [Grand Jury]

[1196] According to Konstantin Kilimnik, Paul Manafort's associate, Page also gave some individuals in Russia the impression that he had maintained his connections to President-Elect Trump. In a December 8, 2016 email intended for Manafort, Kilimnik wrote, "Carter Page is in Moscow today, sending messages he is authorized to talk to Russia on behalf of DT on a range of issues of mutual interest, including Ukraine."[1197]

On December 9, 2016, Page went to dinner with NES employees Shlomo Weber and Andrej Krickovic.[1198] Weber had contacted Dvorkovich to let him know that Page was in town and to invite him to stop by the dinner if he wished to do so, and Dvorkovich came to the restaurant for a few minutes to meet with Page.[1199] Dvorkovich congratulated Page on Trump's election and expressed interest in starting a dialogue between the United States and Russia.[1200] Dvorkovich asked Page if he could facilitate connecting Dvorkovich with individuals involved in the transition to begin a discussion of future cooperation.[1201] [Grand Jury]

[202] [Grand Jury]

[1203]

[1194] Aven 8/2/18 302, at 8; [Grand Jury]

[1195] Page 3/10/17 302, at 4; Page 3/16/17 302, at 3; [Grand Jury] Among other meetings, Page contacted Andrey Baranov, head of investor relations at Rosneft, and they discussed the sale of Rosneft and meetings Baranov had attended with Rosneft CEO Igor Sechin. [Grand Jury]

[1196] [Grand Jury]

[1197] [Investigative Technique]

[1198] Page 3/16/17 302, at 3; Page 3/30/17 302, at 8.

[1199] Weber 7/28/17 302, at 4; Page 3/16/17 302, at 3; [Grand Jury]

[1200] Page 3/16/17 302, at 3; [Grand Jury]

[1201] Page 3/16/17 302, at 3; [Grand Jury]

[1202] [Grand Jury]

[1203] [Grand Jury]

U.S. Department of Justice

~~Attorney Work Product // May Contain Material Protected Under Fed. R. Crim. P. 6(e)~~

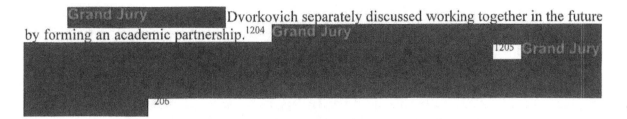

Dvorkovich separately discussed working together in the future by forming an academic partnership.[1204]

7. Contacts With and Through Michael T. Flynn

Incoming National Security Advisor Michael Flynn was the Transition Team's primary conduit for communications with the Russian Ambassador and dealt with Russia on two sensitive matters during the transition period: a United Nations Security Council vote and the Russian government's reaction to the United States's imposition of sanctions for Russian interference in the 2016 election.[1207] Despite Kushner's conclusion that Kislyak did not wield influence inside the Russian government, the Transition Team turned to Flynn's relationship with Kislyak on both issues. As to the sanctions, Flynn spoke by phone to K.T. McFarland, his incoming deputy, to prepare for his call to Kislyak; McFarland was with the President-Elect and other senior members of the Transition Team at Mar-a-Lago at the time. Although transition officials at Mar-a-Lago had some concern about possible Russian reactions to the sanctions, the investigation did not identify evidence that the President-Elect asked Flynn to make any request to Kislyak. Flynn asked Kislyak not to escalate the situation in response to U.S. sanctions imposed on December 29, 2016, and Kislyak later reported to Flynn that Russia acceded to that request.

a. United Nations Vote on Israeli Settlements

On December 21, 2016, Egypt submitted a resolution to the United Nations Security Council calling on Israel to cease settlement activities in Palestinian territory.[1208] The Security Council, which includes Russia, was scheduled to vote on the resolution the following day.[1209] There was speculation in the media that the Obama Administration would not oppose the resolution.[1210]

[1204] Grand Jury

[1205] Grand Jury

[1206] Grand Jury

[1207] As discussed further in Volume I, Section V.C.4, *infra*, Flynn pleaded guilty to making false statements to the FBI, in violation of 18 U.S.C. § 1001, about these communications with Ambassador Kislyak. Plea Agreement, *United States v. Michael T. Flynn*, No. 1:17-cr-232 (D.D.C. Dec. 1, 2017), Doc. 3. Flynn's plea agreement required that he cooperate with this Office, and the statements from Flynn in this report reflect his cooperation over the course of multiple debriefings in 2017 and 2018.

[1208] Karen DeYoung, *How the U.S. Came to Abstain on a U.N. Resolution Condemning Israeli Settlements*, Washington Post (Dec. 28, 2016).

[1209] Karen DeYoung, *How the U.S. Came to Abstain on a U.N. Resolution Condemning Israeli Settlements*, Washington Post (Dec. 28, 2016).

[1210] Michelle Nichols & Lesley Wroughton, *U.S. Intended to Allow Passage of U.N. Draft Critical of Israel*, Reuters (Dec. 21, 2016).

U.S. Department of Justice

~~Attorney Work Product // May Contain Material Protected Under Fed. R. Crim. P. 6(e)~~

According to Flynn, the Transition Team regarded the vote as a significant issue and wanted to support Israel by opposing the resolution.[1211] On December 22, 2016, multiple members of the Transition Team, as well as President-Elect Trump, communicated with foreign government officials to determine their views on the resolution and to rally support to delay the vote or defeat the resolution.[1212] Kushner led the effort for the Transition Team; Flynn was responsible for the Russian government.[1213] Minutes after an early morning phone call with Kushner on December 22, Flynn called Kislyak.[1214] According to Flynn, he informed Kislyak about the vote and the Transition Team's opposition to the resolution, and requested that Russia vote against or delay the resolution.[1215] Later that day, President-Elect Trump spoke with Egyptian President Abdel Fattah al-Sisi about the vote.[1216] Ultimately, Egypt postponed the vote.[1217]

On December 23, 2016, Malaysia, New Zealand, Senegal, and Venezuela resubmitted the resolution.[1218] Throughout the day, members of the Transition Team continued to talk with foreign leaders about the resolution, with Flynn continuing to lead the outreach with the Russian government through Kislyak.[1219] When Flynn again spoke with Kislyak, Kislyak informed Flynn that if the resolution came to a vote, Russia would not vote against it.[1220] The resolution later passed 14-0, with the United States abstaining.[1221]

b. U.S. Sanctions Against Russia

Flynn was also the Transition Team member who spoke with the Russian government when the Obama Administration imposed sanctions and other measures against Russia in response to Russia's interference in the 2016 presidential election. On December 28, 2016, then-President Obama signed Executive Order 13757, which took effect at 12:01 a.m. the following day and

---

[1211] Flynn 11/16/17 302, at 12; Flynn 11/17/17 302, at 2.

[1212] Flynn 11/16/17 302, at 12-14; Flynn 11/17/17 302, at 2.

[1213] Flynn 11/16/17 302, at 12-14; Flynn 11/17/17 302, at 2; Kushner 11/1/17 302, at 3; 12/22/16 Email, Kushner to Flynn; 12/22/16 Email, McFarland to ▮Personal Privacy▮ et al.

[1214] Flynn 11/16/17 302, at 13; Call Records of Michael T. Flynn ▮Grand Jury▮.

[1215] Statement of Offense ¶ 3(d), *United States v. Michael T. Flynn*, No. 1:17-cr-232 (D.D.C. Dec. 1, 2017), Doc. 4 ("*Flynn* Statement of Offense"); Flynn 11/16/17 302, at 12-13.

[1216] Flynn 11/17/17 302, at 2; Flynn 11/16/17 302, at 13.

[1217] *U.N. Vote on Israeli Settlement Postponed, "Potentially Indefinitely"*, Reuters (Dec. 22, 2016).

[1218] Somini Sengupta & Rick Gladstone, *Rebuffing Israel, U.S. Allows Censure Over Settlements*, New York Times (Dec. 23, 2016).

[1219] Flynn 11/16/17 302, at 12-14; Kushner 11/1/17 302, at 3; 12/23/16 Email, Flynn to Kushner et al.

[1220] *Flynn* Statement of Offense ¶ 3(g).

[1221] *Israel's Settlements Have No Legal Validity, Constitute Flagrant Violation of International Law, Security Council Reaffirms*, 7853rd Meeting (PM), United Nations Security Council (Dec. 23, 2016).

U.S. Department of Justice

Attorney Work Product // May Contain Material Protected Under Fed. R. Crim. P. 6(e)

imposed sanctions on nine Russian individuals and entities.[1222] On December 29, 2016, the Obama Administration also expelled 35 Russian government officials and closed two Russian government-owned compounds in the United States.[1223]

During the rollout of the sanctions, President-Elect Trump and multiple Transition Team senior officials, including McFarland, Steve Bannon, and Reince Priebus, were staying at the Mar-a-Lago club in Palm Beach, Florida. Flynn was on vacation in the Dominican Republic,[1224] but was in daily contact with McFarland.[1225]

The Transition Team and President-Elect Trump were concerned that these sanctions would harm the United States's relationship with Russia.[1226] Although the details and timing of sanctions were unknown on December 28, 2016, the media began reporting that retaliatory measures from the Obama Administration against Russia were forthcoming.[1227] When asked about imposing sanctions on Russia for its alleged interference in the 2016 presidential election, President-Elect Trump told the media, "I think we ought to get on with our lives."[1228]

Russia initiated the outreach to the Transition Team. On the evening of December 28, 2016, Kislyak texted Flynn, "can you kindly call me back at your convenience."[1229] Flynn did not respond to the text message that evening. Someone from the Russian Embassy also called Flynn the next morning, at 10:38 a.m., but they did not talk.[1230]

The sanctions were announced publicly on December 29, 2016.[1231] At 1:53 p.m. that day, McFarland began exchanging emails with multiple Transition Team members and advisors about the impact the sanctions would have on the incoming Administration.[1232] At 2:07 p.m., a Transition Team member texted Flynn a link to a New York Times article about the sanctions.[1233] At 2:29

[1222] *Taking Additional Steps to Address the National Emergency With Respect to Significant Malicious Cyber-Enabled Activities*, The White House, Office of the Press Secretary (Dec. 29, 2016).

[1223] *Statement by the President on Actions in Response to Russian Malicious Cyber Activity and Harassment*, The White House, Office of the Press Secretary (Dec. 29, 2016).

[1224] Flynn 11/16/17 302, at 14; McFarland 12/22/17 302, at 3-8; Bannon 2/12/18 302, at 5.

[1225] Flynn 11/17/17 302, at 5; Flynn 1/19/18 302, at 1; McFarland 11/22/17 302, at 3-9.

[1226] Flynn 11/17/17 302, at 3.

[1227] Christine Wang, *US to announce new sanctions against Russia in response to election hacking*, CNBC (Dec. 28, 2016).

[1228] John Wagner, *Trump on alleged election interference by Russia: "Get on with our lives"*, Washington Post (Dec. 29, 2016).

[1229] SF000006 (12/28/16 Text Message, Kislyak to Flynn).

[1230] Call Records of Michael T. Flynn Grand Jury

[1231] Flynn 11/17/17 302, at 2-3; McFarland 12/22/17 302, at 4-5.

[1232] 12/29/16 Email, McFarland to O'Brien et al.; 12/29/16 Email, McFarland to Flynn et al.

[1233] SF000001 (12/29/16 Text Message, Flaherty to Flynn).

U.S. Department of Justice

~~Attorney Work Product~~ // ~~May Contain Material Protected Under Fed. R. Crim. P. 6(e)~~

p.m., McFarland called Flynn, but they did not talk.[1234] Shortly thereafter, McFarland and Bannon discussed the sanctions.[1235] According to McFarland, Bannon remarked that the sanctions would hurt their ability to have good relations with Russia, and that Russian escalation would make things more difficult.[1236] McFarland believed she told Bannon that Flynn was scheduled to talk to Kislyak later that night.[1237] McFarland also believed she may have discussed the sanctions with Priebus, and likewise told him that Flynn was scheduled to talk to Kislyak that night.[1238] At 3:14 p.m., Flynn texted a Transition Team member who was assisting McFarland, "Time for a call???"[1239] The Transition Team member responded that McFarland was on the phone with Tom Bossert, a Transition Team senior official, to which Flynn responded, "Tit for tat w Russia not good. Russian AMBO reaching out to me today."[1240]

Flynn recalled that he chose not to communicate with Kislyak about the sanctions until he had heard from the team at Mar-a-Lago.[1241] He first spoke with Michael Ledeen,[1242] a Transition Team member who advised on foreign policy and national security matters, for 20 minutes.[1243] Flynn then spoke with McFarland for almost 20 minutes to discuss what, if anything, to communicate to Kislyak about the sanctions.[1244] On that call, McFarland and Flynn discussed the sanctions, including their potential impact on the incoming Trump Administration's foreign policy goals.[1245] McFarland and Flynn also discussed that Transition Team members in Mar-a-Lago did not want Russia to escalate the situation.[1246] They both understood that Flynn would relay a message to Kislyak in hopes of making sure the situation would not get out of hand.[1247]

[1234] Call Records of K.T. McFarland [Grand Jury].

[1235] McFarland 12/22/17 302, at 5-6.

[1236] McFarland 12/22/17 302, at 5-6.

[1237] McFarland 12/22/17 302, at 6.

[1238] McFarland 12/22/17 302, at 6.

[1239] SF000001 (12/29/16 Text Message, Flynn to Flaherty).

[1240] SF000001 (12/29/16 Text Message, Flynn to Flaherty).

[1241] Flynn 11/20/17 302, at 3.

[1242] Michael Ledeen is married to Barbara Ledeen, the Senate staffer whose 2016 efforts to locate Hillary Clinton's missing emails are described in Volume I, Section III.D.2, *supra*.

[1243] Flynn 11/17/17 302, at 3; Call Records of Michael Ledeen [Grand Jury].

[1244] Flynn 11/17/17 302, at 3-4; *Flynn* Statement of Offense ¶ 3(c); Call Records of K.T. McFarland [Grand Jury]; Call Records of Michael T. Flynn [Grand Jury].

[1245] Flynn 11/17/17 302, at 3-4

[1246] Flynn 11/17/17 302, at 3-4; *Flynn* Statement of Offense ¶ 3(c); McFarland 12/22/17 302, at 6-7.

[1247] Flynn 11/17/17 302, at 4; McFarland 12/22/17 302, at 6-7.

U.S. Department of Justice

~~Attorney Work Product // May Contain Material Protected Under Fed. R. Crim. P. 6(e)~~

Immediately after speaking with McFarland, Flynn called and spoke with Kislyak.[1248] Flynn discussed multiple topics with Kislyak, including the sanctions, scheduling a video teleconference between President-Elect Trump and Putin, an upcoming terrorism conference, and Russia's views about the Middle East.[1249]   With respect to the sanctions, Flynn requested that Russia not escalate the situation, not get into a "tit for tat," and only respond to the sanctions in a reciprocal manner.[1250]

Multiple Transition Team members were aware that Flynn was speaking with Kislyak that day. In addition to her conversations with Bannon and Reince Priebus, at 4:43 p.m., McFarland sent an email to Transition Team members about the sanctions, informing the group that "Gen [F]lynn is talking to russian ambassador this evening."[1251]   Less than an hour later, McFarland briefed President-Elect Trump. Bannon, Priebus, Sean Spicer, and other Transition Team members were present.[1252] During the briefing, President-Elect Trump asked McFarland if the Russians did "it," meaning the intrusions intended to influence the presidential election.[1253] McFarland said yes, and President-Elect Trump expressed doubt that it was the Russians.[1254] McFarland also discussed potential Russian responses to the sanctions, and said Russia's response would be an indicator of what the Russians wanted going forward.[1255] President-Elect Trump opined that the sanctions provided him with leverage to use with the Russians.[1256] McFarland recalled that at the end of the meeting, someone may have mentioned to President-Elect Trump that Flynn was speaking to the Russian ambassador that evening.[1257]

After the briefing, Flynn and McFarland spoke over the phone.[1258] Flynn reported on the substance of his call with Kislyak, including their discussion of the sanctions.[1259] According to McFarland, Flynn mentioned that the Russian response to the sanctions was not going to be escalatory because they wanted a good relationship with the incoming Administration.[1260] McFarland also gave Flynn a summary of her recent briefing with President-Elect Trump.[1261]

[1248] Flynn Statement of Offense ¶ 3(d).

[1249] Flynn 11/17/17 302, at 3-4; *Flynn* Statement of Offense ¶ 3(c); 12/30/16 Email, Flynn to McFarland.

[1250] Flynn 11/17/17 302, at 1; *Flynn* Statement of Offense ¶ 3(d).

[1251] 12/29/16 Email, McFarland to Flynn et al.

[1252] 12/29/16 Email, Westerhout to Flaherty; McFarland 12/22/17 302, at 7.

[1253] McFarland 12/22/17 302, at 7.

[1254] McFarland 12/22/17 302, at 7.

[1255] McFarland 12/22/17 302, at 7.

[1256] McFarland 12/22/17 302, at 7.

[1257] McFarland 12/22/17 302, at 7.

[1258] McFarland 12/22/17 302, at 7.

[1259] Flynn 11/17/17 302, at 4; *Flynn* Statement of Offense ¶ 3(e).

[1260] McFarland 12/22/17 302, at 8.

[1261] McFarland 12/22/17 302, at 8.

U.S. Department of Justice

~~Attorney Work Product // May Contain Material Protected Under Fed. R. Crim. P. 6(e)~~

The next day, December 30, 2016, Russian Foreign Minister Sergey Lavrov remarked that Russia would respond in kind to the sanctions.[1262] Putin superseded that comment two hours later, releasing a statement that Russia would not take retaliatory measures in response to the sanctions at that time.[1263] Hours later President-Elect Trump tweeted, "Great move on delay (by V. Putin)."[1264] Shortly thereafter, Flynn sent a text message to McFarland summarizing his call with Kislyak from the day before, which she emailed to Kushner, Bannon, Priebus, and other Transition Team members.[1265] The text message and email did not include sanctions as one of the topics discussed with Kislyak.[1266] Flynn told the Office that he did not document his discussion of sanctions because it could be perceived as getting in the way of the Obama Administration's foreign policy.[1267]

On December 31, 2016, Kislyak called Flynn and told him the request had been received at the highest levels and that Russia had chosen not to retaliate to the sanctions in response to the request.[1268] Two hours later, Flynn spoke with McFarland and relayed his conversation with Kislyak.[1269] According to McFarland, Flynn remarked that the Russians wanted a better relationship and that the relationship was back on track.[1270] Flynn also told McFarland that he believed his phone call had made a difference.[1271] McFarland recalled congratulating Flynn in response.[1272] Flynn spoke with other Transition Team members that day, but does not recall whether they discussed the sanctions.[1273] Flynn recalled discussing the sanctions with Bannon the next day and that Bannon appeared to know about Flynn's conversation with Kislyak.[1274] Bannon,

---

[1262] *Comment by Foreign Minister Sergey Lavrov on recent US sanctions and the expulsion of Russian diplomats, Moscow, December 20, 2016*, The Ministry of Foreign Affairs of the Russian Federation (Dec. 30, 2016 (5:32 a.m.)).

[1263] *Statement of the President of the Russian Federation*, Kremlin, Office of the President (Dec. 30, 2016 (7:15 a.m.)).

[1264] @realDonaldTrump 12/30/16 (11:41 a.m.) Tweet.

[1265] 12/30/16 Email, Flynn to McFarland; 12/30/16 Email, McFarland to Kushner et al.

[1266] 12/30/16 Email, McFarland to Kushner et al.

[1267] Flynn 11/17/17 302, at 4.

[1268] Call Records of Michael T. Flynn ▮Grand Jury▮ ; Flynn 11/17/17 302, at 1; Flynn 1/19/17 302, at 3; Flynn Statement of Offense ¶ 3(g).

[1269] Call Records of Michael T. Flynn ▮Grand Jury▮ ; Flynn 11/17/17 302, at 5; Flynn 1/19/17 302, at 3; McFarland 12/22/17 302, at 10.

[1270] McFarland 12/22/17 302, at 10.

[1271] McFarland 12/22/17 302, at 10.

[1272] McFarland 12/22/17 302, at 10.

[1273] Flynn 11/17/17 302, at 5-6.

[1274] Flynn 11/21/17 302, at 1; Flynn 11/20/17 302, at 3; Flynn 1/19/17 302, at 5; *Flynn* Statement of Offense ¶ 3(h).

U.S. Department of Justice

~~Attorney Work Product~~ // ~~May Contain Material Protected Under Fed. R. Crim. P. 6(e)~~

for his part, recalled meeting with Flynn that day, but said that he did not remember discussing sanctions with him.[1275]

Additional information about Flynn's sanctions-related discussions with Kislyak, and the handling of those discussions by the Transition Team and the Trump Administration, is provided in Volume II of this report.

* * *

In sum, the investigation established multiple links between Trump Campaign officials and individuals tied to the Russian government. Those links included Russian offers of assistance to the Campaign. In some instances, the Campaign was receptive to the offer, while in other instances the Campaign officials shied away. Ultimately, the investigation did not establish that the Campaign coordinated or conspired with the Russian government in its election-interference activities.

[1275] Bannon 2/12/18 302, at 9.

V. PROSECUTION AND DECLINATION DECISIONS

The Appointment Order authorized the Special Counsel's Office "to prosecute federal crimes arising from [its] investigation" of the matters assigned to it. In deciding whether to exercise this prosecutorial authority, the Office has been guided by the Principles of Federal Prosecution set forth in the Justice (formerly U.S. Attorney's) Manual. In particular, the Office has evaluated whether the conduct of the individuals considered for prosecution constituted a federal offense and whether admissible evidence would probably be sufficient to obtain and sustain a conviction for such an offense. Justice Manual § 9-27.220 (2018). Where the answer to those questions was yes, the Office further considered whether the prosecution would serve a substantial federal interest, the individuals were subject to effective prosecution in another jurisdiction, and there existed an adequate non-criminal alternative to prosecution. *Id.*

As explained below, those considerations led the Office to seek charges against two sets of Russian nationals for their roles in perpetrating the active-measures social media campaign and computer-intrusion operations. Harm to Ongoing Matter

The Office similarly determined that the contacts between Campaign officials and Russia-linked individuals either did not involve the commission of a federal crime or, in the case of campaign-finance offenses, that our evidence was not sufficient to obtain and sustain a criminal conviction. At the same time, the Office concluded that the Principles of Federal Prosecution supported charging certain individuals connected to the Campaign with making false statements or otherwise obstructing this investigation or parallel congressional investigations.

A. Russian "Active Measures" Social Media Campaign

On February 16, 2018, a federal grand jury in the District of Columbia returned an indictment charging 13 Russian nationals and three Russian entities—including the Internet Research Agency (IRA) and Concord Management and Consulting LLC (Concord)—with violating U.S. criminal laws in order to interfere with U.S. elections and political processes.[1276] The indictment charges all of the defendants with conspiracy to defraud the United States (Count One), three defendants with conspiracy to commit wire fraud and bank fraud (Count Two), and five defendants with aggravated identity theft (Counts Three through Eight). *Internet Research Agency* Indictment. Concord, which is one of the entities charged in the Count One conspiracy, entered an appearance through U.S. counsel and moved to dismiss the charge on multiple grounds. In orders and memorandum opinions issued on August 13 and November 15, 2018, the district court denied Concord's motions to dismiss. *United States v. Concord Management & Consulting LLC*, 347 F. Supp. 3d 38 (D.D.C. 2018). *United States v. Concord Management & Consulting LLC*, 317 F. Supp. 3d 598 (D.D.C. 2018). As of this writing, the prosecution of Concord remains ongoing before the U.S. District Court for the District of Columbia. The other defendants remain at large.

[1276] A more detailed explanation of the charging decision in this case is set forth in a separate memorandum provided to the Acting Attorney General before the indictment.

U.S. Department of Justice

~~Attorney Work Product // May Contain Material Protected Under Fed. R. Crim. P. 6(e)~~

Although members of the IRA had contact with individuals affiliated with the Trump Campaign, the indictment does not charge any Trump Campaign official or any other U.S. person with participating in the conspiracy. That is because the investigation did not identify evidence that any U.S. person who coordinated or communicated with the IRA knew that he or she was speaking with Russian nationals engaged in the criminal conspiracy. The Office therefore determined that such persons did not have the knowledge or criminal purpose required to charge them in the conspiracy to defraud the United States (Count One) or in the separate count alleging a wire- and bank-fraud conspiracy involving the IRA and two individual Russian nationals (Count Two).

The Office did, however, charge one U.S. national for his role in supplying false or stolen bank account numbers that allowed the IRA conspirators to access U.S. online payment systems by circumventing those systems' security features. On February 12, 2018, Richard Pinedo pleaded guilty, pursuant to a single-count information, to identity fraud, in violation of 18 U.S.C. § 1028(a)(7) and (b)(1)(D). Plea Agreement, *United States v. Richard Pinedo*, No. 1:18-cr-24 (D.D.C. Feb. 12, 2018), Doc. 10. The investigation did not establish that Pinedo was aware of the identity of the IRA members who purchased bank account numbers from him. Pinedo's sales of account numbers enabled the IRA members to anonymously access a financial network through which they transacted with U.S. persons and companies. *See* Gov't Sent. Mem. at 3, *United States v. Richard Pinedo*, No. 1:18-cr-24 (D.D.C. Sept. 26, 2018), Doc. 24. On October 10, 2018, Pinedo was sentenced to six months of imprisonment, to be followed by six months of home confinement, and was ordered to complete 100 hours of community service.

B. Russian Hacking and Dumping Operations

1. Section 1030 Computer-Intrusion Conspiracy

a. Background

On July 13, 2018, a federal grand jury in the District of Columbia returned an indictment charging Russian military intelligence officers from the GRU with conspiring to hack into various U.S. computers used by the Clinton Campaign, DNC, DCCC, and other U.S. persons, in violation of 18 U.S.C. §§ 1030 and 371 (Count One); committing identity theft and conspiring to commit money laundering in furtherance of that hacking conspiracy, in violation of 18 U.S.C. §§ 1028A and 1956(h) (Counts Two through Ten); and a separate conspiracy to hack into the computers of U.S. persons and entities responsible for the administration of the 2016 U.S. election, in violation of 18 U.S.C. §§ 1030 and 371 (Count Eleven). *Netyksho* Indictment.[1277] As of this writing, all 12 defendants remain at large.

The *Netyksho* indictment alleges that the defendants conspired with one another and with others to hack into the computers of U.S. persons and entities involved in the 2016 U.S. presidential election, steal documents from those computers, and stage releases of the stolen documents to interfere in the election. *Netyksho* Indictment ¶ 2. The indictment also describes how, in staging

---

[1277] The Office provided a more detailed explanation of the charging decision in this case in meetings with the Office of the Acting Attorney General before the indictment.

U.S. Department of Justice

~~Attorney Work Product // May Contain Material Protected Under Fed. R. Crim. P. 6(e)~~

the releases, the defendants used the Guccifer 2.0 persona to disseminate documents through WikiLeaks. On July 22, 2016, WikiLeaks released over 20,000 emails and other documents that the hacking conspirators had stolen from the DNC. *Netyksho* Indictment ¶ 48. In addition, on October 7, 2016, WikiLeaks began releasing emails that some conspirators had stolen from Clinton Campaign chairman John Podesta after a successful spearphishing operation. *Netyksho* Indictment ¶ 49.

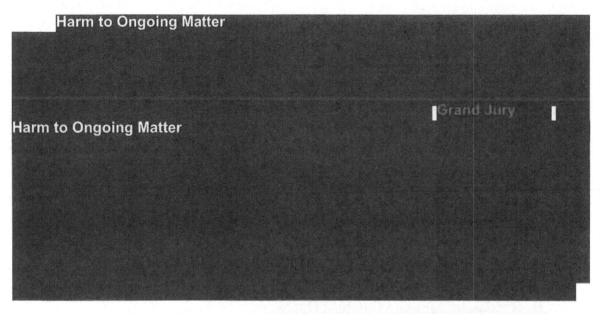

b. *Charging Decision As to* Harm to Ongoing Matter

[1278] The Office also considered, but ruled out, charges on the theory that the post-hacking sharing and dissemination of emails could constitute trafficking in or receipt of stolen property under the National Stolen Property Act (NSPA), 18 U.S.C. §§ 2314 and 2315. The statutes comprising the NSPA cover "goods, wares, or merchandise," and lower courts have largely understood that phrase to be limited to tangible items since the Supreme Court's decision in *Dowling v. United States*, 473 U.S. 207 (1985). *See United States v. Yijia Zhang*, 995 F. Supp. 2d 340, 344-48 (E.D. Pa. 2014) (collecting cases). One of those post-*Dowling* decisions—*United States v. Brown*, 925 F.2d 1301 (10th Cir. 1991)—specifically held that the NSPA does not reach "a computer program in source code form," even though that code was stored in tangible items (*i.e.*, a hard disk and in a three-ring notebook). *Id.* at 1302-03. Congress, in turn, cited the *Brown* opinion in explaining the need for amendments to 18 U.S.C. § 1030(a)(2) that "would ensure that the theft of intangible information by the unauthorized use of a computer is prohibited in the same way theft of physical items [is] protected." S. Rep. 104-357, at 7 (1996). That sequence of events would make it difficult to argue that hacked emails in electronic form, which are the relevant stolen items here, constitute "goods, wares, or merchandise" within the meaning of the NSPA.

Harm to Ongoing Matter

Harm to Ongoing Matter

Harm to Ongoing Matter

U.S. Department of Justice

Attorney Work Product // May Contain Material Protected Under Fed. R. Crim. P. 6(e)

Harm to Ongoing Matter

Harm to Ongoing Matter

279 Harm to Ongoing Matter

Harm to Ongoing Matter

Harm to Ongoing Matter

1279 Harm to Ongoing Matter

U.S. Department of Justice

~~Attorney Work Product // May Contain Material Protected Under Fed. R. Crim. P. 6(e)~~

Harm to Ongoing Matter

2. Potential Section 1030 Violation By PP

Personal Privacy

Personal Privacy

See United States v. Willis, 476 F.3d 1121, 1125 n.1 (10th Cir. 2007) (explaining that the 1986 amendments to Section 1030 reflect Congress's desire to reach "'intentional acts of unauthorized access—rather than mistaken, inadvertent, or careless ones'") (quoting S. Rep. 99-432, at 5 (1986)). In addition, the computer Personal Privacy likely qualifies as a "protected" one under the statute, which reaches "effectively all computers with Internet access." *United States v. Nosal*, 676 F.3d 854, 859 (9th Cir. 2012) (en banc). Personal Privacy

Applying the Principles of Federal Prosecution, however, the Office determined that prosecution of this potential violation was not warranted. Those Principles instruct prosecutors to consider, among other things, the nature and seriousness of the offense, the person's culpability in connection with the offense, and the probable sentence to be imposed if the prosecution is successful. Justice Manual § 9-27.230. Personal Privacy

U.S. Department of Justice

~~Attorney Work Product // May Contain Material Protected Under Fed. R. Crim. P. 6(e)~~

Personal Privacy

C. Russian Government Outreach and Contacts

As explained in Section IV above, the Office's investigation uncovered evidence of numerous links (*i.e.*, contacts) between Trump Campaign officials and individuals having or claiming to have ties to the Russian government. The Office evaluated the contacts under several sets of federal laws, including conspiracy laws and statutes governing foreign agents who operate in the United States. After considering the available evidence, the Office did not pursue charges under these statutes against any of the individuals discussed in Section IV above—with the exception of FARA charges against Paul Manafort and Richard Gates based on their activities on behalf of Ukraine.

One of the interactions between the Trump Campaign and Russian-affiliated individuals— the June 9, 2016 meeting between high-ranking campaign officials and Russians promising derogatory information on Hillary Clinton—implicates an additional body of law: campaign-finance statutes. Schemes involving the solicitation or receipt of assistance from foreign sources raise difficult statutory and constitutional questions. As explained below, the Office evaluated those questions in connection with the June 9 meeting Harm to Ongoing Matter . The Office ultimately concluded that, even if the principal legal questions were resolved favorably to the government, a prosecution would encounter difficulties proving that Campaign officials or individuals connected to the Campaign willfully violated the law.

Finally, although the evidence of contacts between Campaign officials and Russia-affiliated individuals may not have been sufficient to establish or sustain criminal charges, several U.S. persons connected to the Campaign made false statements about those contacts and took other steps to obstruct the Office's investigation and those of Congress. This Office has therefore charged some of those individuals with making false statements and obstructing justice.

1. Potential Coordination: Conspiracy and Collusion

As an initial matter, this Office evaluated potentially criminal conduct that involved the collective action of multiple individuals not under the rubric of "collusion," but through the lens of conspiracy law. In so doing, the Office recognized that the word "collud[e]" appears in the Acting Attorney General's August 2, 2017 memorandum; it has frequently been invoked in public reporting; and it is sometimes referenced in antitrust law, *see, e.g.*, *Brooke Group v. Brown & Williamson Tobacco Corp.*, 509 U.S. 209, 227 (1993). But collusion is not a specific offense or theory of liability found in the U.S. Code; nor is it a term of art in federal criminal law. To the contrary, even as defined in legal dictionaries, collusion is largely synonymous with conspiracy as that crime is set forth in the general federal conspiracy statute, 18 U.S.C. § 371. *See Black's Law Dictionary* 321 (10th ed. 2014) (collusion is "[a]n agreement to defraud another or to do or obtain something forbidden by law"); 1 Alexander Burrill, *A Law Dictionary and Glossary* 311 (1871) ("An agreement between two or more persons to defraud another by the forms of law, or to employ such forms as means of accomplishing some unlawful object."); 1 *Bouvier's Law Dictionary* 352

U.S. Department of Justice

~~Attorney Work Product // May Contain Material Protected Under Fed. R. Crim. P. 6(e)~~

(1897) ("An agreement between two or more persons to defraud a person of his rights by the forms of law, or to obtain an object forbidden by law.").

For that reason, this Office's focus in resolving the question of joint criminal liability was on conspiracy as defined in federal law, not the commonly discussed term "collusion." The Office considered in particular whether contacts between Trump Campaign officials and Russia-linked individuals could trigger liability for the crime of conspiracy—either under statutes that have their own conspiracy language (*e.g.*, 18 U.S.C. §§ 1349, 1951(a)), or under the general conspiracy statute (18 U.S.C. § 371). The investigation did not establish that the contacts described in Volume I, Section IV, *supra*, amounted to an agreement to commit any substantive violation of federal criminal law—including foreign-influence and campaign-finance laws, both of which are discussed further below. The Office therefore did not charge any individual associated with the Trump Campaign with conspiracy to commit a federal offense arising from Russia contacts, either under a specific statute or under Section 371's offenses clause.

The Office also did not charge any campaign official or associate with a conspiracy under Section 371's defraud clause. That clause criminalizes participating in an agreement to obstruct a lawful function of the U.S. government or its agencies through deceitful or dishonest means. *See Dennis v. United States*, 384 U.S. 855, 861 (1966); *Hammerschmidt v. United States*, 265 U.S. 182, 188 (1924); *see also United States v. Concord Mgmt. & Consulting LLC*, 347 F. Supp. 3d 38, 46 (D.D.C. 2018). The investigation did not establish any agreement among Campaign officials—or between such officials and Russia-linked individuals—to interfere with or obstruct a lawful function of a government agency during the campaign or transition period. And, as discussed in Volume I, Section V.A, *supra*, the investigation did not identify evidence that any Campaign official or associate knowingly and intentionally participated in the conspiracy to defraud that the Office charged, namely, the active-measures conspiracy described in Volume I, Section II, *supra*. Accordingly, the Office did not charge any Campaign associate or other U.S. person with conspiracy to defraud the United States based on the Russia-related contacts described in Section IV above.

2. Potential Coordination: Foreign Agent Statutes (FARA and 18 U.S.C. § 951)

The Office next assessed the potential liability of Campaign-affiliated individuals under federal statutes regulating actions on behalf of, or work done for, a foreign government.

a. Governing Law

Under 18 U.S.C. § 951, it is generally illegal to act in the United States as an agent of a foreign government without providing notice to the Attorney General. Although the defendant must act on behalf of a foreign government (as opposed to other kinds of foreign entities), the acts need not involve espionage; rather, acts of any type suffice for liability. *See United States v. Duran*, 596 F.3d 1283, 1293-94 (11th Cir. 2010); *United States v. Latchin*, 554 F.3d 709, 715 (7th Cir. 2009); *United States v. Dumeisi*, 424 F.3d 566, 581 (7th Cir. 2005). An "agent of a foreign government" is an "individual" who "agrees to operate" in the United States "subject to the direction or control of a foreign government or official." 18 U.S.C. § 951(d).

The crime defined by Section 951 is complete upon knowingly acting in the United States as an unregistered foreign-government agent. 18 U.S.C. § 951(a). The statute does not require willfulness, and knowledge of the notification requirement is not an element of the offense. *United States v. Campa*, 529 F.3d 980, 998-99 (11th Cir. 2008); *Duran*, 596 F.3d at 1291-94; *Dumeisi*, 424 F.3d at 581.

The Foreign Agents Registration Act (FARA) generally makes it illegal to act as an agent of a foreign principal by engaging in certain (largely political) activities in the United States without registering with the Attorney General. 22 U.S.C. §§ 611-621. The triggering agency relationship must be with a foreign principal or "a person any of whose activities are directly or indirectly supervised, directed, controlled, financed, or subsidized in whole or in major part by a foreign principal." 22 U.S.C. § 611(c)(1). That includes a foreign government or political party and various foreign individuals and entities. 22 U.S.C. § 611(b). A covered relationship exists if a person "acts as an agent, representative, employee, or servant" or "in any other capacity at the order, request, or under the [foreign principal's] direction or control." 22 U.S.C. § 611(c)(1). It is sufficient if the person "agrees, consents, assumes or purports to act as, or who is or holds himself out to be, whether or not pursuant to contractual relationship, an agent of a foreign principal." 22 U.S.C. § 611(c)(2).

The triggering activity is that the agent "directly or through any other person" in the United States (1) engages in "political activities for or in the interests of [the] foreign principal," which includes attempts to influence federal officials or the public; (2) acts as "public relations counsel, publicity agent, information-service employee or political consultant for or in the interests of such foreign principal"; (3) "solicits, collects, disburses, or dispenses contributions, loans, money, or other things of value for or in the interest of such foreign principal"; or (4) "represents the interests of such foreign principal" before any federal agency or official. 22 U.S.C. § 611(c)(1).

It is a crime to engage in a "[w]illful violation of any provision of the Act or any regulation thereunder." 22 U.S.C. § 618(a)(1). It is also a crime willfully to make false statements or omissions of material facts in FARA registration statements or supplements. 22 U.S.C. § 618(a)(2). Most violations have a maximum penalty of five years of imprisonment and a $10,000 fine. 22 U.S.C. § 618.

b. *Application*

The investigation uncovered extensive evidence that Paul Manafort's and Richard Gates's pre-campaign work for the government of Ukraine violated FARA. Manafort and Gates were charged for that conduct and admitted to it when they pleaded guilty to superseding criminal informations in the District of Columbia prosecution.[1280] The evidence underlying those charges is not addressed in this report because it was discussed in public court documents and in a separate

---

[1280] *Gates* Superseding Criminal Information; Waiver of Indictment, *United States v. Richard W. Gates III*, 1:17-cr-201 (D.D.C. Feb. 23, 2018), Doc. 203; Waiver of Trial by Jury, *United States v. Richard W. Gates III*, 1:17-cr-201 (D.D.C. Feb. 23, 2018), Doc. 204; *Gates* Plea Agreement; Statement of Offense, *United States v. Richard W. Gates III*, 1:17-cr-201 (D.D.C. Feb. 23, 2018), Doc. 206; Plea Agreement, *United States v. Paul J. Manafort, Jr.*, 1:17-cr-201 (D.D.C. Sept. 14, 2018), Doc. 422; Statement of Offense, *United States v. Paul J. Manafort, Jr.*, 1:17-cr-201 (D.D.C. Sept. 14, 2018), Doc. 423.

U.S. Department of Justice

~~Attorney Work Product // May Contain Material Protected Under Fed. R. Crim. P. 6(e)~~

prosecution memorandum submitted to the Acting Attorney General before the original indictment in that case.

In addition, the investigation produced evidence of FARA violations involving Michael Flynn. Those potential violations, however, concerned a country other than Russia (*i.e.*, Turkey) and were resolved when Flynn admitted to the underlying facts in the Statement of Offense that accompanied his guilty plea to a false-statements charge. Statement of Offense, *United States v. Michael T. Flynn*, No. 1:17-cr-232 (D.D.C. Dec. 1, 2017), Doc. 4 ("*Flynn* Statement of Offense").[1281]

The investigation did not, however, yield evidence sufficient to sustain any charge that any individual affiliated with the Trump Campaign acted as an agent of a foreign principal within the meaning of FARA or, in terms of Section 951, subject to the direction or control of the government of Russia, or any official thereof. In particular, the Office did not find evidence likely to prove beyond a reasonable doubt that Campaign officials such as Paul Manafort, George Papadopoulos, and Carter Page acted as agents of the Russian government—or at its direction, control, or request—during the relevant time period.[1282] Personal Privacy

As a result, the Office did not charge PP any other Trump Campaign official with violating FARA or Section 951, or attempting or conspiring to do so, based on contacts with the Russian government or a Russian principal.

Finally, the Office investigated whether one of the above campaign advisors—George Papadopoulos—acted as an agent of, or at the direction and control of, the government of Israel. While the investigation revealed significant ties between Papadopoulos and Israel (and search warrants were obtained in part on that basis), the Office ultimately determined that the evidence was not sufficient to obtain and sustain a conviction under FARA or Section 951.

3. Campaign Finance

Several areas of the Office's investigation involved efforts or offers by foreign nationals to provide negative information about candidate Clinton to the Trump Campaign or to distribute that information to the public, to the anticipated benefit of the Campaign. As explained below, the Office considered whether two of those efforts in particular—the June 9, 2016 meeting at Trump

---

[1281] Harm to Ongoing Matter

[1282] On four occasions, the Foreign Intelligence Surveillance Court (FISC) issued warrants based on a finding of probable cause to believe that Page was an agent of a foreign power. 50 U.S.C. §§ 1801(b), 1805(a)(2)(A). The FISC's probable-cause finding was based on a different (and lower) standard than the one governing the Office's decision whether to bring charges against Page, which is whether admissible evidence would likely be sufficient to prove beyond a reasonable doubt that Page acted as an agent of the Russian Federation during the period at issue. *Cf. United States v. Cardoza*, 713 F.3d 656, 660 (D.C. Cir. 2013) (explaining that probable cause requires only "a fair probability," and not "certainty, or proof beyond a reasonable doubt, or proof by a preponderance of the evidence").

U.S. Department of Justice

~~Attorney Work Product // May Contain Material Protected Under Fed. R. Crim. P. 6(e)~~

Tower ███Harm to Ongoing Matter███—constituted prosecutable violations of the campaign-finance laws. The Office determined that the evidence was not sufficient to charge either incident as a criminal violation.

a. Overview Of Governing Law

"[T]he United States has a compelling interest . . . in limiting the participation of foreign citizens in activities of democratic self-government, and in thereby preventing foreign influence over the U.S. political process." *Bluman v. FEC*, 800 F. Supp. 2d 281, 288 (D.D.C. 2011) (Kavanaugh, J., for three-judge court), *aff'd*, 565 U.S. 1104 (2012). To that end, federal campaign-finance law broadly prohibits foreign nationals from making contributions, donations, expenditures, or other disbursements in connection with federal, state, or local candidate elections, and prohibits anyone from soliciting, accepting, or receiving such contributions or donations. As relevant here, foreign nationals may not make—and no one may "solicit, accept, or receive" from them—"a contribution or donation of money or other thing of value" or "an express or implied promise to make a contribution or donation, in connection with a Federal, State, or local election." 52 U.S.C. § 30121(a)(1)(A), (a)(2).[1283] The term "contribution," which is used throughout the campaign-finance law, "includes" "any gift, subscription, loan, advance, or deposit of money or anything of value made by any person for the purpose of influencing any election for Federal office." 52 U.S.C. § 30101(8)(A)(i). It excludes, among other things, "the value of [volunteer] services." 52 U.S.C. § 30101(8)(B)(i).

Foreign nationals are also barred from making "an expenditure, independent expenditure, or disbursement for an electioneering communication." 52 U.S.C. § 30121(a)(1)(C). The term "expenditure" "includes" "any purchase, payment, distribution, loan, advance, deposit, or gift of money or anything of value, made by any person for the purpose of influencing any election for Federal office." 52 U.S.C. § 30101(9)(A)(i). It excludes, among other things, news stories and non-partisan get-out-the-vote activities. 52 U.S.C. § 30101(9)(B)(i)-(ii). An "independent expenditure" is an expenditure "expressly advocating the election or defeat of a clearly identified candidate" and made independently of the campaign. 52 U.S.C. § 30101(17). An "electioneering communication" is a broadcast communication that "refers to a clearly identified candidate for Federal office" and is made within specified time periods and targeted at the relevant electorate. 52 U.S.C. § 30104(f)(3).

The statute defines "foreign national" by reference to FARA and the Immigration and Nationality Act, with minor modification. 52 U.S.C. § 30121(b) (cross-referencing 22 U.S.C. § 611(b)(1)-(3) and 8 U.S.C. § 1101(a)(20), (22)). That definition yields five, sometimes-overlapping categories of foreign nationals, which include all of the individuals and entities relevant for present purposes—namely, foreign governments and political parties, individuals

---

[1283] Campaign-finance law also places financial limits on contributions, 52 U.S.C. § 30116(a), and prohibits contributions from corporations, banks, and labor unions, 52 U.S.C. § 30118(a); *see Citizens United v. FEC*, 558 U.S. 310, 320 (2010). Because the conduct that the Office investigated involved possible electoral activity by foreign nationals, the foreign-contributions ban is the most readily applicable provision.

U.S. Department of Justice

~~Attorney Work Product // May Contain Material Protected Under Fed. R. Crim. P. 6(e)~~

outside of the U.S. who are not legal permanent residents, and certain non-U.S. entities located outside of the U.S.

A "knowing[] and willful[]" violation involving an aggregate of $25,000 or more in a calendar year is a felony. 52 U.S.C. § 30109(d)(1)(A)(i); *see Bluman*, 800 F. Supp. 2d at 292 (noting that a willful violation will require some "proof of the defendant's knowledge of the law"); *United States v. Danielczyk*, 917 F. Supp. 2d 573, 577 (E.D. Va. 2013) (applying willfulness standard drawn from *Bryan v. United States*, 524 U.S. 184, 191-92 (1998)); *see also Wagner v. FEC*, 793 F.3d 1, 19 n.23 (D.C. Cir. 2015) (en banc) (same). A "knowing[] and willful[]" violation involving an aggregate of $2,000 or more in a calendar year, but less than $25,000, is a misdemeanor. 52 U.S.C. § 30109(d)(1)(A)(ii).

b. Application to June 9 Trump Tower Meeting

The Office considered whether to charge Trump Campaign officials with crimes in connection with the June 9 meeting described in Volume I, Section IV.A.5, *supra*. The Office concluded that, in light of the government's substantial burden of proof on issues of intent ("knowing" and "willful"), and the difficulty of establishing the value of the offered information, criminal charges would not meet the Justice Manual standard that "the admissible evidence will probably be sufficient to obtain and sustain a conviction." Justice Manual § 9-27.220.

In brief, the key facts are that, on June 3, 2016, Robert Goldstone emailed Donald Trump Jr., to pass along from Emin and Aras Agalarov an "offer" from Russia's "Crown prosecutor" to "the Trump campaign" of "official documents and information that would incriminate Hillary and her dealings with Russia and would be very useful to [Trump Jr.'s] father." The email described this as "very high level and sensitive information" that is "part of Russia and its government's support to Mr. Trump-helped along by Aras and Emin." Trump Jr. responded: "if it's what you say I love it especially later in the summer." Trump Jr. and Emin Agalarov had follow-up conversations and, within days, scheduled a meeting with Russian representatives that was attended by Trump Jr., Manafort, and Kushner. The communications setting up the meeting and the attendance by high-level Campaign representatives support an inference that the Campaign anticipated receiving derogatory documents and information from official Russian sources that could assist candidate Trump's electoral prospects.

This series of events could implicate the federal election-law ban on contributions and donations by foreign nationals, 52 U.S.C. § 30121(a)(1)(A). Specifically, Goldstone passed along an offer purportedly from a Russian government official to provide "official documents and information" to the Trump Campaign for the purposes of influencing the presidential election. Trump Jr. appears to have accepted that offer and to have arranged a meeting to receive those materials. Documentary evidence in the form of email chains supports the inference that Kushner and Manafort were aware of that purpose and attended the June 9 meeting anticipating the receipt of helpful information to the Campaign from Russian sources.

The Office considered whether this evidence would establish a conspiracy to violate the foreign contributions ban, in violation of 18 U.S.C. § 371; the solicitation of an illegal foreign-source contribution; or the acceptance or receipt of "an express or implied promise to make a

U.S. Department of Justice

~~Attorney Work Product // May Contain Material Protected Under Fed. R. Crim. P. 6(e)~~

[foreign-source] contribution," both in violation of 52 U.S.C. § 30121(a)(1)(A), (a)(2). There are reasonable arguments that the offered information would constitute a "thing of value" within the meaning of these provisions, but the Office determined that the government would not be likely to obtain and sustain a conviction for two other reasons: first, the Office did not obtain admissible evidence likely to meet the government's burden to prove beyond a reasonable doubt that these individuals acted "willfully," *i.e.*, with general knowledge of the illegality of their conduct; and, second, the government would likely encounter difficulty in proving beyond a reasonable doubt that the value of the promised information exceeded the threshold for a criminal violation, *see* 52 U.S.C. § 30109(d)(1)(A)(i).

i. Thing-of-Value Element

A threshold legal question is whether providing to a campaign "documents and information" of the type involved here would constitute a prohibited campaign contribution. The foreign contribution ban is not limited to contributions of money. It expressly prohibits "a contribution or donation of money or *other thing of value*." 52 U.S.C. § 30121(a)(1)(A), (a)(2) (emphasis added). And the term "contribution" is defined throughout the campaign-finance laws to "include[]" "any gift, subscription, loan, advance, or deposit of money or *anything of value*." 52 U.S.C. § 30101(8)(A)(i) (emphasis added).

The phrases "thing of value" and "anything of value" are broad and inclusive enough to encompass at least some forms of valuable information. Throughout the United States Code, these phrases serve as "term[s] of art" that are construed "broad[ly]." *United States v. Nilsen*, 967 F.2d 539, 542 (11th Cir. 1992) (per curiam) ("thing of value" includes "both tangibles and intangibles"); *see also, e.g.*, 18 U.S.C. §§ 201(b)(1), 666(a)(2) (bribery statutes); *id.* § 641 (theft of government property). For example, the term "thing of value" encompasses law enforcement reports that would reveal the identity of informants, *United States v. Girard*, 601 F.2d 69, 71 (2d Cir. 1979); classified materials, *United States v. Fowler*, 932 F.2d 306, 310 (4th Cir. 1991); confidential information about a competitive bid, *United States v. Matzkin*, 14 F.3d 1014, 1020 (4th Cir. 1994); secret grand jury information, *United States v. Jeter*, 775 F.2d 670, 680 (6th Cir. 1985); and information about a witness's whereabouts, *United States v. Sheker*, 618 F.2d 607, 609 (9th Cir. 1980) (per curiam). And in the public corruption context, "'thing of value' is defined broadly to include the value which the defendant subjectively attaches to the items received." *United States v. Renzi*, 769 F.3d 731, 744 (9th Cir. 2014) (internal quotation marks omitted).

Federal Election Commission (FEC) regulations recognize the value to a campaign of at least some forms of information, stating that the term "anything of value" includes "the provision of any goods or services without charge," such as "membership lists" and "mailing lists." 11 C.F.R. § 100.52(d)(1). The FEC has concluded that the phrase includes a state-by-state list of activists. *See Citizens for Responsibility and Ethics in Washington v. FEC*, 475 F.3d 337, 338 (D.C. Cir. 2007) (describing the FEC's findings). Likewise, polling data provided to a campaign constitutes a "contribution." FEC Advisory Opinion 1990-12 (Strub), 1990 WL 153454 (citing 11 C.F.R. § 106.4(b)). And in the specific context of the foreign-contributions ban, the FEC has concluded that "election materials used in previous Canadian campaigns," including "flyers, advertisements, door hangers, tri-folds, signs, and other printed material," constitute "anything of value," even though "the value of these materials may be nominal or difficult to ascertain." FEC Advisory Opinion 2007-22 (Hurysz), 2007 WL 5172375, at *5.

These authorities would support the view that candidate-related opposition research given to a campaign for the purpose of influencing an election could constitute a contribution to which the foreign-source ban could apply. A campaign can be assisted not only by the provision of funds, but also by the provision of derogatory information about an opponent. Political campaigns frequently conduct and pay for opposition research. A foreign entity that engaged in such research and provided resulting information to a campaign could exert a greater effect on an election, and a greater tendency to ingratiate the donor to the candidate, than a gift of money or tangible things of value. At the same time, no judicial decision has treated the voluntary provision of uncompensated opposition research or similar information as a thing of value that could amount to a contribution under campaign-finance law. Such an interpretation could have implications beyond the foreign-source ban, *see* 52 U.S.C. § 30116(a) (imposing monetary limits on campaign contributions), and raise First Amendment questions. Those questions could be especially difficult where the information consisted simply of the recounting of historically accurate facts. It is uncertain how courts would resolve those issues.

ii. Willfulness

Even assuming that the promised "documents and information that would incriminate Hillary" constitute a "thing of value" under campaign-finance law, the government would encounter other challenges in seeking to obtain and sustain a conviction. Most significantly, the government has not obtained admissible evidence that is likely to establish the scienter requirement beyond a reasonable doubt. To prove that a defendant acted "knowingly and willfully," the government would have to show that the defendant had general knowledge that his conduct was unlawful. U.S. Department of Justice, *Federal Prosecution of Election Offenses* 123 (8th ed. Dec. 2017) ("*Election Offenses*"); *see Bluman*, 800 F. Supp. 2d at 292 (noting that a willful violation requires "proof of the defendant's knowledge of the law"); *Danielczyk*, 917 F. Supp. 2d at 577 ("knowledge of general unlawfulness"). "This standard creates an elevated scienter element requiring, at the very least, that application of the law to the facts in question be fairly clear. When there is substantial doubt concerning whether the law applies to the facts of a particular matter, the offender is more likely to have an intent defense." *Election Offenses* 123.

On the facts here, the government would unlikely be able to prove beyond a reasonable doubt that the June 9 meeting participants had general knowledge that their conduct was unlawful. The investigation has not developed evidence that the participants in the meeting were familiar with the foreign-contribution ban or the application of federal law to the relevant factual context. The government does not have strong evidence of surreptitious behavior or efforts at concealment at the time of the June 9 meeting. While the government has evidence of later efforts to prevent disclosure of the nature of the June 9 meeting that could circumstantially provide support for a showing of scienter, *see* Volume II, Section II.G, *infra*, that concealment occurred more than a year later, involved individuals who did not attend the June 9 meeting, and may reflect an intention to avoid political consequences rather than any prior knowledge of illegality. Additionally, in light of the unresolved legal questions about whether giving "documents and information" of the sort offered here constitutes a campaign contribution, Trump Jr. could mount a factual defense that he

187

U.S. Department of Justice

~~Attorney Work Product // May Contain Material Protected Under Fed. R. Crim. P. 6(e)~~

did not believe his response to the offer and the June 9 meeting itself violated the law. Given his less direct involvement in arranging the June 9 meeting, Kushner could likely mount a similar defense. And, while Manafort is experienced with political campaigns, the Office has not developed evidence showing that he had relevant knowledge of these legal issues.

iii. Difficulties in Valuing Promised Information

The Office would also encounter difficulty proving beyond a reasonable doubt that the value of the promised documents and information exceeds the $2,000 threshold for a criminal violation, as well as the $25,000 threshold for felony punishment. *See* 52 U.S.C. § 30109(d)(1). The type of evidence commonly used to establish the value of non-monetary contributions—such as pricing the contribution on a commercial market or determining the upstream acquisition cost or the cost of distribution—would likely be unavailable or ineffective in this factual setting. Although damaging opposition research is surely valuable to a campaign, it appears that the information ultimately delivered in the meeting was not valuable. And while value in a conspiracy may well be measured by what the participants expected to receive at the time of the agreement, *see, e.g.*, *United States v. Tombrello*, 666 F.2d 485, 489 (11th Cir. 1982), Goldstone's description of the offered material here was quite general. His suggestion of the information's value—*i.e.,* that it would "incriminate Hillary" and "would be very useful to [Trump Jr.'s] father"—was non-specific and may have been understood as being of uncertain worth or reliability, given Goldstone's lack of direct access to the original source. The uncertainty over what would be delivered could be reflected in Trump Jr.'s response ("*if it's what you say* I love it") (emphasis added).

Accordingly, taking into account the high burden to establish a culpable mental state in a campaign-finance prosecution and the difficulty in establishing the required valuation, the Office decided not to pursue criminal campaign-finance charges against Trump Jr. or other campaign officials for the events culminating in the June 9 meeting.

c. Application to Harm to Ongoing Matter

Harm to Ongoing Matter

i. *Questions Over Whether* Harm to Ongoing Matter

Harm to Ongoing Matter

Harm to Ongoing Matter

Harm to Ongoing Matter

U.S. Department of Justice

~~Attorney Work Product // May Contain Material Protected Under Fed. R. Crim. P. 6(e)~~

ii. Willfulness

As discussed, to establish a criminal campaign-finance violation, the government must prove that the defendant acted "knowingly and willfully." 52 U.S.C. § 30109(d)(1)(A)(i). That standard requires proof that the defendant knew generally that his conduct was unlawful. *Election Offenses* 123. Given the uncertainties noted above, the "willfulness" requirement would pose a substantial barrier to prosecution.

iii. Constitutional Considerations

Finally, the First Amendment could pose constraints on a prosecution. Harm to Ongoing Matter

iv. Analysis as to HOM

4. False Statements and Obstruction of the Investigation

The Office determined that certain individuals associated with the Campaign lied to investigators about Campaign contacts with Russia and have taken other actions to interfere with the investigation. As explained below, the Office therefore charged some U.S. persons connected to the Campaign with false statements and obstruction offenses.

a. *Overview Of Governing Law*

False Statements. The principal federal statute criminalizing false statements to government investigators is 18 U.S.C. § 1001. As relevant here, under Section 1001(a)(2), it is a crime to knowingly and willfully "make[] any materially false, fictitious, or fraudulent statement or representation" "in any matter within the jurisdiction of the executive . . . branch of the Government." An FBI investigation is a matter within the Executive Branch's jurisdiction. *United States v. Rodgers*, 466 U.S. 475, 479 (1984). The statute also applies to a subset of legislative branch actions—*viz.*, administrative matters and "investigation[s] or review[s]" conducted by a congressional committee or subcommittee. 18 U.S.C. § 1001(c)(1) and (2); *see United States v. Pickett*, 353 F.3d 62, 66 (D.C. Cir. 2004).

Whether the statement was made to law enforcement or congressional investigators, the government must prove beyond a reasonable doubt the same basic non-jurisdictional elements: the statement was false, fictitious, or fraudulent; the defendant knew both that it was false and that it was unlawful to make a false statement; and the false statement was material. *See, e.g., United States v. Smith*, 831 F.3d 1207, 1222 n.27 (9th Cir. 2017) (listing elements); *see also* Ninth Circuit Pattern Instruction 8.73 & cmt. (explaining that the Section 1001 jury instruction was modified in light of the Department of Justice's position that the phrase "knowingly and willfully" in the statute requires the defendant's knowledge that his or her conduct was unlawful). In the D.C. Circuit, the government must prove that the statement was actually false; a statement that is misleading but "literally true" does not satisfy Section 1001(a)(2). *See United States v. Milton*, 8 F.3d 39, 45

U.S. Department of Justice

~~Attorney Work Product // May Contain Material Protected Under Fed. R. Crim. P. 6(e)~~

(D.C. Cir. 1993); *United States v. Dale*, 991 F.2d 819, 832-33 & n.22 (D.C. Cir. 1993). For that false statement to qualify as "material," it must have a natural tendency to influence, or be capable of influencing, a discrete decision or any other function of the agency to which it is addressed. *See United States v. Gaudin*, 515 U.S. 506, 509 (1995); *United States v. Moore*, 612 F.3d 698, 701 (D.C. Cir. 2010).

Perjury. Under the federal perjury statutes, it is a crime for a witness testifying under oath before a grand jury to knowingly make any false material declaration. *See* 18 U.S.C. § 1623. The government must prove four elements beyond a reasonable doubt to obtain a conviction under Section 1623(a): the defendant testified under oath before a federal grand jury; the defendant's testimony was false in one or more respects; the false testimony concerned matters that were material to the grand jury investigation; and the false testimony was knowingly given. *United States v. Bridges*, 717 F.2d 1444, 1449 n.30 (D.C. Cir. 1983). The general perjury statute, 18 U.S.C. § 1621, also applies to grand jury testimony and has similar elements, except that it requires that the witness have acted willfully and that the government satisfy "strict common-law requirements for establishing falsity." *See Dunn v. United States*, 442 U.S. 100, 106 & n.6 (1979) (explaining "the two-witness rule" and the corroboration that it demands).

Obstruction of Justice. Three basic elements are common to the obstruction statutes pertinent to this Office's charging decisions: an obstructive act; some form of nexus between the obstructive act and an official proceeding; and criminal (*i.e.*, corrupt) intent. A detailed discussion of those elements, and the law governing obstruction of justice more generally, is included in Volume II of the report.

b. *Application to Certain Individuals*

i. *George Papadopoulos*

Investigators approached Papadopoulos for an interview based on his role as a foreign policy advisor to the Trump Campaign and his suggestion to a foreign government representative that Russia had indicated that it could assist the Campaign through the anonymous release of information damaging to candidate Clinton. On January 27, 2017, Papadopoulos agreed to be interviewed by FBI agents, who informed him that the interview was part of the investigation into potential Russian government interference in the 2016 presidential election.

During the interview, Papadopoulos lied about the timing, extent, and nature of his communications with Joseph Mifsud, Olga Polonskaya, and Ivan Timofeev. With respect to timing, Papadopoulos acknowledged that he had met Mifsud and that Mifsud told him the Russians had "dirt" on Clinton in the form of "thousands of emails." But Papadopoulos stated multiple times that those communications occurred before he joined the Trump Campaign and that it was a "very strange coincidence" to be told of the "dirt" before he started working for the Campaign. This account was false. Papadopoulos met Mifsud for the first time on approximately March 14, 2016, after Papadopoulos had already learned he would be a foreign policy advisor for the Campaign. Mifsud showed interest in Papadopoulos only after learning of his role on the Campaign. And Mifsud told Papadopoulos about the Russians possessing "dirt" on candidate Clinton in late April 2016, more than a month after Papadopoulos had joined the Campaign and

U.S. Department of Justice

~~Attorney Work Product // May Contain Material Protected Under Fed. R. Crim. P. 6(e)~~

been publicly announced by candidate Trump. Statement of Offense ¶¶ 25-26, *United States v. George Papadopoulos*, No. 1:17-cr-182 (D.D.C. Oct. 5, 2017), Doc. 19 ("*Papadopoulos* Statement of Offense").

Papadopoulos also made false statements in an effort to minimize the extent and importance of his communications with Mifsud. For example, Papadopoulos stated that "[Mifsud]'s a nothing," that he thought Mifsud was "just a guy talk[ing] up connections or something," and that he believed Mifsud was "BS'ing to be completely honest with you." In fact, however, Papadopoulos understood Mifsud to have substantial connections to high-level Russian government officials and that Mifsud spoke with some of those officials in Moscow before telling Papadopoulos about the "dirt." Papadopoulos also engaged in extensive communications over a period of months with Mifsud about foreign policy issues for the Campaign, including efforts to arrange a "history making" meeting between the Campaign and Russian government officials. In addition, Papadopoulos failed to inform investigators that Mifsud had introduced him to Timofeev, the Russian national who Papadopoulos understood to be connected to the Russian Ministry of Foreign Affairs, despite being asked if he had met with Russian nationals or "[a]nyone with a Russian accent" during the campaign. *Papadopoulos* Statement of Offense ¶¶ 27-29.

Papadopoulos also falsely claimed that he met Polonskaya before he joined the Campaign, and falsely told the FBI that he had "no" relationship at all with her. He stated that the extent of their communications was her sending emails—"Just, 'Hi, how are you?' That's it." In truth, however, Papadopoulos met Polonskaya on March 24, 2016, after he had joined the Campaign; he believed that she had connections to high-level Russian government officials and could help him arrange a potential foreign policy trip to Russia. During the campaign he emailed and spoke with her over Skype on numerous occasions about the potential foreign policy trip to Russia. *Papadopoulos* Statement of Offense ¶¶ 30-31.

Papadopoulos's false statements in January 2017 impeded the FBI's investigation into Russian interference in the 2016 presidential election. Most immediately, those statements hindered investigators' ability to effectively question Mifsud when he was interviewed in the lobby of a Washington, D.C. hotel on February 10, 2017. *See* Gov't Sent. Mem. at 6, *United States v. George Papadopoulos*, No. 1:17-cr-182 (D.D.C. Aug. 18, 2017), Doc. 44. During that interview, Mifsud admitted to knowing Papadopoulos and to having introduced him to Polonskaya and Timofeev. But Mifsud denied that he had advance knowledge that Russia was in possession of emails damaging to candidate Clinton, stating that he and Papadopoulos had discussed cybersecurity and hacking as a larger issue and that Papadopoulos must have misunderstood their conversation. Mifsud also falsely stated that he had not seen Papadopoulos since the meeting at which Mifsud introduced him to Polonskaya, even though emails, text messages, and other information show that Mifsud met with Papadopoulos on at least two other occasions—April 12 and April 26, 2016. In addition, Mifsud omitted that he had drafted (or edited) the follow-up message that Polonskaya sent to Papadopoulos following the initial meeting and that, as reflected in the language of that email chain ("Baby, thank you!"), Mifsud may have been involved in a personal relationship with Polonskaya at the time. The false information and omissions in Papadopoulos's January 2017 interview undermined investigators' ability to challenge Mifsud when he made these inaccurate statements.

U.S. Department of Justice

~~Attorney Work Product // May Contain Material Protected Under Fed. R. Crim. P. 6(e)~~

Given the seriousness of the lies and omissions and their effect on the FBI's investigation, the Office charged Papadopoulos with making false statements to the FBI, in violation of 18 U.S.C. § 1001. Information, *United States v. George Papadopoulos*, No. 1:17-cr-182 (D.D.C. Oct. 3, 2017), Doc. 8. On October 7, 2017, Papadopoulos pleaded guilty to that charge pursuant to a plea agreement. On September 7, 2018, he was sentenced to 14 days of imprisonment, a $9,500 fine, and 200 hours of community service.

ii. ▓▓▓▓▓

iii. Michael Flynn

Michael Flynn agreed to be interviewed by the FBI on January 24, 2017, four days after he had officially assumed his duties as National Security Advisor to the President. During the interview, Flynn made several false statements pertaining to his communications with the Russian ambassador.

First, Flynn made two false statements about his conversations with Russian Ambassador Kislyak in late December 2016, at a time when the United States had imposed sanctions on Russia for interfering with the 2016 presidential election and Russia was considering its response. *See Flynn* Statement of Offense. Flynn told the agents that he did not ask Kislyak to refrain from escalating the situation in response to the United States's imposition of sanctions. That statement was false. On December 29, 2016, Flynn called Kislyak to request Russian restraint. Flynn made the call immediately after speaking to a senior Transition Team official (K.T. McFarland) about what to communicate to Kislyak. Flynn then spoke with McFarland again after the Kislyak call to report on the substance of that conversation. Flynn also falsely told the FBI that he did not remember a follow-up conversation in which Kislyak stated that Russia had chosen to moderate its response to the U.S. sanctions as a result of Flynn's request. On December 31, 2016, Flynn in fact had such a conversation with Kislyak, and he again spoke with McFarland within hours of the call to relay the substance of his conversation with Kislyak. *See Flynn* Statement of Offense ¶ 3.

U.S. Department of Justice

~~Attorney Work Product // May Contain Material Protected Under Fed. R. Crim. P. 6(e)~~

Second, Flynn made false statements about calls he had previously made to representatives of Russia and other countries regarding a resolution submitted by Egypt to the United Nations Security Council on December 21, 2016. Specifically, Flynn stated that he only asked the countries' positions on how they would vote on the resolution and that he did not request that any of the countries take any particular action on the resolution. That statement was false. On December 22, 2016, Flynn called Kislyak, informed him of the incoming Trump Administration's opposition to the resolution, and requested that Russia vote against or delay the resolution. Flynn also falsely stated that Kislyak never described Russia's response to his December 22 request regarding the resolution. Kislyak in fact told Flynn in a conversation on December 23, 2016, that Russia would not vote against the resolution if it came to a vote. *See Flynn* Statement of Offense ¶ 4.

Flynn made these false statements to the FBI at a time when he was serving as National Security Advisor and when the FBI had an open investigation into Russian interference in the 2016 presidential election, including the nature of any links between the Trump Campaign and Russia. Flynn's false statements and omissions impeded and otherwise had a material impact on that ongoing investigation. *Flynn* Statement of Offense ¶¶ 1-2. They also came shortly before Flynn made separate submissions to the Department of Justice, pursuant to FARA, that also contained materially false statements and omissions. *Id.* ¶ 5. Based on the totality of that conduct, the Office decided to charge Flynn with making false statements to the FBI, in violation of 18 U.S.C. § 1001(a). On December 1, 2017, and pursuant to a plea agreement, Flynn pleaded guilty to that charge and also admitted his false statements to the Department in his FARA filing. *See id.*; Plea Agreement, *United States v. Michael T. Flynn*, No. 1:17-cr-232 (D.D.C. Dec. 1, 2017), Doc. 3. Flynn is awaiting sentencing.

iv. Michael Cohen

Michael Cohen was the executive vice president and special counsel to the Trump Organization when Trump was president of the Trump Organization. Information ¶ 1, *United States v. Cohen*, No. 1:18-cr-850 (S.D.N.Y. Nov. 29, 2018), Doc. 2 ("*Cohen* Information"). From the fall of 2015 through approximately June 2016, Cohen was involved in a project to build a Trump-branded tower and adjoining development in Moscow. The project was known as Trump Tower Moscow.

In 2017, Cohen was called to testify before the House Permanent Select Committee on Intelligence (HPSCI) and the Senate Select Committee on Intelligence (SSCI), both of which were investigating Russian interference in the 2016 presidential election and possible links between Russia and the presidential campaigns. In late August 2017, in advance of his testimony, Cohen caused a two-page statement to be sent to SSCI and HPSCI addressing Trump Tower Moscow. *Cohen* Information ¶¶ 2-3. The letter contained three representations relevant here. First, Cohen stated that the Trump Moscow project had ended in January 2016 and that he had briefed candidate Trump on the project only three times before making the unilateral decision to terminate it. Second, Cohen represented that he never agreed to travel to Russia in connection with the project and never considered asking Trump to travel for the project. Third, Cohen stated that he did not recall any Russian government contact about the project, including any response to an email that

U.S. Department of Justice

~~Attorney Work Product // May Contain Material Protected Under Fed. R. Crim. P. 6(e)~~

he had sent to a Russian government email account. *Cohen* Information ¶ 4. Cohen later asked that his two-page statement be incorporated into his testimony's transcript before SSCI, and he ultimately gave testimony to SSCI that was consistent with that statement. *Cohen* Information ¶ 5.

Each of the foregoing representations in Cohen's two-page statement was false and misleading. Consideration of the project had extended through approximately June 2016 and included more than three progress reports from Cohen to Trump. Cohen had discussed with Felix Sater his own travel to Russia as part of the project, and he had inquired about the possibility of Trump traveling there—both with the candidate himself and with senior campaign official Corey Lewandowski. Cohen did recall that he had received a response to the email that he sent to Russian government spokesman Dmitry Peskov—in particular, that he received an email reply and had a follow-up phone conversation with an English-speaking assistant to Peskov in mid-January 2016. *Cohen* Information ¶ 7. Cohen knew the statements in the letter to be false at the time, and admitted that he made them in an effort (1) to minimize the links between the project and Trump (who by this time was President), and (2) to give the false impression that the project had ended before the first vote in the Republican Party primary process, in the hopes of limiting the ongoing Russia investigations. *Id.*

Given the nature of the false statements and the fact that he repeated them during his initial interview with the Office, we charged Cohen with violating Section 1001. On November 29, 2018, Cohen pleaded guilty pursuant to a plea agreement to a single-count information charging him with making false statements in a matter within the jurisdiction of the legislative branch, in violation of 18 U.S.C. § 1001(a)(2) and (c). *Cohen* Information. The case was transferred to the district judge presiding over the separate prosecution of Cohen pursued by the Southern District of New York (after a referral from our Office). On December 7, 2018, this Office submitted a letter to that judge recommending that Cohen's cooperation with our investigation be taken into account in sentencing Cohen on both the false-statements charge and the offenses in the Southern District prosecution. On December 12, 2018, the judge sentenced Cohen to two months of imprisonment on the false-statements count, to run concurrently with a 36-month sentence imposed on the other counts.

v.

196

U.S. Department of Justice

~~Attorney Work Product // May Contain Material Protected Under Fed. R. Crim. P. 6(e)~~

Harm to Ongoing Matter

Harm to Ongoing Matter

Harm to Ongoing Matter

vi. Jeff Sessions

As set forth in Volume I, Section IV.A.6, *supra*, the investigation established that, while a U.S. Senator and a Trump Campaign advisor, former Attorney General Jeff Sessions interacted with Russian Ambassador Kislyak during the week of the Republican National Convention in July 2016 and again at a meeting in Sessions's Senate office in September 2016. The investigation also established that Sessions and Kislyak both attended a reception held before candidate Trump's

U.S. Department of Justice

Attorney Work Product // May Contain Material Protected Under Fed. R. Crim. P. 6(e)

foreign policy speech at the Mayflower Hotel in Washington, D.C., in April 2016, and that it is possible that they met briefly at that reception.

The Office considered whether, in light of these interactions, Sessions committed perjury before, or made false statements to, Congress in connection with his confirmation as Attorney General. In January 2017 testimony during his confirmation hearing, Sessions stated in response to a question about Trump Campaign communications with the Russian government that he had "been called a surrogate at a time or two in that campaign and I didn't have – did not have communications with the Russians." In written responses submitted on January 17, 2017, Sessions answered "[n]o" to a question asking whether he had "been in contact with anyone connected to any part of the Russian government about the 2016 election, either before or after election day." And, in a March 2017 supplement to his testimony, Sessions identified two of the campaign-period contacts with Ambassador Kislyak noted above, which had been reported in the media following the January 2017 confirmation hearing. Sessions stated in the supplemental response that he did "not recall any discussions with the Russian Ambassador, or any other representatives of the Russian government, regarding the political campaign on these occasions or any other occasion."

Although the investigation established that Sessions interacted with Kislyak on the occasions described above and that Kislyak mentioned the presidential campaign on at least one occasion, the evidence is not sufficient to prove that Sessions gave knowingly false answers to Russia-related questions in light of the wording and context of those questions. With respect to Sessions's statements that he did "not recall any discussions with the Russian Ambassador . . . regarding the political campaign" and he had not been in contact with any Russian official "about the 2016 election," the evidence concerning the nature of Sessions's interactions with Kislyak makes it plausible that Sessions did not recall discussing the campaign with Kislyak at the time of his statements. Similarly, while Sessions stated in his January 2017 oral testimony that he "did not have communications with Russians," he did so in response to a question that had linked such communications to an alleged "continuing exchange of information" between the Trump Campaign and Russian government intermediaries. Sessions later explained to the Senate and to the Office that he understood the question as narrowly calling for disclosure of interactions with Russians that involved the exchange of campaign information, as distinguished from more routine contacts with Russian nationals. Given the context in which the question was asked, that understanding is plausible.

Accordingly, the Office concluded that the evidence was insufficient to prove that Sessions was willfully untruthful in his answers and thus insufficient to obtain or sustain a conviction for perjury or false statements. Consistent with the Principles of Federal Prosecution, the Office therefore determined not to pursue charges against Sessions and informed his counsel of that decision in March 2018.

vii. Others Interviewed During the Investigation

The Office considered whether, during the course of the investigation, other individuals interviewed either omitted material information or provided information determined to be false. Applying the Principles of Federal Prosecution, the Office did not seek criminal charges against any individuals other than those listed above. In some instances, that decision was due to evidentiary hurdles to proving falsity. In others, the Office determined that the witness ultimately provided truthful information and that considerations of culpability, deterrence, and resource-preservation weighed against prosecution. *See* Justice Manual §§ 9-27.220, 9-27.230.

Made in the USA
Middletown, DE
26 April 2019